THIS
WORKING
LIFE

LISA LEONG +
MONIQUE ROSS

Hardie Grant

BOOKS

Published in 2022 by Hardie Grant Books, an imprint of Hardie Grant Publishing

Hardie Grant Books (Melbourne)
Wurundjeri Country
Building 1, 658 Church Street
Richmond, Victoria 3121

Hardie Grant Books (London)
5th & 6th Floors
52–54 Southwark Street
London SE1 1UN

hardiegrantbooks.com

A catalogue record for this book is available from the National Library of Australia

This Working Life
ISBN 978 1 7437 9806 5

10 9 8 7 6 5 4 3 2 1

Cover and text design by Julia Murray
Illustrations by Julia Murray
Cover images courtesy of iStock: Devonyu/stock colors/chictype/mustafa güner/Arina Bogachyova/yoyagerix/fumumpa/sandipruel/SasinParaksa/oleghz
Typeset in Proxima Nova Light by Kirbyjones
Printed in Australia by Griffin Press, part of Ovato, an Accredited ISO AS/NZS 14001 Environmental Management System printer.

The paper this book is printed on is certified against the Forest Stewardship Council® Standards. Griffin Press holds FSC® chain of custody certification SGSHK-COC-005088. FSC® promotes environmentally responsible, socially beneficial and economically viable management of the world's forests.

Hardie Grant acknowledges the Traditional Owners of the country on which we work, the Wurundjeri people of the Kulin nation and the Gadigal people of the Eora nation, and recognises their continuing connection to the land, waters and culture. We pay our respects to their Elders past and present.

Foreword

In 1999, as I was sitting in the cloying Boston summer heat with rows and rows of my classmates graduating from Harvard Business School – a day I could never have imagined as a young girl growing up in Geelong, Australia – I remember being struck by the following words of advice shared by our Dean: 'No success in business will ever make up for a failure at home.' Wow, I remember thinking. That's so right. (And sheesh, *no pressure*!)

More than twenty years later, as a full-time working mother of three, and an ambitious, curious person who truly loves the work I do, these words have at times guided – and also haunted – me. How *do* I succeed in my work but not let it consume me? How do I really define success anyway? How do I balance chasing some of these dreams with the deeply held desire to be a great friend, wife, mother and community member? Or as Lisa Leong and Monique Ross ask us to reflect on in the pages herein, 'Who am I really when the "On Air light" is off?'

This book is a gift, taking us on a journey to answer 'what *really* drives me?' and once I can identify that, '*how* do I design the career and life I most deeply want?'

Equally pragmatic and grounded, inspiring and insightful, *This Working Life* pushes us to action – asking us not to just work harder (tried that one!) but to experiment, and tinker and play our way to The Working Life we most truly want to have.

As we come out of the upheaval and pressures of COVID-19, the invitation offered feels especially timely. To find more meaning and joy. To reduce pressure and burnout. To re-define what 'success' means for each of us as individuals.

An invitation to offer more grace to ourselves.

An invitation to find *our* sunshine.

Enjoy.

Sarah Harden, CEO of Hello Sunshine

CONTENTS

02

TIME TO TINKER 108

03

04

Introduction

'Whatever you do,' the doctor said, 'don't google it.' So, of course, I googled it. Then I sat in bed and cried. The natural next step was to look up story after story about people who'd suffered the same condition. People who could never go back to work again. Who were bedridden. Forever in pain. I cried a lot that week. What had I done?

It was 2013 and I was working in a very important role as an executive at a global law firm in Hong Kong. I knew it was very important because my calendar was bursting with back-to-back meetings and my inbox was overflowing. I was ticking all the boxes of success (or what I thought was success). Jetting around Asia in business class every week? Tick. Cross-cultural team of eighteen? Tick. Home owner with a mortgage? Double tick.

I couldn't see it then, but I was pushing way too hard. I was running off cortisol and adrenaline on top of cortisol and adrenaline. I had energy, but it was wildly shooting out in all directions. Big red flags were waving, but I was looking straight through them. I mean, my attempt at finding balance involved training for an Olympic-distance triathlon. So I was squeezing a heavy regime of running, swimming and cycling into my life with my very important job. Absolutely *nailing* work–life balance, right?

I'd been in the job for about a year and a half when we went on our first big family holiday – and I completely crashed. I got shingles, a debilitating illness that causes a horrible, blistering rash. Even worse, after the shingles passed I had postherpetic neuralgia, where your nerves are so frayed and raw and damaged that you suffer searing pain. I couldn't hug my husband or my four-year-old daughter. When she'd run up for a cuddle, I'd panic and cry out, 'No!' That's how scared I was of the pain. Even the touch of the breeze on my skin hurt.

Thankfully, I was luckier than some of the people I read about on those tearful Google quests. After a month, armed with seven different types of painkillers, I went back to work. I was managing the pain, soldiering on ... but I hadn't really recovered. Cue copious amounts of alcohol, late nights and minimal sleep. My relationship with my husband Darcy, my creative soulmate and head cheerleader, was breaking down. I was in a work hole – exhausted, isolated, running on empty. My resilience was demolished, and all those ticked boxes weren't doing anything to help.

Somewhere along the way, without knowing it, I'd taken a wrong turn. My life was in chaos and my future was clouded in uncertainty.

A forced stop

Fast-forward to today.

I am obsessed with work. I'm also really curious about it. I genuinely want to understand why it is the way it is and how we might change it for the better.

Joining forces with my producer Maria 'Magic' Tickle, I host *This Working Life*, an ABC Radio show that explores these questions ('... until next week, keep workin'!'). As the COVID-19 crisis challenged and changed how we work, the show started to feel not only helpful, but essential.

Once again life was in chaos and the future was clouded in uncertainty. But this time it wasn't just me. This was felt by people the world over – maybe ... probably ... by *you*.

I heard from people who suddenly had the rug pulled out from under their lives because of the pandemic. People whose carefully laid plans evaporated overnight. People whose very secure jobs suddenly felt very insecure. People who were going: 'Hang on a minute. All of my assumptions about my career and work and success might not be right.' People who no longer wanted to work full-time to only live part-time. People who were realising that inertia had been leading them down the path for so long that they didn't even know why they were walking anymore.

There was a collective feeling of being stuck, frustrated, bored, weary – that deep kind of weary that has moved itself into your bones, built a home and started raising a family there. There was also a collective feeling of not knowing how to get unstuck.

Through the magic of radio, I was able to stand beside people, in the dark and cold, and ask some big questions with them. And there was one question that kept popping up: 'Lisa, what should I do next? How do I approach my work and career in these chaotic and uncertain times?'

I didn't know what to say, so I did as I always do. I asked more questions.

Over time a thought bubble emerged: chaos and uncertainty have always been part of our lives, but now we need to build them in. We should stop planning like there will ever be a 'normal' where stability is guaranteed. We need to have a plan that centres on agility – some other way of navigating that doesn't require 'zero wind, calm conditions and pleasant temperatures'.

Finding the sunshine in life is one of my superpowers. It's not that I don't see the darkness, oh Nelly I do, but I try to feel my way around for the crack that lets the light through.

When I had shingles, deep down in that damp pit of struggle, I found the light peeking in. Getting sick was a forced stop, and in that pause, as unwelcome as it was, I had a realisation that changed everything: my head had taken over and I'd forgotten about my heart.

I realised that what I know matters and what I do matters, but *who I am* matters more. I needed to reconnect with my whole self and bring that whole self to work, but first I needed to figure out who this 'whole self' was.

The pandemic has also been a kind of forced stop. It robbed many people of their autonomy and agency and sense of normalcy, and brought unemployment, financial insecurity, daily disruptions, illness and a pervasive feeling of uncertainty about the future. It led to what many experts described as 'collective grief', and left our reserves running low.

I wonder if, perhaps, the light in all this darkness is the chance to reflect on your career, and the role of work in your life. The chance to reconnect with the joy and meaning work can provide, and move forward with even more intention. The chance to see choices and opportunities where you may not have seen them before. The chance to make changes if you want to, be it small tweaks or setting yourself on an entirely new course.

Maybe, just maybe, that's the little ray of sunshine in this COVID shitshow. (See, I told you it's a superpower!)

Your life is a lab

For years now, I have thought of my life as a lab: a place where I can run tests and tweak and experiment. I absolutely love this mindset because it takes the pressure off.

When you see every day as Lab Day, you learn about yourself from the things that happen, instead of reverting to 'well, I'm shit at that' or 'I'm a failure' or 'I'm an imposter and soon everyone will discover that I don't actually know what I'm doing'. Instead, you foster a curiosity that lets you go: 'Oh, I learned something new today.'

I was a lawyer for seven years and I think some people could look at me now and think I've wasted a law degree. But it's not a waste at all. It was really cool and I got to explore all these different parts of myself – bits I liked and bits I didn't like. My degree gave me this concept of Lab Day. I did law and science, but I wasn't the best scientist. I was so bad that I once sparked the evacuation of an organic chemistry lab. Really. I didn't read the manual properly. In fairness, the handbook was really big and boring, so I completely missed the giant image of the skull and crossbones on the back ... and the part that said the whole experiment had to be done in a fume cupboard. So I got to the final stage, a week into this thing, and all of a sudden the air was full of black smoke and toxic fumes and panicked cries to evacuate. That day made me famous on campus – and I also learned something valuable.

It wasn't about reading the manual (though I suppose that's important too, especially when you're playing around with poison). Nope, the lesson that stuck with me was about why we experiment. Proving a hypothesis wrong is often just as useful as proving it right. A negative result is critical information that helps lead you to the right answer. It's all valuable.

I look at my career in the same way. Every day, in my lab, I learn something that helps me develop it a little bit more. It doesn't have to be perfect the first time. In fact, it's better if it's not.

Every day is Lab Day. Remember this. We will refer back to this philosophy throughout this book, and you can fall back on it when you need to.

The journey ahead

I know from experience that changing jobs (or careers) doesn't actually solve anything if you aren't connected to yourself. Whatever dissatisfaction or frustration you're feeling just ends up following you around.

I went from law to radio, then back to law, then back to radio – all while trying to find the right fit for me. You've got to do the work on yourself first, and that's where we're going to start in this book.

In Part 1, we'll go back to basics and figure out who you are. What makes your heart sing? What do you value? What has your career looked like up until now? This is the fertile ground from which we can grow something beautiful.

Don't worry if you're reading this and thinking, 'I don't know who I am or what I want to do'. For now, just allow yourself a bit of space to unfurl and expand. If you do know who you are and what you want, perhaps you can open your imagination to more possibilities. It's pretty deep work and it might sound daunting, but I've got your back.

In Part 2, it's time to tinker. We'll explore different ways to craft your job, how to start earning income from multiple revenue streams and how to completely reinvent your career. No matter which stage you're at, you'll learn how to turn the job you have into a job you love. You'll also learn how to leave a job without being sucked into an identity crisis.

In Part 3, we start to play. We'll examine how you show up in the world of work, and how bringing more humanity to that space can make you more effective and more connected. We'll introduce you to the idea of work–life coherence and to routines that can supercharge your work day. We'll also explore how nature can help you tap into your full potential. And because there's more to life than work, you'll also get some tips on how to switch off – *really* switch off – and become more present.

We'll turn the spotlight on the not-so-fun stuff that many of us have to grapple with in our careers: I'm talking imposter thoughts, stress and burnout. We'll build up some resilience that will help us when it all gets super tough.

In Part 4, we enter a more liminal space – the space between where we are, and where we are going next. We'll take everything we've learned about who we are and what we love and learn how to apply it in the workplace. We sow the seeds for the Second Renaissance. Yep, you heard it right. We're not mucking around. We're here for meaningful change.

A squad of explorers

I like to think of myself as an explorer rather than an expert. I don't know everything, because nobody knows everything, so I've pulled together a valiant squad for this book – you're part of it now too – to explore all of the big questions together.

Our squad is made up of some of the world's leading experts and thinkers, and a community of people with real-world wisdom, who have generously shared their personal stories and hard-won learnings from their life experiences.

Some of the people in our squad might surprise you. Enter Little Green, a fabulously talented young indie musician also known as Amy Nelson. She literally gave this book a soundtrack, and her songs will accompany us through these pages.

Also in the squad is Monique Ross, a journalist and writer who linked arms with me for the lively barn dance of writing this book. Monique worked at the ABC for more than a decade, and just as we started putting pen to paper (or fingertips to keyboards) she hit the accelerator on a huge career shift and sped off in a wild new direction: she became a forest bathing guide. Her work in forest bathing is about helping people to slow down, awaken their senses and immerse themselves in nature. It's a way to support the health, wellbeing and connectedness of both people and the planet.

Monique brings a really interesting perspective; she's living a lot of the stuff we're writing about and she will help guide us through this book.

At the end of each chapter, she'll invite you to do a Sit Spot, inspired by a simple and powerful forest bathing practice. The idea is to find a place to simply sit and do nothing, to become part of the scenery and let the world unfold around you. Start thinking about a place you can easily return to – a spot in your garden, a nearby park, or even just looking out your window. For each Sit Spot, Monique will offer a reflection that will help you soak up what you have learned.

There's no right or wrong way to approach this; the point is to take a moment to pause and absorb. Even the most intrepid explorers need to take a breath every now and then.

A gentle privilege check

As you read my story, and those of others in this book, keep in mind that there are elements of privilege at play. I have felt empowered to make choices in my life which may not feel possible for everyone due to family circumstances, education, socio-economic status, health or disadvantage.

When I first left my legal career to take a punt at radio presenting, even though I was in my early thirties, I was freshly single with zero obligations and minimal possessions. Everything I owned fit in one suitcase. (No joke: when I broke up with my English boyfriend at the time, I rang up my school friend, Lucy McCullagh, who invited me to stay on her couch while I sorted out my life. I packed up the couch every morning by putting everything I owned back into the suitcase. I ended up living with her until I left London – nearly 18 months later!)

Monique doesn't have kids (unless you count the fur babies), so she is in a different financial position than someone who is supporting a family, and has been able to make different choices as a result.

There is power in admitting when we've had a leg up in life, or had advantages or opportunities that have made our lot a bit easier than the next person's. It doesn't mean we have lived a pampered life of luxury, or that we're ignorant or that things have been plain sailing.

The truth is, we don't all work for the same reasons. Some of us are lucky enough to find a calling; we'd want to do our work whether we were paid for it or not, because we love it. Some of us might not see our work as a calling, but we can find ways to enjoy most of what we do. For others, work is just a pay cheque, or a necessity, and fulfilment comes from other areas of life.

Why you work can influence the amount of agency you feel you have to craft your career. I have met many people who feel like they don't have any agency at all. If that is you, my compassionate challenge is to get curious and test the boundaries of that assumption.

There are definitely people out there working three jobs and fighting for shifts and just barely keeping the lights on and food in the fridge. If you are grinding it out to make ends meet, you may not feel like you have any room to make changes. But there are also a lot of people working hard – *too hard* – for things that aren't essential to their lives at all.

We focus so much on financial affluence. But what about time affluence? What about creative affluence? What about energy affluence?

If you focus on who you are and peel back the layers on what you think you want, you might just discover that you have more flexibility than you think, and perhaps more influence to make some changes. Stay open to that possibility as we move forward.

Get on the front foot

We don't want this book to be something you read, then put on a shelf and promptly forget about. We want this book to be helpful in your life: something you carry with you and dog-ear and mark up and come back to over and over.

Monique often talks about the objectification of nature – our tendency to see it as something we can look at but not touch, like a piece of art in a museum. But really, the earth wants to feel our touch, and know our stories. It is yearning to connect with us.

So, too, is this book longing to connect with *you*, and you'll get the most out of it if you come prepared to engage. We want you to explore the ideas in this book in a practical way. We'll give you lots of facts and theories and ideas, and then ask you to roll up your sleeves and test them out for yourself.

It won't always feel frictionless; there won't always be instant gratification. In places it will take time and effort, and you will need to go deep. That doesn't mean it's going to feel heavy or awful. There is a lot of fun to be had in the deep places, and the rewards there are so much greater than those to be found by skimming along on the surface. The reward isn't only in the outcome; the process is a gift in and of itself. It's all data.

No matter what stage you're at in your career, the time to act is now. The way we work is rapidly changing, and the best defence is a good offence. This book will unlock a trove of tips, tools and strategies to help you move forward in a brave new direction.

Remember: what you know matters and so does what you do. But *who you are* matters more. So let's dive in with a really big, potent, important question: who are you?

01

LET'S GO INSIDE

We start by standing still.

Standing still, and going deep.

Often we think about our careers in terms of: 'Is *the job* right for me?' But, if you let it, the question slowly but deftly circles back to you.

Am I the right person for this job? What value am I adding? Do I even like it? What makes me happy? Why don't I know anymore?

Change starts at the individual level – what the business world sometimes calls a 'systems thinking approach'. In a system, every element is interrelated. If you change one part of the system, the whole system changes. The change starts with you, and meaningful change is underpinned by an understanding of who you are, why you are and how you've got to where you're standing now.

That is why, before we go out and explore the world of work, we're going to do some reflective work. We're going to shake the giant tree of our lives and see what falls out, what wakes up, what flies away.

We're going to explore our upbringing and what it tells us about who we have become.

We'll pinpoint our values and learn how they can help guide our next steps.

We'll map our career highs and lows, learn how to find spots of sunshine in the darkest corners of life, and begin to build a better relationship with failure.

We'll unearth our superpowers and begin to see ourselves as a Category of One.

This reflective work will give you your bearings and help you navigate forward. It will illuminate the path towards a meaningful destination so you don't end up looping back to this familiar point, wondering how you wound up here, again.

Are you ready? Take a big breath, followed by the longest exhale you've done all day.

Let's start by standing still, together.

CHAPTER 1

Your future begins in your past

As a young boy, my dad found himself in the frightening grip of a guerilla war. It was the 1950s, and a communist uprising was targeting the destruction of Malaya's economic wealth, based largely on its extensive rubber plantations and tin mining. His hometown, Ampang, was a poor rural area with mainly Chinese inhabitants. It was close to the jungle and the surrounding forests were filled with rubber plantations – and it was the eye of the storm that became known as the Malayan Emergency.

My dad would listen as communists emerged in the night to execute those who opposed them. He remembers hearing gunfire, and quickly switching off the lights in the family's coffee shop. Everyone squatted down low to avoid stray bullets and stayed very still until the danger passed. Sometimes they stayed like that for the whole night. Sometimes he'd see the trucks of British soldiers carrying out the bodies of communists shot in the jungle nearby. They put them on the lawn of the police station opposite the coffee shop. The bodies lay there, tied to poles. It seemed like it always happened just after a thunderstorm. My dad, not even ten years old, vowed to leave the turbulence of Ampang behind and to never live in an environment like that ever again.

By the new decade, he had arrived in Melbourne. Dad adored the beautiful suburban landscape that now surrounded him: peaceful and green. He said this period had a profound impact on his life and is one of the reasons he became an architect and embraced his career so enthusiastically. He believed he was able to influence the environment in which we lived; he could use his imagination to create a happy place for people to enjoy.

Much later in his life, Dad reflected to me that it's interesting to see how your future is rooted in your childhood. How your early experiences shape the person you become, and your innermost dreams and desires and aspirations.

I can see his childhood reflected in his work. Dad doesn't like dark rooms – that's a reaction to the dim interiors of his home in Ampang and the chaos of the conflict unfolding around him. His architecture and landscape design were influenced by Zen – uncluttered and minimalist, bright and open. These calm environments, far removed from violence in the night, speak to the core of him.

Dad was right when he said our futures are rooted in our childhoods. And our childhoods don't have to be as terrifying and traumatic as his was to have a profound impact on our identity and on the career choices we make.

My own childhood was fairly run of the mill. We lived in the same family home, did the same activities on the weekend and went on summer holidays to the same rental accommodation at the beach each year. But looking back on it all these years later, some things start to line up.

Going back in time to answer a big question

We need to know who we are before we can become who we want to be.

'Who are you?' is a big and complex question. There are answers to be found in our values, our interests, our formative experiences, the highs and lows and in-betweens of our careers to this point. We'll get to all of that. But first, we need to go back in time.

Right back.

Back to our upbringing – and even back to the experiences our parents had before we were born. There are clues to be found there, clues that can help us understand how we got to where we are now, and get us closer to where (and who) we want to be.

We don't often stop to take stock of how our parents moulded us, but they are generally the number one influence on our career choices.

Looking back, I can see how my parents shaped the way I think about and approach my work. It wasn't that they directed me down a certain road or pressured me to choose a particular career. It was subtler than that.

Dad, for example, gave me this drive to find a profession that suits me at a soul level. He found something that spoke to the core of him, and subconsciously, I have been in search of the same.

The way his career ended also had a profound impact on me.

My dad had a long and distinguished career in architecture, serving as the Chief Design Architect with the Australian Government for thirty years. He is a loyal, passionate and disciplined person. In fact, he was awarded the Australian Public Service Medal in the 1997 Queen's Birthday Honours (like an Order of Australia for public servants), the first overseas-born Malaysian Chinese to get such an honour for service to architecture from the Australian Government. He felt proud and lucky given his start in life as a scrawny kid who left Malaysia in the '60s.

He instilled in me a focus on one career — one job that you pour yourself into. That was, until that job eroded and then disappeared entirely. When Dad was in his forties, due to the privatisation of some government departments, his architectural and design department was disbanded. It was gutting for a person who was so passionate about public works and design. Even though it was death by a thousand (budget) cuts, the chronic stress of uncertainty and the shock of seeing something disbanded was too much for my dad to bear. He wasn't in the mindset to switch to something new.

In the early 2000s I was in London working for a law firm when my brother came to visit. He arrived at my door with some devastating news: Dad had suffered a stroke.

Thankfully, Dad is still alive. But the stroke paralysed his whole right side. He can no longer use his right hand, which is the hand he draws with. Incredibly, he managed to find that crack where the light gets in: he felt grateful that the stroke happened after he had retired and that he could utilise the incredible advancements in computer technology to relearn how to express his creativity through the digital world.

Watching Dad's experience, a few lessons began to crystallise in my subconscious.

We need to be nimble and proactive with our careers. No job, not even a full-time government job, is 'safe' from the vestiges of life. We need to be conscious about the role of work in our lives — and find the sunshine in our work, our relationships and in ourselves.

Who is in the car with you?

So, how do you start unpacking the way your parents have shaped your life, worldview and choices? (I talk about 'parents' here, but it equally applies to anyone who played a pivotal role in your life during your formative years: a guardian, sibling, or even a role model. Feel free to mentally switch up the word 'parents' to one that's a better fit for your life.)

Karen Bremner, a career coach and counsellor, says it is helpful to think of your career as a journey in a car. You're in the driver's seat, but there are other people sitting in there with you — parents, relatives, friends, teachers, neighbours.

Some of them are cheerleaders; they'll support you and help you get wherever you want to go. Others are gentle influences; they will share their opinions and offer guidance, but ultimately let you make your own choices. Others are back-seat drivers, shouting out a 'better' route and trying to grab the wheel.

Everyone in the car wants what is best for you. The problem is, they assume it's the same as what is best for them. This is because we tend to think everyone else is just like us, even though we are all very different.

'It's important to become aware of who is in the car with you and how much power you have given them,' Karen says. 'At the end of the day, it's your career. You have to take the steering wheel, because wherever you end up has to be somewhere you are happy to be. There's no point driving somewhere just because everybody else loves it. You end up sitting there going, "Why am I even here? I don't want to be here!"'

This is a reality for many people. Maybe you became a doctor because everyone else in your family is in the medical field, or went into the family business because that path always felt entrenched.

▸ If everyone in your family went to university, there may have been a silent expectation that you would too.
▸ If nobody in your family completed tertiary education, you may have chosen a hands-on or trade-based career instead.

- If your parents worked hard to give you the 'best schooling', you may have felt pressure to choose a 'worthy' career path.
- If your parents struggled to make ends meet, you may have sought out a high-earning job.
- If you had a sibling who excelled academically, you may have felt that you didn't measure up and avoided an academic path so there could be no comparison between you.
- If your parents were workaholics, you may value a job with flexibility so you can spend more time with family.
- If you had a parent who loved their job, you may have sought out a similar role.
- If you didn't have stability at home, you may highly value that in your career now.

Underlying beliefs and behaviours

Our parents influence our choices through the underlying beliefs that we often inherit from them.

For example, I absorbed my egalitarian beliefs from my parents, along with my belief that being grateful is important in life (which drives me to give back to my community). I believe wholeheartedly in lifelong learning, because my parents taught me that education matters.

I need to always be on time or, better yet, early. I get this from my dad, who is extremely punctual. I only recently discovered why while reading his autobiography. Even though his widowed mother was busy running the local cafe and raising ten children, she was very particular about his safety. She made his brother take him from school to the bus station, but his brother had to cycle many kilometres to pick Dad up so he was often late. Fearing he'd been forgotten, Dad would hide behind the palm trees near the school, away from the gaze of his friends, and cry. My dad has said that this feeling of distress is why he grew up to be so particular about being on time – and his beliefs and behaviours were passed on to me.

I was surprised to realise this link. For most of my life, I had thought punctuality was just 'who I am'.

Karen says we often accept beliefs or assumptions without questioning them because we are completely unaware of them. We don't even realise that these beliefs and assumptions can steer us in a particular direction.

Examples might be what we believe about:

▶ what's appropriate for men or women (e.g. engineering vs nursing)
▶ the meaning of 'hard work'
▶ the value of a 'realistic' or 'worthy' career compared to something 'creative'
▶ the importance of unpaid work in society
▶ how much career 'success' matters to your identity, and what success looks like to you
▶ following a certain path because you're good at it, even if you don't really enjoy it.

Sometimes these influences are buried so deep that they are just normal to us. It's not helpful to label any of this as 'good' or 'bad' – it just is. There is no point looking back with regret or blame, but if things are not working for us, seeing how our past choices have been influenced can help empower us to make different ones now.

A source of inspiration

Your parents' experiences, even before you were born, can have a ripple effect on your life. We can look to Monique for an example of this. She says her mum's career has shaped the way she approaches major career decisions.

Monique's mum, Tricia, grew up in Hillston, a tiny country town in the farther reaches of the Riverina region of New South Wales. Perched on the banks of the Lachlan River, it is a place of wheat and wool and rich red soils. Her family made do with what they had, which wasn't always that much – 'bread and duck under the table' was often on the menu.

Tricia graduated high school and set her sights on a world beyond the dusty expanse of the outback. She did a teaching diploma (it seemed like a better fit than the alternative of nursing) but absolutely hated it – she didn't have the patience to wrangle a room full of kindergarten kids. Towards the end of her qualification, the requirements changed. She'd need to upgrade to a degree to work as a teacher – another year of study. Tricia decided instead to walk away, knowing she'd only be miserable in the role.

Decades later, this decision would have a huge impact on Monique when she was weighing up whether to make a big career move out of media. She had fallen into the trap of the sunk cost fallacy.

What's that, you ask? Have you ever realised thirty minutes into a movie that you're not digging it, but you watch it to the end anyway? This is because of the sunk cost fallacy. We stick with a behaviour because we've already invested time, money or energy into it. Monique had invested many years into building a career in the media – maybe if she just threw herself into it even more, she'd rediscover that spark?

But then she remembered her mum.

'Imagine if she'd actually become a teacher,' Monique says. 'Yeah, she gave a few years of her life to the diploma, but it's nothing compared to investing the rest of her life in something she didn't love.'

Looking at her mum's experience, Monique felt less pressure to make the 'right' decision in career terms, or to stick with something just because she'd invested a lot in it. Instead, she was able to make a decision that felt right for her. She called time on the ABC after almost twelve years in the building.

'Mum showed me that it's OK to change directions, even if it means a big "step back". Being happy in what you do actually really matters.'

A work ethic is born (again)

As Monique journeyed back to the past, she realised how much of her work philosophy is directly connected to her parents. Her own work ethic closely mirrors that of her dad (who once said he got his work ethic from his own father).

Monique's dad, Colin, also did a teaching diploma; he met Tricia while on his rural placement in Hillston. He worked for many years as a teacher librarian in the same school Monique attended. He was a quiet man of quick wit, and a bit of an unsung tech pioneer.

'When our school first got computers, way back in the ancient days of yore, that was because of my dad. He spearheaded that,' Monique recalls. 'He maybe didn't understand the technology, but he understood that it was going to be important.'

Monique admired her dad and the other teachers he was friends with. She loved talking to them and hanging with the adults. 'In Year 4 I even wrote a song about one of my teachers,' she says. 'I sang it at our primary school talent quest, in front of everyone: Mr Cam, you're the man, you're always there to lend a hand. You guide, you help, you understand, oh Mr Cam, you're the man!' You don't have to stretch your imagination too far to see how this kid wound up being mercilessly bullied.

In high school Monique would often eat lunch with her dad in the library, surrounded by high shelves full of books. This is where she connected with language and storytelling — and where her dad taught her the most important career lesson she's ever learned: 'The only thing that matters is doing your very best.'

Her parents didn't pressure her to do any one thing in particular, but they did want her to pick something and give it her all. To put in the effort to achieve something, no matter what it was. Even if she wasn't very good at it ('hello, maths and science!') she would try her hardest. That mattered more than the grades. 'I was bullied for trying in school, for doing my best,' Monique says. 'And Dad helped me see that it was a strength, even if other people didn't see it yet.'

As an adult, when Monique watched her dad struggle with chronic pain and depression, she sometimes heard him mutter the same advice to himself: the only thing that matters is doing your very best, whatever that means to you today. Sometimes for her dad that meant just getting out of bed in the morning. But it was his best, and that's all you can ask of yourself.

Monique says this advice absolutely underpins her work ethic. She doesn't ever want to be someone who casually phones it in, regardless of how mundane the task is. That's not her style (as much as she'd like it to be sometimes). Even as a moody teenager, she was a hard worker. While at school she worked as a Subway 'sandwich artist' (she assures me this is a real role) and she became a store manager in the gap between graduation and uni. 'Even then, I took so much pride from doing a good job. I cared that bit more than most other kids.'

Visualise your lineage

Karen Bremner suggests using a genogram as a useful tool to identify patterns within your family and to tease out the ways they may have shaped your career choices.

Grab a piece of paper and draw up a family tree. Take it back to your grandparents if you can. You can include aunts and uncles if you want, as well as people not related to you but who you were close to as a kid.

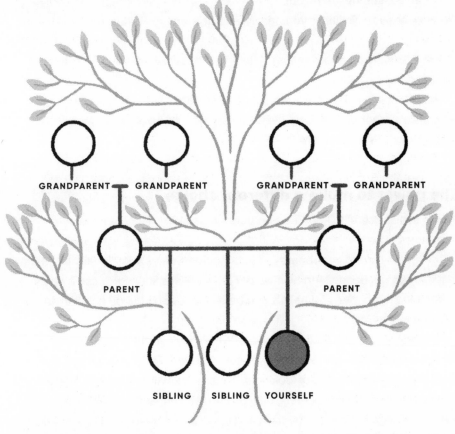

For each person you've listed, answer each of these questions as best as you can, from your observations over the years.

▸ What is (or was) their work and in what field? Is it paid or unpaid work?
▸ What are their strengths and skills?

- What is important to them? What values drive them in their work?
- How do they feel about their work: do they enjoy it or not? Are they OK with that or is it a source of disappointment?
- What are their beliefs about the role of work in their life?

Then take a step back. Ask yourself:

- Do any patterns emerge?
- What has been important in your family?
- What beliefs, assumptions or expectations did they have that might have been passed down to you?
- How are you similar to your family, and how are you different?

'There is something about seeing all this on a page, where you can suddenly join the dots,' says Karen.

You can start to think about what a good life looks like to you, and what a successful career means to you. You can start to see if you have been chasing your dream, or someone else's.

The power to make a different choice

Why is this all useful to know? Karen puts it beautifully: 'Once you have awareness, you have choice.'

Taking the time to interrogate our upbringing gives us some qualitative data that can help us understand how we got to where we are now. It can help us understand our underlying beliefs and behaviours, and change any that no longer serve us.

'The first step is just getting clear on, "What's my current programming? What are the things I am taking for granted as truth?" Then you can see that there might be other ways of looking at it,' Karen explains. 'It sounds like one of those tacky motivational posters, but you can reinvent any day. Any day, you're free to start again. So you look back and take stock, but you don't get stuck in the past. You look back so you can move forward, so you can start building a picture of what it is you actually want to move towards.'

Think about a big organisation. A lot of the time there's something really dumb that everyone is doing, which can be traced back to a decision made twenty years ago in circumstances that don't apply anymore. But everyone still does it because it's how it's always been done, even if it's a waste of time, money and energy. It feels baked in, but if we designed it, we can redesign it.

'You made the best decision you knew how to at the time. Now you can do better. Now you can make a different decision,' says Karen.

You can make a different choice, be it small or big.

Now that I know the link between my father's history and my being early to everything, I can examine my belief that 'we should not be late to things' and ask: when does it serve me, and when does it not?

It doesn't serve me when I am stuck in traffic and putting too much stress and pressure on myself. An old friend died after running across the road for a bus because he was late to work. It all matters.

If you have driven your career to a place you're not happy in, you can take charge and steer yourself towards a better location. Don't worry if you don't know where you'd rather be instead — we will explore that soon. This is just the beginning of our journey into our identity, and we are nowhere near the end.

There have been myriad experiences between then and now: experiences that have shaped your values; highs and lows that have made a huge impact on who you are and moulded your experience of work. So buckle up: that's where we're heading to next.

SIT SPOT

Desire lines are the paths we walk because they feel right, even if they deviate from the official route set out by another. That bit of worn grass between the planned curves of a concrete path? That's a desire line.

What would it mean, in this moment, to realise that there is no 'right' path through your life? What would it mean to create your own desire lines to follow forward?

CHAPTER 2

Get rooted

H ow do you weigh up decisions about your career? How do you choose what to do next; whether to embrace an opportunity or turn it down, to stay or to go, to listen to your head or your gut? When you ask yourself a question and divergent choices arise, how do you work out which answer is right for you?

Perhaps you make a list of all the pros and cons, diligently noting down the arguments for and against a particular path. Perhaps you consider how each possibility will help you move towards a long-term goal, like landing a big promotion. Perhaps you ask your friends for advice, or even throw caution to the wind and toss a coin: heads for yes, tails for no.

However you do it, it's highly possible that your decision is, at least in part, based on external factors such as societal views of what success looks and feels like. This might be why, despite deeply yearning for more family time, you accept a high-paying job knowing it comes hand in hand with demanding overtime. Because that position means you've *made it*, right?

Success has become synonymous with money and power, but it's a narrow definition. Arianna Huffington likens the obsession with money and power to sitting on a two-legged stool: sooner or later, you're going to fall off.[1] It's not sustainable.

In times of uncertainty and upheaval, using these external factors as a guide feels fraught. So what can we look to instead? Perhaps, we need to go inward. There is a lot of research being done in the area of values – those pillars of your worldview which guide your attitudes and actions, beliefs and behaviours.

I believe our values can be helpful shepherds in life. They can provide a measuring stick for a definition of success that is unique to you and ensure that where you end up is true to who you are.

According to Greta Bradman, broadcaster, psychologist and the founder of values-based tech start-up Eiris Inc., we all have two sets of values: core values and threat-based values (more on these soon).

'Our values are only as useful as they are prioritised and actioned,' Greta says. 'This is not about being an evangelist with one's values. This is about allowing them to serve us, in service of our version of a life well lived.'

If you can run your choices in life through your values system, you can bring more intention and awareness to the decisions you make. You can hook into your values during testing times or when you need an incentive to stick to the right path. You can prioritise the things that are actually important to you, instead of the things you think should be important to you.

Be like a tree

We can think of our values as being the roots of a tree, prying and pushing into the soil of our lives. Roots serve as an anchor; they're the reason trees don't topple over in a storm. They are strong and tenacious and, given time, some roots will even grow through rock. They are the reason trees can reach up tall into the sky. Without roots, no growth is possible.

The root systems of trees are dazzlingly complex and diverse. They can run remarkably deep – a wild fig at the Echo Caves in South Africa holds the Guinness World Record for having the greatest root depth, at some 120 metres. Many trees stretch their roots out wide, extending well beyond the reach of their individual branches. The root system of a mature oak can total hundreds of kilometres in length. This means the roots of trees standing together in a forest eventually intersect and intermingle. They connect.

Scientists like ecologist Suzanne Simard have shown that trees even communicate with each other through their roots, via a complex underground network of fungi often called the 'wood wide web'. They share nutrients and resources. They alert each other to threats. They help each other thrive.

Our roots give us strength and stability. They anchor us to who we truly are and provide a nourishing foundation for our lives. They can provide a point of connection with others. So when we need direction in life, it's helpful to ground down and be like a tree, and to remember what it is that we stand for.

To get rooted, so that we can continue to grow, we need to unearth our values.

Beliefs, motivations, goals

Values can sometimes feel like a nebulous concept, particularly if you are not familiar with working with them. Greta helped me get under the hood in a practical way.

As she studied the research of Shalom Schwartz, the social psychologist who created the theory of basic human values, it became evident to her that our values are a composite of three factors. According to Greta, these factors are 'our beliefs, based on past experiences; our motivations, based on current needs; and our goals, based on future desires and aspirations.'

We all have many different values, and at any given moment particular values can activate.

'When a value is activated, we have an emotional response,' Greta explains. 'The feelings we experience can be either positive, if an event or experience is congruent with our values, or our feelings can be negative, if what is occurring is incongruent with our values. Sometimes, we can experience both at once, which can feel confusing.'

Sometimes our values rub up against each other in an uncomfortable way.

Say, for example, one of your dominant values is family. You want to be there for your kids and your partner, be present at mealtimes and connect with them in a genuine way. But you also have a drive for success and achievement in your career, which is just as valid.

'Recognising the tension between those values that are important to you is a powerful gateway to being more intentional around how you prioritise your values at a given moment,' Greta says. 'You can't hold all your values as equally important all the time. Getting intentional can help you wade through the discomfort of confusing feelings, when you're sitting with values that would suggest different actions depending on which you prioritise.'

This can help you circumnavigate some of the guilt you may feel around prioritising one value over another.

You can value family while at the same time valuing the fulfilment you get from your work and the way your work enables you to provide for your family. Both are legitimate values and you can choose how and when one may take priority.

'You can get really real and get really intentional around that prioritisation in smaller moments, not just the big moments,' Greta says. 'You can stop and really think about "What is my values prioritisation in this context? What really fits with me?" And then make a decision. Make a choice as to how you act in this moment, given that prioritisation.'

REFLECTION

Unearth your core values

Your values, and how you prioritise them, can shift as you grow. What mattered most to you as a fresh graduate is probably different to what matters most to you now. I wonder what my 21-year-old self would have listed as her values. She probably didn't value listing values for a start. I've found that my core values have crystallised with age, and some latent values have risen to the surface. So even if you have a good grasp on what your values are, it can be useful to refresh your understanding from time to time.

Pinpointing your values can feel like a daunting task, and while it does take some time and thought, it's exciting to uncover them: peeling back the layers of ourselves to get to the gift inside.

'The idea that we can sit down and just magically come up with our values and superimpose them onto ourselves is not really the way that it works,' Greta says. 'We need to put the time in, and treat it as an iterative process. It's a little bit like Michelangelo's *David* – chipping away and uncovering what is there.'

Greta has developed a values elicitation process over several years, and she took Monique and me through it. (We dubbed it a 'valicitation'.)

1. Take a look at the list below. This is Greta's list of fifty-one common values. Make a note of the values that are important to you (or circle them in the book; I love the idea that you'll mark up your copy as you go). Pick up to twenty or so. If your values are not on this list, add them in. That's what the blank spaces are for. I added 'joy' to mine.

   Focus on things that are actually important to you, not things you think 'should' matter, or things that matter to other people. There are no right or wrong values to pick. (Remember: no one's going to see this except you so it's OK to be honest.)

Acceptance	Accountability	Achievement	Adaptability	Adventure
Altruism	Authenticity	Awareness	Balance	Beauty
Collaboration	Communication	Community	Compassion	Connection
Contribution	Control	Courage	Creativity	Curiosity
Excellence	Fairness	Family	Freedom	Friendliness
Gratitude	Health	Humility	Humour	Independence
Influence	Integrity	Intelligence	Leadership	Learning
Legacy	Love	Loyalty	Mastery	Novelty
Openness	Persistence	Pleasure	Respect	Responsibility
Security	Sincerity	Spirituality	Wealth	Wisdom
Work ethic				

2. Once you have your list of values, it's time to start narrowing them down. Put the values into a Top 10. Then narrow them down again into a Top 5. Your Top 5 are your core values – what you should come back to when you need to get rooted.
3. The next step is to come up with a definition of what each value means to you. You may even like to rework the name of each value to something that resonates with you. The idea is that you end up with something unique that you can easily bring to mind whenever you need to. For example, Greta values persistence and determination, which she names 'Little Red Engine'.

4. To go even deeper, have a go at inserting one of your core values into this sentence and answering the question: 'What does _____ mean to me?'

So if one of your values is 'wealth', you might do something like this.

What does wealth mean to me?

Wealth → don't have to ask others for money → can buy whatever I want → independence

Wealth → gives me a sense of pride to have nice things → makes me feel accomplished

Wealth → have a safety net so I'm less worried about money when things feel uncertain → gives me a sense of security

Voila! You've unearthed some deeper meaning about your value.

You may find that your values have some overlap. Greta says you can group similar values together under one umbrella. Monique grouped learning and work ethic under persistence; and community, family and openness fell under the banner of connection.

My list of values is written up on my wall at home: health, connection, curiosity, freedom and joy. Monique's are authenticity, freedom, connection, persistence and gratitude. It's interesting to see how much overlap there is between us, which is perhaps why we work so well together despite being such outwardly different people. We are also a strong team because of where our values differ. Take my value of joy and Monique's value of persistence as an example. If we both just *persisted* with the process of writing this book, it may not have been as fun, and if it was all joy, we may never have finished at all.

It's useful to note the values of any team you may be in and use that to inform your approach to collaborating. It can help you understand why someone works differently to you or thrives under different workflows.

Survival values

The core values you have just unearthed are what Greta calls 'thriving' values. They're aspirational and tend to be focused around the collective and the greater good for humanity. But Greta says we also have 'surviving' values that are less spoken about.

'These come to the fore when we feel under threat, or when our needs around safety and security are not met,' Greta says. 'These survival values may overlap with our core values but have some key differences. These threat-based values are focused on keeping ourselves and our nearest and dearest safe and secure, even if it is at the expense of the collective. It's about hunkering down and surviving. They may manifest in our focusing on our own wealth or power for our own benefit even when it is at the expense of others or things we hold as important when we're not under threat.'

When you are feeling under threat in some way – say, you're stressed about job security – your survival values activate and you might make a decision that doesn't really land for you. You do something which feels incongruent to how you think about the world. For example, you might claim credit in the moment for an idea that wasn't actually yours, even though you hold honesty and transparency as core values. You might buy coffee in a takeaway cup because it's convenient, even though you value sustainability.

'It's not about pillorying yourself for your behaviour or your actions. It's about noticing those moments in which a different value has come to the fore,' Greta says. 'I've had people say, "I'm clearly just full of shit. You know those values that I thought were so important to me? I had a bad day and they went out the window."'

This is normal. We all have survival values and they don't mean our thriving values are not authentic and real. Rather than beating yourself up about them when they arise, use your survival values as an opportunity to pause, then bring more intention back to your decision-making.

While it is OK for certain values to take priority at certain times, Greta says paying attention to our thriving values is important for the longer term.

'[Thriving values] really pertain to mental health and wellbeing. The more that we're focused on our threat-based values, the shorter our time horizon becomes in terms of what we're prioritising outcomes for. At such times, we tend to sacrifice the longer term for short-term safety.'

Values-based decision-making

Our values are only useful if we prioritise them and action them, as Greta points out. If they don't translate into our behaviour, they just ... sit there, gathering dust. Now that you know your values, you can use them to shape your decisions.

When you need to make a decision, big or small, come up with two or three alternative choices you could make. Ask yourself:

- ▸ How does each choice align with my core values?
- ▸ On that basis, which choice am I going to make?

This is how you get down into what is most important to you and negotiate the way you prioritise your values. It can help you avoid getting sidetracked with things like, 'Oh it would be such a good opportunity', and 'I feel like I should do this'. You can park all the new and shiny stuff, and look at how the choices you can make actually serve your values.

This reminds me of an interview I did on *This Working Life* with Abigail Forsyth,[2] the inventor and managing director of KeepCup, the reusable coffee cups that kickstarted a global movement. She is extremely values driven, and one of her core values is sustainability.

When KeepCup was set to expand into the UK market, Abigail faced a big decision. She would save loads of money by manufacturing the products in Australia and then shipping them to London to sell – but the carbon footprint would be huge. Even though it was cheaper to manufacture in Australia, it did not meet the long-term goals and values of her business. She didn't have to think too hard to decide to manufacture in the UK, despite the higher cost. 'It was really important to us that the solution we had didn't exacerbate the problem,' she says. 'We were making a long-term bet on the future of the business and our products.'

For me, that is a powerful example of living by your values.

Five values to help you navigate your career

When I speak about innovation, I often refer to five values that help underpin an innovation mindset:

COURAGE CURIOSITY CREATIVITY

COMPASSION CONNECTION

These same values are critical to navigating your career in times of chaos, because they help you hone the experimental mindset you need to make changes.

They have emerged in my life time and time again. To show you how useful they can be, and tangible ways they can be put into action, let's look to a few examples from my career.

COURAGE

You've got to have courage to have a flourishing career.

My move from law to radio required me, at times, to dig deep into the bucket of bravery. When I decided to follow my heart into full-time radio, I collected all the best bits from my volunteer work at a hospital radio show. I cut together a demo tape and sent it out to all the radio stations around London and beyond. In reply, I got a stack of rejection letters. I was crushed. Then the rumination and catastrophising started. What was I thinking? Of course they wouldn't give me a gig. Who'd want my bogan voice on their radio station?

But I had a glimmer of an idea. At 6 am one Saturday, I found myself in the outskirts of London, shivering in the cold and sleet, staring at the door of Liberty Radio, the city's largest AM commercial radio station. I was listening on my portable radio to the program director, who was presenting the breakfast show live inside.

I stared up at the doorbell. Willing myself to press it. To cold-call. He stopped talking to play a song. This was my chance. My mind was racing through a multiple choice of worst-case scenarios.

Q: If I ring this bell, will he:

a. ignore me
b. embarrass me
c. shout at me
d. call the police and have me arrested

Then it dawned on me: the risk of doing nothing is greater than the risk of doing something. I'd been conditioned (as so many of us have) to ask myself, 'What is the worst thing that could happen?' But that wasn't the right question to ask in this moment. The right question was, 'But what if it works?'

I pressed the doorbell. Lo and behold, his voice crackled through the intercom. My heart beat heavily in my chest. Could he hear it?

'Hello! I'm Lisa Leong. I'm a radio DJ.' (I may have been exaggerating just a little.) 'I was wondering if I could make you a cup of coffee this morning?'

There was a long pause. Then he said, 'OK.' The door buzzed. I pushed the door open. I saw a flight of stairs. I climbed up, knees shaking. Where is the kitchen? How does he take his coffee? I made an instant white coffee and took it into the studio. He waved at the guest chair so I sat down. I watched in awe as he presented his show. In between breaks, he chatted to me. And then I left.

The next day, Sunday at 6 am, I did it again. Pressed that doorbell, pushed the door, walked up the stairs and made him a cup of coffee. But this time he started talking to me on the air. Like a radio duo. I was on the air across London! I did this for a few weekends running until he was so sick of me he gave me my own Sunday afternoon radio show. I asked him if I could co-present with my radio partner in crime, Zoe 'Mackalack' Mack, a vibrant and creative radio host, and he said yes. (More on creative collaboration to come.)

That's how I learned the power of being courageous.

CURIOSITY AND CREATIVITY

I have an innate and enduring curiosity. I love this value, and it's at the centre of how I approach my work life. It's about constant experimentation. Each day at work, you're stress-testing your choices. How does it feel? How does it fit? What needs further exploration?

Sometimes the way forward involves a bit of creativity and a leap of faith. In 2003, when I was fresh out of the Australian Film Television and Radio School (AFTRS) in Sydney, I got my first full-time paid radio gig. A new radio station, Hot Tomato, was launching on the Gold Coast, and I was one of two midnight-to-dawn announcers. Yep, the (not so) highly coveted graveyard shift!

On launch day, the program director called me into their office and said: 'Tonight, I want a caller on with you every time I hear your voice on air.'

'Impossible,' fired back the lawyer voice in my head. We were a brand-new radio station — literally hours old — and it was a midnight slot. So I had no listeners, and therefore no callers. But I thought, 'OK, I need to get curious. What is the art of the possible here?'

I asked my husband to help. We brainstormed and Darcy said: 'Who are your fellow workers of the night? We need to link the night crew.' We came up with a list: taxi drivers, bakers, petrol station attendants, restaurant staff, hotel workers, cleaners, the local 7-Eleven …

At 11 pm that night, Darcy drove me to a taxi rank. I got out of the car and walked to the top of the taxi queue. I leaned in through the driver's window. 'Hi, I'm Lisa Leong from Hot Tomato, your new radio station on the Gold Coast. What's your name and number, please? Listen to me tonight on the radio. I'll call you and get you on the air.' I went down the taxi rank until my notepad was full with names and numbers. Then hubby drove me to work.

It was midnight. The song was ending and it was time to set up my shift. 'Hi, it's two past midnight on 102.9 Hot Tomato. I'm Lisa Leong and I'll be with you from midnight to dawn. I need a coffee to get me through to the end. Call me if you can recommend the best coffee in town.'

No one called. So I pulled out my list and called the first number. Ted. I recorded him telling me about the best coffee in town, then chopped it up and put it on the air. Ted listened to hear his voice and his mates listened to have a laugh. I worked my way down the list for the show and I got a caller on every time I was on the air.

Over the next few weeks we hit the bakers, then hoteliers, then service stations. We covered the Gold Coast night workers – and created an audience. Curiosity and creativity helped me find a solution that didn't exist.

COMPASSION AND CONNECTION

This boils down to connecting with other people from a place of authenticity and understanding. I believe we need to weave these values deep into the fabric of what we do, in life and in work. We come up with the best ideas and solutions together, not alone.

Through this book we'll explore how these values can help you progress your career. But for now, I want to share the story of how I woke up to their importance.

In 2013, when I had that terrible case of shingles and wound up with postherpetic neuralgia, I was on seven different painkillers a day, crying nonstop in bed. One day I had a long phone conversation with my friend Tristan Forrester. It was four years after Tristan had done a Vipassanā meditation retreat and he asked me, 'Have you ever thought about doing meditation for your pain?'

I was cynical. As a busy 'Type A', my first reaction was 'I don't have time to sit down and do nothing'. But I was desperate, so I started researching. I came at it from a scientific perspective. I started with the work of Jon Kabat-Zinn, a scientist working at the University of Massachusetts Medical School, who had studied the Zen mindfulness tradition and pioneered it in the West. He had a hypothesis that patients could benefit from undertaking mindfulness in conjunction with their treatment. From his work, he created an eight-week mindfulness for stress reduction program. I signed up immediately.

Suffice to say I found it incredibly difficult. But I went to all the classes and stuck with it as much as I could (even though I always fell asleep in the horizontal mindfulness sessions ... and I snore), and by jingo, it made a difference. It helped me with the pain, and it also impacted my life in some surprising ways.

I made mindfulness part of my daily routine, a habit, and I started getting some telling feedback. First my brother Andrew said, 'What happened to you? You seem a lot nicer now.' (He would benefit from some mindfulness and tact classes.)

Then my team noticed. A colleague said, 'You are much more present when I talk with you. Did you know that when I came in for my one-on-one meetings, you were so distracted, you used to send out emails on your BlackBerry to the team, including me, when I was speaking.' I was busy multitasking, and it was obvious to my team that I wasn't fully listening.

Then clients told me that our conversations had become really meaningful. I was asking important questions and connecting with them – and they were grateful for it.

Mindfulness didn't just help me with my pain, or even with my stress. It changed the way I experience the world and my relationships with other people. Before I had been full of my own distracting thoughts and ideas, and all my stuff got in the way. But when I am fully present in the moment, without judgement, I form deeper connections with people. They have lasting impact because they're underpinned by authenticity and compassion.

These connections have helped me on so many different levels in my career. They're to thank for the career I have today.

A good kind of addiction

The more you use values-based decision-making, the more natural it will feel.

It may start out as a very conscious process, but eventually it becomes intuitive. Greta says it can even become addictive.

'Values can offer a stand-in for courage, particularly over time. Courage is when we are afraid but we go in there and we do it anyway. The addictive bit comes in because you start making what look like really courageous decisions, because they feel like they're in line with your values, and then you realise that actually it felt good – really good.'

Now, let's all go and get deeply rooted, so that we can continue to grow.

SIT SPOT

The sun and the moon shine so differently, but they each light up the sky.

What would it mean, in this moment, to give yourself permission to define success in a way that is authentic to you?

CHAPTER 3

Who are you when the On Air light switches off?

've amassed a rather eclectic troupe of all-singing, all-dancing nicknames over the years.

When I worked in London, the tax office incorrectly registered me under the name Lisa Le Pong. It was a pain to try and change, so some people from London call me Le Pong.

In Hong Kong, we needed to nominate a Chinese name for our work in China. I am super loud, so some funny person thought it would be cool for me to be called Jing Hua, which apparently translates as 'Quiet Flower'. So a number of people call me Quiet Flower.

My middle name starts with an S, so my name looks like this on paper: Lisa S. Leong. At college, my friend Alex Campbell made the jump from S. Leong to Sleong ... to Schlong ... and finally to Schlonga! It caught on to the point that some people didn't know my real name. Even my law firm colleagues called me Schlonga. To this day, old friends will walk up to me from a distance, shouting, 'Helloooo, Schlonga!'

My daughter calls me Mama, so for a time I blogged under the name Big Mama. My family sometimes call me 'Bony M' – I'm skinny, so when they hug me, my bones stick out and stab into them. I also have a rap alter ego, Lil Lisa. (Told you these nicknames were all-singing, all-dancing!)

When I was a radio presenter at SAFM, my on-air name was Lethal Lisa, after 'Lethal Leigh Matthews', the Hawthorn football player. It became quite the persona. I wasn't famous by any stretch of the imagination, but I was dipping a tiny part of my left pinky toe into that pool. I'd meet people who'd know more about me than I did about them, which was a bizarre and slightly uncomfortable feeling. But they knew the persona, not the person. They knew Lethal Lisa.

You might know that feeling. If you're a doctor, or engineer, or CEO, or manager, or whatever, you might be used to going into a room where people know your role and feel that they know you because of it. We can start to feel like we *are* that job. So much of our identity gets tied up in what we do for a living.

Steve Ahern, the former head of radio at the Australian Film Television and Radio School, once advised our cohort to think deeply about this question: 'Who do you want to be when the On Air light switches off?' He was referring to the bright red light in a studio which alerts people that you're broadcasting or recording.

In the media there are no guarantees, and one day, that light will switch off. So, you can't get too hung up on the persona – 'Lethal Lisa of SAFM'. You have to know who's behind the work persona and who you are beyond work.

That advice has stayed with me. In 2010, after nearly a decade of following my radio dreams, Lethal Lisa switched off the mic. I went back to law, working as a business development manager at my old law firm Freehills so my family could move back to Melbourne. But after a while, I began to feel like my work identity had become my whole identity. I'd lost touch with who I was outside of work. In 2016 I booked myself into a weekend health retreat in south-east Queensland with my friend Jenni. I needed a moment to reset. And something magical happened.

For the whole weekend, nobody asked me what I did for work. It wasn't something we were forbidden from talking about, but we were all burnt-out executive types who didn't want to think about work, let alone talk about it. So I was just ... Lisa. There was a moment when I was sitting with others, taking in the view of the lush emerald hinterland, the afternoon sun beaming down on us, the air clean and crisp. We were all laughing, massive deep belly laughs, mostly about the therapy things we could do at the retreat and how strange some of them were. (Equine therapy and sound baths were in the mix. And no, not together.) I felt unguarded and honest and joyous. And I thought, 'Oh, here I am. This is me. They don't care what I do, they don't know what my day job is. They like me just for being me.' It was there that I was reminded that I exist without my job title – that I am whole and complete without it. I loved that feeling. I wanted to be me again. Just Lisa.

We all have our own On Air light at work, even if it's not the literal flashing red light of a radio studio. Who are you when your On Air light switches off? It's an important question to ask and to keep on exploring.

Nonlinear careers

The way we work is rapidly changing. In this era of unprecedented global disruption, a 'job for life' is becoming increasingly rare. Gone are the days of a planned career structure, a progressive rise in income and security, and a shiny gold watch at retirement. (Though perhaps, as my dad's experience shows, this was never a certainty anyway.)

These days we're zigzagging around different roles and even different industries. The average Australian will stay in a job for about 3.4 years and have as many as seven career changes in their lifetime. Social researcher Mark McCrindle estimates that generation alpha, the demographic cohort born between 2010 and 2025, will have eighteen separate jobs in their lifetime across six separate careers.[1]

Nonlinear careers have shaken off their stigma and become the new normal. It means my LinkedIn profile looks very comfortable among other 'slashies' (people who put their multiple hats on their profile, separated by slashes – like 'blogger/fashion icon/podcaster').

The nonlinear career path isn't always logical and it isn't always predictable, but it all eventually comes together. The late Apple co-founder Steve Jobs put it well: 'You can't connect the dots looking forward; you can only connect them looking backward. So you have to trust that the dots will somehow connect in your future.'[2]

The trend away from linear careers has only been accelerated by COVID-19. The pandemic has been devastating for businesses and workers. The International Labour Organization says the equivalent of 255 million full-time jobs were lost in 2020 as a result of the pandemic,[3] and the long-term

economic impact could ripple for years. Some jobs that once felt entirely secure now feel very fragile, even to people who've effectively grown up in them. We can no longer future-proof our jobs and we can't plan ahead. We have to be fluid and adaptive. We need a different mindset. We need to broaden our horizons.

Where do we start? Thinking about what you want to do might seem like the obvious answer, but perhaps there is a better question to ask. Maybe it's less about *what* you want to do, and more about *who* you want to be. Who are you, and what can that tell you about what you should do next?

I know that's a really big question, but we have already started answering it by exploring our generational legacies and our values. We're going to build on that now, by unpacking our careers to this point.

Pattern interrupt

By exploring the highs and lows that have led us to this moment, and illuminating any turning points in our careers and identities, we can uncover more clues to guide us forward.

At my school it felt natural to become either a doctor or a lawyer, and I set my sights on the latter. The law eventually took me to London, where I was one of the early ecommerce (internet) lawyers. I was working for entrepreneurs during the internet bubble that rose up from the popularisation of the world wide web, and for a while it was so much fun.

One of my highlights was working on the rollout of digital interactive music television across Europe. The project was led by two Danish bankers. They

were super tall, super dashing and super Danish. It was rumoured that they partied with the Danish princess (not Mary – this is before her time). And there I was, their 5-foot-nothing Aussie-Asian super lawyer! I did feel cool by association, I admit.

But in 2000 came chaos. The bubble burst, the financiers lost their money, and it all became a lot harder for everyone. I saw tech clients lose their funding and their businesses. Because I worked in a huge law firm, I was able to be redeployed pretty easily and I started working on big mergers and acquisitions. Basically my job was to scour contracts to make sure that what someone was buying was what they thought they were buying. So I'd sit in this airless, windowless room filled with wall-to-wall documents, and go through each one. I'd take a folder, review the thick contract documents, then move on to the next folder. It was folders and folders and hours and hours of sitting there under fluorescent lights. Through that experience and the pause in the flow of exciting client work, I took time to take stock.

I realised that I was waiting for someone to tap me on the shoulder and say, 'Oi, Lisa! You're not meant to be a lawyer. Let me whisk you away, I know what you need to do.' But, of course, nobody does that. Instead, inertia was leading me ... nowhere. I decided I needed to proactively choose each day instead of just letting the next day 'happen'. No one was going to magically beam me into my perfect job. I had to tap myself on the shoulder.

I also realised that money isn't everything. (Money is, of course, *something*, as I discovered when I was sleeping on a mattress on the floor of a rental room while chasing my radio dreams, but it is far from the only thing that has value.) There was a part of me that wasn't feeling entirely fulfilled as a lawyer and I was aware I was pouring all of me into my law firm. I did the work I was meant to do – and more: client seminars, presentations, chairing internal meetings. But what if I took that 10 per cent of energy that went above and beyond the actual requirements of my job and put it somewhere else? I'd still be doing my job but moving some of my discretionary time away.

I decided to put some of my energy into something community-minded. A friend suggested I volunteer in a hospital. In London, the hospitals are so big that many of them have their own hospital radio. And there it was, in the middle of Charing Cross Hospital – a full-blown radio station! Big mics, big radio desk with a confusing amount of faders and lights and cables. It was very exciting. I'd never wanted to be a radio presenter before, though I was a dedicated radio listener.

I ended up training to be a DJ and started volunteering on the 'Monday Night Bingo' show. I would pull out bingo balls and sometimes get to do the calls on air. 'Legs 11!' When I had accumulated enough volunteer hours, I got into the presenter training program, then got my own hospital radio show. I created Thursday Night Therapy with Lisa Leong, and interviewed anyone I found interesting, which was (and still is) everyone I knew. I'd get my (mainly lawyer) friends who were part of comedy groups (Mick, Tim and Tim) or doing a marathon (Sophie) or playing viola (Deirdre) or writing a sell-out West End play (Mel) to come on. And my radio show became a hit. (I'm not sure if it was because I had a somewhat captive audience.)

I well and truly caught the radio bug. I decided there and then (without too much consideration) to leave the law and become a radio DJ.

Looking back, I realised the devastating news about my dad's stroke occurred around the time of my volunteering at hospital radio. I didn't consciously leave my identity as a lawyer as a consequence of that, but I wonder whether it subconsciously helped me give myself that tap on the shoulder.

Career cold case

If a storm of uncertainty suddenly looms over your career and you have no idea what you want to do next, you might be asked the question: 'Well, what are you passionate about?'

It is very common to then draw a blank. 'What *am* I passionate about? I have no idea.'

Perhaps a useful framing is to view your career as a cold case. You are a detective who needs to go back in time to find the teeny tiny clues that have remained latent until now.

I have often found my clues thanks to something I call a Life Flow Exercise. I first came up with this reflective tool in 2001, when I felt stuck in that airless, windowless room. Back then I called it a Happiness Graph. It was a completely amazing original idea that, like so many other completely amazing original ideas, turned out to be not that original at all.

It's actually a pretty well-known approach to tapping into what you love and value, and is most often called a Lifeline Exercise. Organisational psychologist Roger Schwarz has a great version of it in his book *The Skilled Facilitator Fieldbook*, and Christina Gerakiteys, the co-CEO of SingularityU Australia, also has a beautiful way of doing it.

My approach these days is a blend of my original Happiness Graph and a few different versions of the Lifeline Exercise.

Life Flow Exercise

In the spirit of treating every day as Lab Day, have a crack at a Life Flow Exercise yourself. Give yourself a bit of time to do this — at least half an hour is ideal. We refer back to this exercise several times throughout the book (it's a gift that really does keep on giving), so it's worth taking the time to do it before reading on.

Let's step through it.

1. Get a piece of paper; the bigger the better. A3 is great if you have it, or you can tape a few smaller pieces together (Monique used the back of a few old bills). I also make a cup of chai tea at this stage.
2. Down the left-hand side, draw a vertical line. When I first did this, I called it my happiness line, but it's actually your emotional highs and lows. Across the bottom, draw a horizontal line, representing time.
3. Along the time line, mark out your life in five-year increments, from when you were born up until the present year. Use longer or shorter increments depending on your age.
4. Plot the highs and lows of your life on your graph. Think about your life as a whole, not just your work life. It can be helpful to ask yourself these questions:

   ▸ What have been the significant milestones or turning points?
   ▸ What has been challenging or frustrating for you?
   ▸ What were your childhood passions? What did you love at school?

EMOTIONAL HIGHS/LOWS

TIME

You might capture your experiences of:

- work, education and volunteering
- relationships and family
- health and wellbeing
- life milestones like moving house or travelling
- creative pursuits, hobbies and passions.

You can reveal as much or as little as you want to. You might find that you do one version now and then come back and reveal a bit more down the track.

You'll end up with a visual representation of what we call the 'peaks' and 'troughs' of your life. There's no right or wrong way for your graph to look. Remember, life is a lab, and these are all data points that will help lead you to an answer.

5. For every peak and trough, make some bullet points about why this was a peak or a trough. What were the circumstances of each moment? How did it impact you?

6. Once you're done plotting your points, step back and take a big-picture look.

- Are there any themes that unite the peaks?
- Are there any patterns that run through all the troughs?
- What lessons emerge for you?
- Are there any dots that can be connected?

These questions can help you begin to pinpoint what you want (or do not want) in your career, and give you insight into what you're being called to do. Let's look to my Life Flow Exercise as an example.

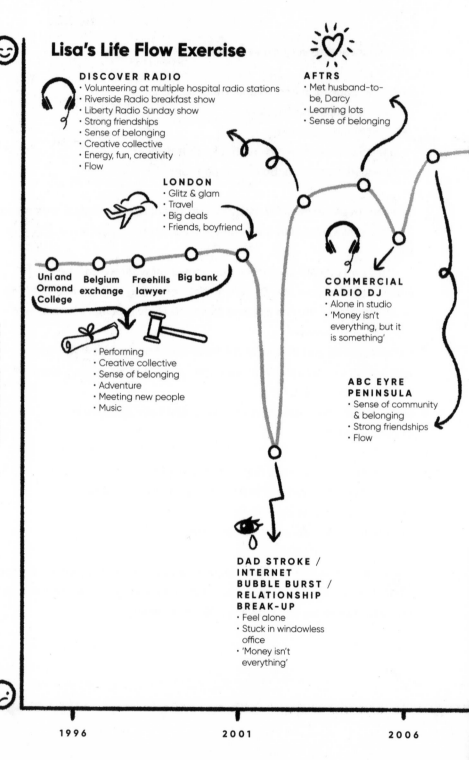

Lisa's Life Flow Exercise

DISCOVER RADIO
- Volunteering at multiple hospital radio stations
- Riverside Radio breakfast show
- Liberty Radio Sunday show
- Strong friendships
- Sense of belonging
- Creative collective
- Energy, fun, creativity
- Flow

AFTRS
- Met husband-to-be, Darcy
- Learning lots
- Sense of belonging

LONDON
- Glitz & glam
- Travel
- Big deals
- Friends, boyfriend

Uni and Ormond College **Belgium exchange** **Freehills lawyer** **Big bank**

- Performing
- Creative collective
- Sense of belonging
- Adventure
- Meeting new people
- Music

COMMERCIAL RADIO DJ
- Alone in studio
- 'Money isn't everything, but it is something'

ABC EYRE PENINSULA
- Sense of community & belonging
- Strong friendships
- Flow

DAD STROKE / INTERNET BUBBLE BURST / RELATIONSHIP BREAK-UP
- Feel alone
- Stuck in windowless office
- 'Money isn't everything'

HAPPINESS LEVEL

1996   2001   2006

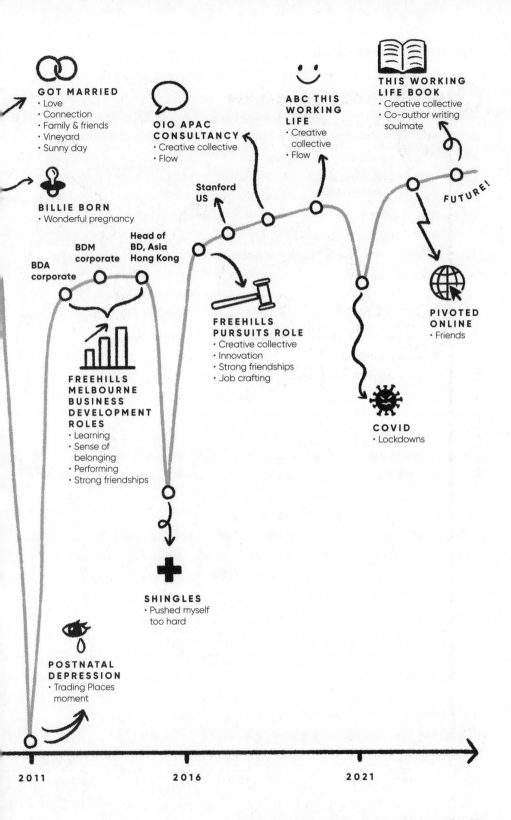

GOT MARRIED
· Love
· Connection
· Family & friends
· Vineyard
· Sunny day

BILLIE BORN
· Wonderful pregnancy

OIO APAC
CONSULTANCY
· Creative collective
· Flow

ABC THIS
WORKING
LIFE
· Creative
  collective
· Flow

THIS WORKING
LIFE BOOK
· Creative collective
· Co-author writing
  soulmate

Stanford
US

FUTURE!

BDA
corporate

BDM
corporate

Head of
BD, Asia
Hong Kong

PIVOTED
ONLINE
· Friends

FREEHILLS
PURSUITS ROLE
· Creative collective
· Innovation
· Strong friendships
· Job crafting

FREEHILLS
MELBOURNE
BUSINESS
DEVELOPMENT
ROLES
· Learning
· Sense of
  belonging
· Performing
· Strong friendships

COVID
· Lockdowns

SHINGLES
· Pushed myself
  too hard

POSTNATAL
DEPRESSION
· Trading Places
  moment

2011

2016

2021

My Life Flow learnings

Take a moment to look at my Life Flow Exercise. It's helped illuminate some very important lessons in my life.

I've got my time on secondment at a big bank as a peak experience at work. It was 1999 and I was the lead lawyer for the newly formed internet bank unit.

It was the heady days of the world wide web and the bank cleared out a whole floor for this new fandangled venture into the online realm. I loved the diverse mix of people. It felt like they'd plucked the top creatives from across the universe to set up digital banking. My manager at the bank was a senior lawyer, Jennifer, who saw my potential and encouraged me to dig deep and be my best work self.

I also had something of a revelation while I was working there: work value is not about hours clocked. It's about contribution and impact. I was used to putting in crazy long hours at my law firm and pretty much worked every weekend on big deals. When I first arrived on secondment, I sat at my desk and powered through my work. My new colleagues would come up to my desk at 5.30 pm and ask me why I was still around. 'I'm working,' I'd cry as they 'dragged' me to the pub. I loved the energy so much. The pub too.

At the lower end of my Life Flow Exercise, the dotcom bust that led to that airless room was a trough and it helped propel me in the direction of radio. These were the days of Lethal Lisa at SAFM. I worked super hard to get that 'capital city gig' – it's a big deal in radio – but my 'dream job' in commercial radio ended up being a surprising trough.

I did a late-night Australian music show and then weekend breakfast. You generally work six-day weeks in radio. The weekend shifts were usually six hours, so I would be on air from 6 am until midday. After about six months, I started getting sad after my shifts. Sometimes I cried. How could this be happening?

When I stepped back and looked at the themes of my Life Flow Exercise, it became clear. All of my peaks share some common elements that are missing from my troughs:

- ▸ collaborative connection with creative, loving people
- ▸ meeting new people and exploring their ideas
- ▸ joy and freedom.

Even though I thought radio was my dream job, I realised that I enjoyed certain aspects of radio, not 'all radio'. You see, during those weekend shifts the radio station was super quiet. I was pretty much alone in a dark, padded studio. Just like those airless, windowless offices in London. Even though it was a totally different industry, I had ended up in a similar place. D'oh!

It was never as simple as 'law bad, radio good'. The problem for me was never the industry, it was the job I was doing within it. I just didn't know it until I hit those troughs. Drawing out the themes of my Life Flow Exercise showed me that I had to find a job centred around connection. Around people.

With that realisation, my next radio move was to the ABC as the breakfast radio presenter for ABC Eyre Peninsula, based in Port Lincoln. This was a dream job and one of my peak career experiences. I would interview up to seven people each day, which played to my sense of curiosity and connection. I loved working closely with my wonderful ABC crew, including Emma Pedler, newsreader Tim Jeanes, and rural reporters Brooke Neindorf and Melanie Tait (an old friend from London). I also made strong friendships with others in the media such as Jodie Hamilton, Jess Wade and Billie Harrison from the local paper, the *Port Lincoln Times*. The Eyre Peninsula community was wonderful, super welcoming and supportive, and I found myself doing my dream MC gigs, such as hosting the famous annual Tuna Toss competition, calling the sheep shearing at local festivals like the Wudinna Show, and making keynote speeches to the senior citizens clubs and RSLs. My heartland!

The future is the past

I can see clear clues in my childhood that line the path to my present. I can link what I loved then with what I love now in a very tangible way.

Some of my happiest memories from school involved performing. In Grade 6 I was the Fox in the musical *Chanticleer*, enticing the poor ego-centred Rooster to fall into my terrible trap. Later that year I beamed proudly as I belted out a number as the 'Christmas Star' in the musical nativity play. I remember looking at my autograph book where one of the teachers had written: 'Lisa, you have a golden voice.' I felt chuffed.

In Year 12, our year level did some graduation performances for the rest of the school. We got a group together to lip-sync to Guns N' Roses. I was Axl Rose, the lead singer, rocking out to 'Welcome to the Jungle'. As the music started, the girls in the school hall screamed their heads off. They stamped their feet so loudly that it felt like the whole world was rumbling. I did my best Axl swagger onto the stage and the crowd went nuts. It was so much fun; everyone was in the moment, swaying together. It felt electric and connecting.

Out of school, my first job was at Safeway in the supermarket's liquor department. I was mostly happy just to do my set hours and then get back to college – armed with a slab of beer, of course. I never went out of my way to excel or take any extra responsibility. But I do remember being flooded with happiness when they let me 'broadcast' through their loudspeaker: 'Hey customers, slabs walking out the door for $18.99 today. Get in quick!' I loved it.

See how these memories now feel like clues, things I should pay attention to in my career cold case? These clues hint at building connection through love, joy and laughter (even through a Safeway loudspeaker). That's exactly what I have come to value in my career.

This is why we go back so far in our Life Flow Exercise – back to when we were children and less aware of the weight of societal expectations. That's why we've spent this time thinking about our parents and our upbringing. That's why we need to think about who we are, beyond our identity at work.

Because even if you have deep expertise in something that you've done for yonks, there might be a part of you that's longing to wake up from hibernation. And that can make all the difference.

SIT SPOT

Many plants go dormant in winter – still alive, but no longer growing. Leaves yellow and droop, or drop off completely. Flowers no longer bloom.

Come spring, they erupt in life, ready to grow again.

What forgotten parts of yourself might you be able to remember, in this moment? What parts of yourself have been waiting for the spring?

CHAPTER 4

The gift of struggle

I n the 1980s movie *Trading Places*, two complete strangers – a rich broker and a street hustler – have their lives 'swapped' as part of an elaborate bet by two callous millionaires.

It's hilarious to watch Dan Aykroyd and Eddie Murphy flailing about as they get a taste of how the other half lives (and while some of the gags are problematic, the movie's commentary on socio-economics, class structure and corporate greed is more relevant than ever).

I have also had a *Trading Places* moment. My life was swapped with that of a complete stranger. Really. The only thing was, the stranger was *me*. And it never came close to being funny.

One moment I was a radio presenter. The next I was in a dressing gown, standing in a line under fluoro lights, shuffling closer to the perspex glass window, picking up my meds in a little plastic cup. No life in my eyes. No way out. Each minute ticking away.

I was in an institution for women suffering from postpartum psychosis.

I'd arrived there in the wake of a scene that belonged on the silver screen: I'd whipped off most of my clothes and bolted down the street, shouting insensible nothings to no one in particular. As I was running, I was somehow out of my body, looking at myself and thinking, 'Oh dear, that person has completely lost it. They are going to lock her up!' That's what happened, too.

I'd started getting symptoms a couple of days after my daughter Billie was born. I wasn't sleeping – at all. My body was racked with panic. I was worried I wasn't caring for my daughter properly and all the preparation I'd done didn't seem to help. Then I started hallucinating.

I was terrified that people were trying to kill me. The doctor who prescribed my medication was definitely in on it. So too the pharmacist, with his mocking eyes and sinister side glances. Even, I realised with a shock, my husband Darcy. My body kept my mind on alert, lest I fall victim to their murderous plot. The sleeplessness continued, followed closely by panic attacks. More drugs were prescribed. Then came the sprint down the road and the hospitalisation.

I was released after a few months and we moved in with my parents for support. I was no longer having psychotic episodes, but instead I slid into a deep hole of depression. It was darker than I could have imagined. I couldn't get out of bed. Darcy would have to pick me up and take me to have a shower and brush my teeth. Medication wasn't working so we decided I needed to go to another in-patient program. I recall seeing an in-patient who had managed to get out of the hole. She was smiling and I looked at her with empty eyes. I couldn't imagine smiling again.

My superpower is finding the sunshine, but there I was, sobbing uncontrollably, wondering, 'Where is the fucking sunshine in this?'

After a period where I wasn't responding to the meds program, Darcy and I faced a big decision: should I try electroconvulsive therapy (ECT)? It's a pretty drastic measure (though not as bad as it's made out to be in the movies), but we were desperate.

I was wheeled into an operating theatre and put under general anaesthetic. I remember waking up and then heading into the kitchen. Usually I'd sit quietly, eyes down, but this time my old self marched in. I looked around the room and announced: 'I just did ECT. Amazing! Highly recommend!' Then I pivoted in a joyful skip and headed back to my room. It was literally as dramatic as that.

I wasn't able to leave the clinic until I completed the program, but in that moment I got my old life back.

Inside every struggle is a gift

My *Trading Places* moment began with a click of the fingers (and, I suspect, a combination of sleep deprivation and chemical imbalance). Luckily, I was swapped back. I was able to feel joy, connection and love once again. I don't take that for granted and I have reflected a lot over the years on what the experience taught me.

When I interviewed Bobby Herrera on *This Working Life*,[1] he gave me a great lens through which to look at struggle. Bobby is one of thirteen kids. His family emigrated from Mexico to the US in the 1960s, with little to their name. Today he's the CEO of HR staffing firm Populus Group, a $500 million organisation.

He has a simple philosophy: inside every struggle is a gift. He believes the hard times somehow shape or prepare us for what comes next, and we can mine them for learning gold. 'There's not one thing we've learned in our life that's worthwhile where struggle didn't precede the wisdom,' he says. 'Every struggle teaches us something. That's the gift.'

It's an incredibly powerful perspective to take in the face of things that can be quite painful. I don't think we can begin to see the gift until we're well clear of the struggle. When we're in struggle's thick grip, we're just trying to survive. I certainly couldn't have taken a step out of my deep hole to go, 'Don't worry, there's a valuable learning opportunity here.'

It might take many years and a lot of work and healing for the gift to take shape. But given time, it usually emerges, popping up in your life on a random afternoon. It did for me. The gift of my struggle is that I learned true empathy.

I now know that it doesn't take much for a *Trading Places* moment to happen. Our fortunes can turn on a dime and we can find ourselves suddenly walking in shoes that don't fit our feet. I try to remember this in the way I approach my work and come at all of my relationships from a place of empathy.

We have two choices when faced with chaotic and uncertain times: to turn away from people or turn towards them. My *Trading Places* moment taught me that the only option for me is to turn towards others.

Shaped by opposing forces

We are talking about struggle in a book that is (largely) about work because we are shaped by our struggles as much as we are by our successes.

Sometimes our struggles are directly linked to work: stress, burnout, redundancy, job loss (we will cover all this and more), and sometimes our struggles exist beyond the realm of work. In either case, they often tend to spill over the edges; they can't be neatly contained in one area of our lives. It is useful to acknowledge that we will all struggle and to bring some awareness to this.

Bobby's story resonated with many *This Working Life* listeners, including Sophie Moloney, the CEO of Sky TV New Zealand.

Sophie says it helped her to understand that the hard times she has encountered throughout her life, including a struggle with body image and an eating disorder (which started in her teenage years and continued into early adulthood), actually *meant something*. It wasn't all for nothing, a cruelty devoid of meaning that she just had to survive. It shaped her into the person she is today — and she is proud to be that person. She is resilient and strong and deeply empathetic. Without that struggle, she might not be the same person. She might not be as effective a leader. What a powerful realisation to have.

'Everyone has been through something,' she says. 'You never know what someone is dealing with or going through, and I am always trying to stay mindful of that because I recall what it's like to not be comfortable or content in your own skin.'

Sophie shows that while we can't change the past, we can choose our reaction in the here and now.

A new perspective

To say COVID has been a struggle for many of us is a huge understatement. But it has also helped us realise what's important to us, and what truly matters.

Software company Atlassian's Dominic Price had a hideous 2020. In February he was diagnosed with early-stage bowel cancer. A week later he had his colon removed. That same day, his sister, who had been fighting breast cancer for six years, found out that doctors were ceasing all treatment. His sister — his best friend — had a matter of months left to live. She lived in Manchester, on the other side of the world from Dominic's home in Sydney.

'Post-surgery I wasn't officially allowed to travel due to COVID restrictions, but I managed to get an exemption and I was on one of very few flights out to Manchester in April to look after my sister and her two boys,' Dominic recalls.

A few weeks later, she died in his arms. When Dominic flew home, he had to face fourteen days in mandatory quarantine. It was a low point in 'this weird-ass rollercoaster of life'.

It was here that he realised that nobody was going to come in and rescue him. Dominic chose to fight the downward spiral. 'Without faking stuff or having this false positivity, how do I find the spiral up?'

Left alone with his thoughts, he started thinking about where happiness comes from. How do we find happiness in a world full of so much struggle?

Dominic realised that his job travelling the world was glamorous and full of status, but it had come at a cost. Partly by design, he had kept commitment and relationships at arm's length with 'all these reasons that were actually excuses'.

'I saw that as like, "OK, I'm forty-two and single. Do I want to be fifty-two and single … because that's like being the creepy uncle who is a little bit weird and still goes out drinking and wears leather pants at night!"'

In that hotel quarantine room, he decided to open himself up to letting someone into his life.

'So sure as shit – I mean this is completely like what Hollywood serves up – the very first person I went on a date with the week after I got out of quarantine moved in three months ago. I found my soulmate and she's absolutely amazing.'

Dominic's struggle came with a chance to slow down and take stock of his life. But that wasn't the only gift.

'It's our sole purpose to unleash other people's potential. How can I use my story to give them permission to share their story, or to live their best life, or confront their own demons and challenges?'

Dominic decided to share his truth to give people permission to do the same. He delivered a powerful TEDx Talk[2] 'not just for my own selfish benefit, but to enable other people to handle their own challenges, constraints, nightmares'.

'Everyone's got a story, everyone's got some shit going on, and we don't see it. We see the mask, but we don't see the chaos behind the camera. I wanted to give people a chance to talk about that.'

Double down on being human

It is true that you never know what someone is grappling with behind closed doors (or off the Zoom screen). We tend to keep our struggles hidden away, especially from colleagues, perhaps because we don't want to seem unprofessional.

Monique's biggest struggle involved her dad. When he was sick, with chronic pain and depression, she took on a carer role, which wasn't easy to do in person as they lived two hours apart. She commuted back and forth a couple of times a week around her shifts, and spent a lot of time on the phone to him and the people in his support network. All the time, she was worried about her dad. It was all-consuming and it started impacting her work.

At the time Monique was working for ABC News Digital, sub-editing and publishing articles, and curating the 'bulletins' for the national news website. This job required her to be across what was happening in the news, not just on the day, but the broader context in which a story was unfolding. She had to know what was 'big news' versus what was a minor development; what was old news and what was new. When she started a shift at 4.30 am, she had to know what had happened the night before. When she started a shift at 5 pm, she had to know what had happened that day. It was part of the job, but Monique didn't have the space to do all of that. She was too tired.

That showed up in the way Monique dealt with her colleagues. Years later, during a boozy dinner, one person would reveal that they had initially been terrified of Monique. She was shocked as several others around the table admitted the same: she had seemed aloof, uninterested, intimidating and unapproachable.

Monique thinks part of it was that she was new to the role and she took it very seriously. (When people met her outside of work, they were suddenly like, 'Oh! You're actually pretty friendly.') But looking back now, she wonders how much of it was because she was quietly struggling with a heavy load. She didn't have much left to give to anyone else.

'It took a while but when I finally opened up, other people did too. They told me about their own mental health issues, or how a loved one was also struggling, or that they were grieving,' she says.

If you traded places with any of your colleagues, you'd probably be surprised at what they're dealing with beneath the surface, and vice versa.

How much easier would some work days be if we could just tell people what we're up against?

Monique's dad took his own life a bit over a year later. Her boss, Stuart Watt, travelled to the funeral. Her colleagues climbed down into her very dark hole and sat with her – among the devastation and regrets and 'what-ifs' and questions that will never be answered and words left unsaid – until she was ready to claw her way out. One even drove her to therapy, waited for an hour while she bared the shattered pieces of her heart, and then drove her home. That newsroom knows the pain of suicide too well; it lost two talented young journalists to depression in the decade Monique was there.

The gift of all this struggle, at least for Monique, is that she softened. She stopped hiding the hurt and shared it instead – and she wasn't alone.

'Stuart built an incredible culture where mental health is talked about fairly openly,' she says. 'You can be honest about needing a "mental health day". I could be open about having anxiety and struggling with grief. It's a place where if you need to reduce your workload or take time off to cope with other life stuff, you can just say that.'

That doesn't mean there is nobody struggling in silence. Our demons thrive in the dark, and the insidious nature of shame and stigma continues to haunt mental health issues. But Monique says, 'We have a powerful example of what it looks like to form connections around who you are, not just what you do – even when who you are is a bit messy and complicated.'

And really, we are all messy and complicated. It's part of being human.

REFLECTION

Unearth the gift in your struggle

Think back to a time in your life when you have struggled or faced a challenge. You might refer back to your Life Flow Exercise and look at the troughs.

To unearth the gift in your struggle, ask yourself:

- ▶ How did you respond to the struggle at the time?
- ▶ What did you learn from the situation?
- ▶ How do you apply those learnings in your life now?
- ▶ How did your experience shape the way you look at the world?

The gift of my struggle is that I learned the true meaning of empathy.

Sophie's experience shaped her into a humble and deeply human leader.

Dominic opened his life up to love.

Monique softened around the edges and became a warmer person.

What is the gift in your struggle?

Reshape your story

If you have faith that even in moments of struggle there has been value, you can go back into the narrative of your life in the role of an editor. You can't erase the struggle, but you can reshape the story you tell about it. You can know that the pain preceded wisdom; that, in some way, it shaped or prepared you for what was to come.

I want my story to make me feel more joyful and loving, not sad and bitter and twisted. I've learned more from the low points than I have from the peaks. So I choose to look for the lessons.

Sometimes there's a lot of emotion to trudge through before the lessons become apparent, a lot of deep work to be done. Sometimes you have to trade places with a stranger, against your will, and fight your way back to yourself.

But there are lessons there, waiting on the other side. In the struggle, there is a gift.

SIT SPOT

Australia is a land that knows the ferocity of bushfires, and many native plants have evolved to survive them. Banksias need the heat and smoke of a fire to germinate. Eucalypts can regrow from burnt trunks. Even the most blackened of landscapes eventually give way to shoots of green.

What would it mean, in this moment, to trust that you, too, have evolved to survive fire?

CHAPTER 5

Harness your superpowers

When you received a report card at school, did your attention (or perhaps your parents' attention) turn straight to your lowest marks? When you get feedback at work, do you fixate on the one thing your colleague or manager says you could do better, rather than the handful of things they say you're a superstar at? If I asked you to think about something you'd like to improve, would you come back with an answer involving something you're not too crash hot at?

Our conditioning leads us to focus on our weaknesses, and we tend to see weaknesses as more changeable than strengths,[1] so we view them as the greatest opportunity for development. But research shows that playing to our strengths has much more impact than focusing on fixing perceived weaknesses.[2] The world's best leaders aren't so because they display a 'lack of weaknesses' – instead, they display 'profound strengths'.

So perhaps we should forget about improving the things we're not so good at (yay!) and focus instead on strengthening our strengths (double yay!).

When we magnify our strengths, they can become superpowers.

First, know your strengths

You need to know your strengths before you can grow them. This can
be trickier than it sounds. Our strengths aren't always as obvious as our
weaknesses because we're simply not used to paying as much attention
to them. But focusing on and amplifying your strengths has been linked
to improved mental and physical health, self-acceptance, resilience and
progression towards your goals.[3]

In a moment we'll step through an approach to drawing out your
strengths, but first, let's have a look at some examples. Monique and I
asked a few of our friends about their strengths and they came back with
the following answers:

- a positive, can-do attitude
- being a collaborative leader who empowers their team
- bringing a sense of lightness and levity
- serving as a 'bridge' between different teams
- being a great coach
- the ability to quickly understand a problem and focus on a solution,
  rather than attributing blame
- being approachable, even on a bad day
- having grit and tenacity
- the ability to read people's emotions and adjust communication style
  accordingly
- calming things down so everyone can reach an agreement
- showing up with intentional presence
- speaking and writing eloquently
- multitasking and being organised
- being gently persuasive
- forgiveness – not holding a grudge
- putting things in a nutshell
- being able to work with many different types of people and teams
- giving honest and constructive feedback, regardless of someone's level
  of seniority.

Do you see yourself mirrored in any of those examples? Did you read any
point and think, 'Oh, I think I do that well too'? Or perhaps a different strength
emerged in your mind. Keep it there as you read on.

It is also worth noting that your strengths aren't something you're born with; they're something you can actively grow. My friend Deirdre Dowling, a professional viola player, has a beautiful way of describing her strengths: she calls them 'developed passions'.

I love this way of thinking about our strengths: as things we have put time and energy and effort into cultivating.

Let's take Deirdre's classical music career as an example. She wasn't a child prodigy; she didn't wake up at five years old and just *play*. 'I had many things that I loved as a kid. I loved nature. I loved riding horses. I loved hanging out with my friends. I also loved playing music. It was just one of the things that was there. Yes, I had a proclivity for it. But it was a developed passion. I had to work really hard over many years,' she says.

Before we dive into a reflection, there's one more thing to say about strengths: they're not about what you're good at versus what you're bad at. You can be really good at something and at the same time be completely bored by it, or even hate doing it. That is still a kind of strength, but it's not the kind that we want to be our superpower.

In Marcus Buckingham's book *Go Put Your Strengths to Work*, he suggests figuring out what energises you rather than turning to the dichotomy of good and bad. Something is a strength if:

- it makes you feel successful
- you're drawn to it, even if you don't know why
- it fully engages you; when doing it, you often find yourself in a flow state
- after doing the activity, you feel energised, fulfilled and powerful.

It's no fun flogging your weaknesses, but it's just as awful to get stuck doing something *only* because you're good at it. Your strengths – and ultimately your superpowers – should align with what lights you up inside.

Think about the strength you've identified in your mind. Does it make you feel strong, authentic and engaged?

What are your strengths?

Now that you have a few examples under your belt, work on drawing out more of your own strengths. These three simple steps will help you find and focus on them.

TAKE A STRENGTHS TEST

A good starting point is the VIA Survey of Character Strengths,[4] a free online self-assessment tool that I've found really helpful. It only takes about ten minutes to complete, so why not have a crack at it now? I like this one because it focuses on who you are as a whole person, rather than just on who you are at work.

There are twenty-four character strengths listed, which we all possess to varying degrees. The strengths fall under six broad virtue categories:

WISDOM / COURAGE / HUMANITY / JUSTICE / TEMPERANCE / TRANSCENDENCE

Creativity	Perspective	Judgement	Curiosity
Honesty	Bravery	Fairness	Humour
Zest	Perseverance	Teamwork	Love
Kindness	Leadership	Social intelligence	Love of learning
Forgiveness	Hope	Prudence	Appreciation of beauty & excellence
Humility	Spirituality	Self-regulation	Gratitude

When I did the survey recently, my biggest strengths were love (relationships with others), humour and creativity. Monique's came back as love, gratitude and perspective.

Take a moment to do the test and reflect on your results. Which of your strengths make you feel energised, or excited? They're strengths worth honing. How might you do this in a work context?

LOOK BACK IN TIME

Next take a moment to think about your proudest achievements in life and the skills you use in your current career. It might help to look back at your Life Flow Exercise.

Ask yourself these questions:

▶ What skills did you use to get to where you are today?
▶ How have you overcome challenges in life?
▶ What do people come to you for because they know you're great at it?

Think about these questions in a lateral way. If people are constantly talking your ear off, you might be a good listener. If people consistently come to you for advice, you might be a good problem-solver.

CROWDSOURCE IT WITH THE THREE WORD EXERCISE

For the last step, we go a little bit rogue in our reflection, and get other people in on the act. This is because the people you're surrounded by often see your strengths very clearly and through a different lens than you do.

Dorie Clark, a consultant and the author of *Reinventing You*, suggests using the Three Word Exercise as a way to figure out your personal brand (aka your reputation).[5] That aligns beautifully for us here, because it's built on your strengths.

So what does this involve? It's simple. Reach out to your family, friends and colleagues with the question: 'If you had to describe me in three words, what would they be?'

Odds are, people aren't going to tell you anything shocking, but you will learn what people think is most distinctive about you, and that can be very powerful.

'We might know all these things about ourselves. But we have no idea what other people think is important or special or meaningful about us, and when you figure that out, it begins to give you a trail of breadcrumbs that you can follow so that you can understand what it is that you do differently or better than other people,' Dorie explains. When I did this, I got responses like: curious, intuitive, creative, happy, hopeful. Yeah!

The exercise may also identify things that you wouldn't have thought of, or reveal patterns in the responses. When Monique did this, some words were repeated many times over: generous, welcoming, creative, authentic. The whole exercise felt like a warm hug and it helped her see herself as others do. At the end of it, she felt exactly like one friend had described her: 'a bad-ass'.

From strengths to superpowers

After that reflection exercise, you should have a much better idea of your strengths. Now, let your superpowers loose!

Your superpowers most likely stem from the strengths that resonate with you, but superpowers are more than strengths. Superpowers are about what *you* bring to your strengths.

While strengths usually revolve around a particular skill or trait, your superpowers are about *how* you utilise those strengths, and *how* all your strengths combine. Superpowers take in the broader context: how you think, feel and behave. This means your superpowers are unique to you. Other people may share the same strengths but they don't utilise them quite like you do, because there is only one you.

One of my biggest strengths is my curiosity – learning new ideas and insights excites me – but my superpower is that I am most curious about the human being behind the idea. I very rarely meet someone who I don't want to learn more about. I can see something in everyone to be curious about. Even if they can't see that spark in themselves, I can help them tap into it through my curiosity.

When I met former bank boss Andrew Thorburn, he used the beautiful phrase 'finding the sunshine'. And that's how I see it: my superpower is finding the sunshine in others, and in work.

Connection is another strength of mine, and my resulting superpower is making connections between seemingly disparate concepts, and people.

Superpowers at work

When you work from your superpowers, you're more engaged and energised – and more effective as a result. You bring a way of thinking that enhances everything you touch. To draw out your superpowers, think about each of your strengths and the context around *how* you utilise them.

That *thing* you bring to your role that isn't found in a manual or the job description? That's probably a superpower! For example, I ask different types of questions because of my unique curiosity.

To think about your superpowers in the context of your career and what you bring to your role or your team, ask yourself:

- ▶ What makes your approach unique?
- ▶ How do your strengths work together, or help each other?
- ▶ What would be missing from your workplace if you left?
- ▶ What do people recognise you for?

New York consulting firm SYPartners looked at the archetypes of great leaders and came up with a list of different superpowers.[6] They range from empathy to systems thinking (understanding all of the pieces of a process) to creative thinking, grit and decisiveness.

All superpowers are valuable at work. When we are aware of each other's unique qualities, it enables a true diversity of thought and creates a collaborative environment where people and teams flourish.

To play to your superpowers at work, think about the following questions:

- ▶ Can you be included on any teams or projects that need your superpowers?
- ▶ Can you do any training or learning to develop them?
- ▶ Can you collaborate with people who will stretch and challenge you?
- ▶ Can you teach your skills to someone else, honing your knowledge at the same time?

Monique gives us a good example of how your superpowers can be built over time. One of her strengths is writing; she's an incredible weaver of words. Her superpower is being able to take a huge volume of complex information, find the threads that connect all the different parts, then distil it down and patch it together in a way that makes sense – 'making words fit good', she jokes.

I saw this superpower in her when we worked on digital content together at Radio National, and you can see its progression in her Life Flow Exercise.

Monique's Life Flow Exercise

HAPPINESS LEVEL

ABC JOB
- Grateful
- Stretch and growth
- Felt skilled
- Great mentors

FINISHED HIGH SCHOOL
- Sweet relief
- Hard work was rewarded (validated work ethic)
- Sense of accomplishment

UNI
- Learning new things
- Still on fringes but started to find 'my people'
- Academic achievement

HIGH SCHOOL
- Felt alone like an outsider
- Didn't fit in
- Discovered a love of language, taking solace in English

HSC
- Stressful but enjoyed studying and writing practice essays

PARENTS SEPARATED
- Felt deep empathy for both
- Confusing time

SUBWAY
- Store manager!
- Leadership position
- Empowering
- But hated hospo!

1996   2001   2006

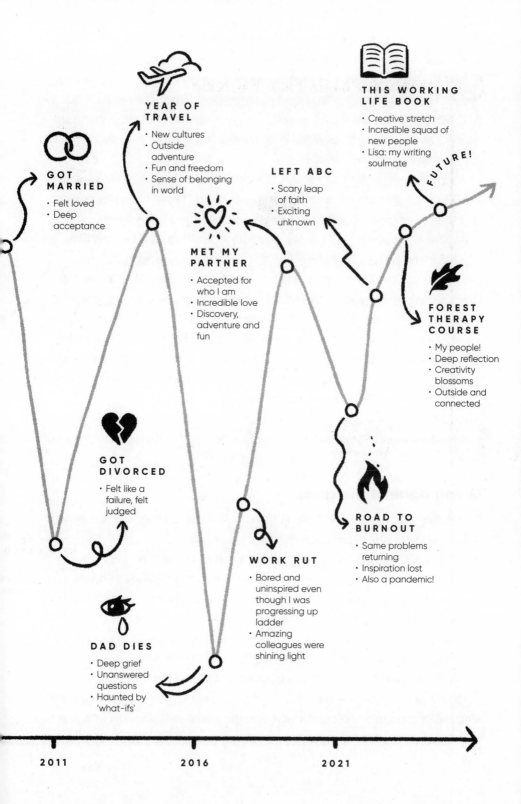

GOT MARRIED
- Felt loved
- Deep acceptance

YEAR OF TRAVEL
- New cultures
- Outside adventure
- Fun and freedom
- Sense of belonging in world

THIS WORKING LIFE BOOK
- Creative stretch
- Incredible squad of new people
- Lisa: my writing soulmate

LEFT ABC
- Scary leap of faith
- Exciting unknown

FUTURE!

MET MY PARTNER
- Accepted for who I am
- Incredible love
- Discovery, adventure and fun

FOREST THERAPY COURSE
- My people!
- Deep reflection
- Creativity blossoms
- Outside and connected

GOT DIVORCED
- Felt like a failure, felt judged

WORK RUT
- Bored and uninspired even though I was progressing up ladder
- Amazing colleagues were shining light

ROAD TO BURNOUT
- Same problems returning
- Inspiration lost
- Also a pandemic!

DAD DIES
- Deep grief
- Unanswered questions
- Haunted by 'what-ifs'

2011   2016   2021

Writing and language are common elements in many of her peaks. In school, she loved debating, writing poetry and short stories, and English classes. This helped to shape her career – what she studied for her HSC, the electives she chose at uni and the path she sought out after graduation. The peaks in her ABC career revolve around those times she was able to write more than she did on a typical day, such as working on special projects or being seconded to roles involving more wordsmithing.

Writing makes her feel successful. She's drawn to it. She often finds herself in a flow state. And after writing, she feels energised, fulfilled and powerful. It's an interest that developed into a strength and became a superpower.

Another superpower you can see developing in Monique's Life Flow Exercise is her leadership style. Because she's often felt like an outsider in life, she values places where she feels a sense of genuine inclusion – look at her Life Flow Exercise and how often themes of acceptance and belonging pop up.

Monique's strength is connection, but her life experience means she utilises it in a way that transforms it into a superpower. She makes people feel heard and valued, and as a result they do their best work. It's a superpower that really shines during times of change management. She can win hearts and minds in a tender way that's all about bringing people in.

Can you see those superpowers reflected in Monique's Life Flow Exercise?

If you look back at your own Life Flow Exercise, what superpowers emerge?

Going against the grain

Sometimes your superpowers aren't obvious. Sometimes they rise up strong from something you've long been told is a weakness.

Megumi Miki is a leadership consultant, a card-carrying introvert, the quietest member of her Japanese family and the author of *Quietly Powerful*. Megumi started the Quietly Powerful movement to bring attention to a skill set that is often overlooked and undervalued. She says that the vast majority of us still think a good leader is someone who embodies an alpha hero style – a confident-looking person who seemingly has all the answers, paints a vivid vision and showers inspiring words upon us. But it's not the only way.

Quieter leaders can be great listeners and coaches, and skilful influencers. Megumi says people feel comfortable sharing ideas and concerns with them because they create a space that empowers people to step up. They have the ability to take diverse ideas and people's feelings into account and think through different parts of complex decisions. Their humble and reflective nature is their secret weapon – especially in uncertain times.

How you think can also be a superpower. Author and researcher Clem Bastow was diagnosed as autistic when she was thirty-six, and says she has come to see her autism as the key to some of her successes and strengths; not the icing on the cake, but the whole cake itself. Her laser-sharp focus, her wit, and the way she sees the world – literally in a different way to other people – are her superpowers. 'The particular way I have of thinking is quite creative and it is very much about finding these seemingly disparate links between things,' she says.

I read Clem's brilliant memoir *Late Bloomer* and had to ask about her Vin Diesel story (yes, that Vin Diesel!), because it's such a great example of this superpower in action.

Clem was working as an entertainment writer in LA and she went along to the press junket for 2013 sci-fi film *Riddick*. Several reporters were sitting around a table, with about fifteen minutes between them to ask questions, so it was 'on for young and old'. Often the actors radiate boredom; they're asked the same dull questions over and over again ('What was it like working with this director?' and 'How great is the cast?'). But Clem had a secret weapon. She knew Vin Diesel was a fan of Dungeons and Dragons – 'he's been playing since he was twelve' – and so was she.

Aha! A chance to genuinely connect on common ground. And it worked. His eyes widened with excitement and they ventured deep into nerd territory together. 'We had this really beautiful moment of connection,' Clem says. She now recognises her approach to interviewing as a 'classic autistic thing' – find someone's special interest and ride that wave.

This story also reveals another superpower: Clem's deep empathy. 'I was always thinking, "What would I most like to talk about if somebody interviewed me?"' she says. 'I always felt like it was a bit of a public service. I wanted to make their day better. I wanted to talk about something that I felt they would find entertaining.'

Megumi and Clem show that superpowers don't have to fit with the typical idea of 'strength'. Our superpowers are as diverse as we are and the world is a better place for it.

Soundtrack

Remember that soundtrack I mentioned? Well, it is time for our first musical moment. Monique and I talked with Little Green about superpowers and she came up with this incredible song. Her superpowers are absolutely shining! (Scan the QR code to listen, or search for the song name on Spotify.)

OAK TREE

Turning inward to find my roots
Facing forward to the woods
Turning to the old oak trees
Shadow on my baby leaves

Everyone is taller than me
And stronger than me oh I cry
Everyone has prettier leaves
I hide away as they shine

But nobody can see what I see
On the floor of the forest each night
Might not be as tall as my friends
But I know I'm unique and I'll find

My superpower

Made mistakes as I grew up
All the oak trees had enough
Took my sunlight made me starve
I grew stronger in the dark

Everyone is taller than me
And stronger than me oh I cry
Everyone has prettier leaves
I hide away as they shine

But nobody can see what I see
On the floor of the forest each night
Might not be as tall as my friends
But I know I'm unique and I'll find

My superpower

Turning inward I found my roots
I'm an oak tree in the woods
Found my place between the sky
And the earth that needs me to thrive

Everyone is taller than me
But now I know that it's alright
Everyone has prettier leaves
But mine are made up of my life

And nobody can see what I see
On the floor of the forest each night
Might not be as tall as my friends
But I know I'm unique and my mind

Is my superpower

With our superpowers combined

So, let's shift our focus from the things we're not so good at to the things we are, and to the things that energise us and make us feel strong.

Our strengths can become superpowers.

When all of your superpowers combine, they form a package so distinctive that you exist in a Category of One.

No idea what I mean by that? Read on ...

SIT SPOT

The mantis shrimp packs a punch so powerful that it briefly heats the surrounding water to the temperature of the Sun's surface.

Bees can sense the electric field of a flower and use it to find pollen. The wood frog handles intense cold by freezing its own blood.

Dung beetles can pull more than 1000 times their body weight; lyrebirds can imitate any sound they hear; reindeer can see UV light.

What would it mean, in this moment, to trust that every creature on earth has superpowers – including you?

CHAPTER 6

Category of One

Nobody else is coming at this thing we call life from the exact same place as you, or in the exact same way. There is no one else with your family, your history, your experiences, your superpowers, your body, your brain, your heart.

You are unique.

Category of One is a business term, which author Joe Calloway explains well: 'Don't strive to be a leader in your category. Create a different category and be the only one in it.' It is often used in relation to companies like Google, Amazon and Apple. They have effectively created a league of their own and they constantly nurture it.

As a thought experiment, what would it be like to apply this concept to your life? How would you live, and work, if you considered yourself to be a Category of One?

An infinite game

Embracing this concept requires a monumental shift away from the way most of us have been conditioned to think. It requires us to shake up our mindset about the role of competition in our working lives. It requires us to play a different game.

Religious scholar James P. Carse describes two different games we play in life: finite and infinite.

Finite games are played for the purpose of winning. The players are known, the rules of engagement are fixed and the end point is clear. Think chess, football or a TV game show.

Infinite games are played for the sole purpose of perpetuating the play. The players might come and go, the boundaries can shift, and there is no defined end point. In this type of game there are no winners or losers; there is only ahead and behind. Life itself is perhaps the best example here. There's no such thing as being 'the best' at life or beating anyone else at living. It's an infinite game, played with the purpose of keeping on playing. Your friendships and relationships are infinite games – as is your work.

The problem, as motivational speaker Simon Sinek argues in his book *The Infinite Game*, is that not everyone recognises which game they're in. So while work is an infinite game, many people and businesses are playing it with a finite mindset. They're playing to win, to be the best, to beat the competition.

This finite game mindset often begins in childhood and carries into our adult lives. It means many workplaces, be it intentional or not, create an environment where employees compete against each other for jobs, bonuses, promotions, status and recognition. It can lead to people hoarding information and ideas, micromanagement, and short-term thinking.

It's a zero-sum game.

Some workplaces can be entirely set up to pit employees against one another. The *New York Times*, after examining workplace policies across corporations, banks, law firms and tech companies, called brutal competition the defining feature of the upper-echelon workplace.[1]

Stack ranking, for example, has been ubiquitous at large companies for years. It forces managers to rank all of their employees on a bell curve. Only a small percentage of employees, say 10 per cent, can be designated as top performers. A set number must be labelled as low performers and are often performance-managed or pushed out, giving the system the nickname 'rank and yank'.

In this type of dog-eat-dog environment, employees don't have an incentive to share ideas or collaborate. At its most extreme, they may sabotage others to get ahead.

Finite games also exist within the infinite one. In a work context, this might be meeting your KPIs, giving a presentation or making a successful pitch. The trick is realising that these are simply parts of the infinite game.

You can't ever 'win' at work. What does that even mean? Even if you get that promotion or score that bonus … the game continues. There's no real end point, is there? The legacy of unnecessary competition has pushed many of us into playing the wrong game.

We need to adjust our mindset for the game we are actually in.

Play your own game

If we are each a Category of One playing in an infinite game, then we're not actually in competition with anyone else in the world. We can leave behind the idea that our value is measured by how well we outperform others. We don't have to keep trying to do better than her, or striving to achieve more than him. We don't need to compare.

This is true in work and in life. It seems folly to compare someone else's projected 'exterior' to our whole, lived 'interior'. Our interior world contains our history, experiences, machinations, mumblings, grumblings, ruminations, mistakes, imperfections — and wonder, awe, hope, ideas, wishes, dreams. We can't really know what another person's life is like, to be in their body, with their experience.

I try not to hold myself up to that kind of comparison. I can't remember ever being seriously jealous of anyone else (though my family say I have the world's worst memory, so this could be totally untrue). I've always been different so it has always seemed like a dumb idea to even try to compare myself. If you won't ever be the norm (whatever that is), then you might as well go for it in terms of being different.

This mindset can help us even in moments where opportunity is scant. Say you're going for a marketing job and you've been shortlisted along with two other people. If all three people are a Category of One, that doesn't mean three positions will magically appear and everyone goes home happy. But you'll stand more of a chance if you go in with open arms and curiosity, and bring your unique ideas and experiences.

It's not that you're suddenly elevated above everyone and everything. You can't waltz into the office tomorrow and announce, 'Darling, don't you know who I am? I'm a Category of One. I've transcended the competition!' This isn't about ego.

You still need to try. You still need to operate in the real world. But perhaps you can change how you flow through it, and I believe if you can do this, you will see that there is more abundance than you might realise.

When you are constantly focused on competition, life starts to resemble a finite pie. When one person takes a big piece, there's less for everyone else. It means you worry about everyone, you stop helping others, you feel jealous when they succeed. You might compete for resources even when you don't have to. You might stay put in a job for longer than you want to, because you're afraid there aren't enough opportunities to go around. You hold yourself back. You become paralysed.

Life is actually an infinite pie: someone else taking a large piece doesn't mean there is less for you. There is abundance. If you believe this, you can cultivate a deep sense of personal worth and security. There is enough to go around.

REFLECTION

Cultivate abundance through gratitude

Practising gratitude is a widely recognised way to shift towards an abundance mindset. When you focus on what you have, instead of what you don't have, you naturally pull yourself out of the scarcity mindset. Energy flows where attention goes. I first heard this from Dan Siegel, a professor of psychiatry at UCLA, and it's so true.

For the next week (and beyond, if you like), keep a gratitude journal. At the beginning or end of each day, write down three things you are genuinely grateful for. If you get stuck, remember the simple things that are easy to overlook: the first sip of your morning coffee, a hot shower, the crisp air on a daily walk, fresh basil picked from the garden, the affection of a pet or loved one.

At the end of the week, take a moment to reflect. Where in your life are you abundant?

I started a gratitude journal in 2016 while on a family holiday to Queensland. Our daughter Billie developed a chest infection during the trip, which then turned into pneumonia. She was coughing quite violently, and it didn't help that we were staying in a hotel room that stank of cheap bleach. I took a short walk outside just to get out of the room and ended up in a little knick-knack shop, where I handed over the money for a gratitude diary.

Each page had the line: 'Today, I am grateful for ...' So each day, I paid attention to the answers.

Sunday 10 Jan: I am happy + grateful for my lovely home where I can make nourishing food, sleep restfully at night on my comfy bed + pillow. I have a beautiful kitchen and meditation corner. And it doesn't smell like cheap bleach. I am happy and grateful that Billie's health is getting better and better.

I have continued to develop my gratitude practice to illuminate the abundance in my life. During tough times, it helps me to reorientate myself towards the essence and away from trivialities and irritants — the negative cognitive bias that our brains are wired for. On a shitty day, you can read through your journal and remember that it isn't always bad.

One of a kind

The grand experiment is to use each day to explore the boundaries of yourself through work. How would you run this grand experiment differently as a Category of One?

Remind yourself of everything you have learned so far. Remind yourself of who you truly are. Your uniqueness is what makes you valuable.

Even if you don't believe it yet, let yourself entertain the idea that there might be something to this Category of One thought experiment. Allow yourself to focus on where you are going, not who you are trying to beat.

Play an infinite game in a league of your own.

SIT SPOT

A flower doesn't compare itself to a bird. It just blooms.
A bird doesn't compare itself to a flower. It just flies.
What would it be like, in this moment, to accept that
you do not need to compete?

CHAPTER 7

Fail like a scientist: Every day is Lab Day

Most of us spend our whole lives avoiding failure. We pick up the pace if we sense it lurking behind us, cross to the other side of the road to avoid eye contact, or change direction entirely rather than risk crossing its path — even if it means we never get to the place we want to go.

Failure by its very definition is a lack of success, even the opposite of it. It's associated with words like inadequate, flawed, collapsed, defeated. A screw-up. A let-down. It hits deeper than a mere mistake or a simple slip-up. Failure is personal. It can hold us back and stop us from taking chances with our careers, even though, so often, the risk of doing nothing is ultimately greater than the risk of doing something.

I'm not saying we should all rush out and actively start failing at things. But as we start to transition from our reflective internal state and move our attention outward, it is worth bringing awareness to our mindset towards change and failure. Can we get a little more comfortable with the idea, so that it's not so fear inducing, so that it doesn't hold us back?

Scientists have a useful way of looking at failure. In a lab, a failed experiment isn't a failure at all. It's an opportunity to learn something, to develop further – another data point that helps lead you to the right answer. It is inevitable, and it has empirical value. A scientist wants to determine the outer boundaries of their thinking and you need a 'fail' to find that out. And if the experiment fails, the *experiment* fails. *You* don't fail. *You* are not a failure.

As you know, I studied organic chemistry at uni and it's fairly safe to say I wasn't the best scientist in a practical sense (remember that evacuated lab?). But I did learn the mindset of a scientist, which has helped me navigate my career – and my life. Now I try to treat every day as Lab Day. Every day I wonder: what will I learn today in terms of my beliefs, my choices, my work life? How can I develop it just a little bit more? What are the outer boundaries?

Along with throwing on a metaphorical white coat, there are a few other approaches that have helped me reframe failure throughout my career and shaped the way I look at my work:

- ▸ growth mindset
- ▸ fast fail
- ▸ applied improv.

These aren't silver bullets that will instantly transform your relationship with failure. Embracing failure is something that takes (a lot of) time and (a lot of) practice. But there's a philosophy around this: things are neither good nor bad, but thinking makes it so. These mindsets can help you bring more awareness to how you think about failure, and what could happen if you changed that thinking – even just a little.

They can also help you stop the expert's mindset from seeping into places where it doesn't belong.

The expert's mindset

Even if you've never heard of the expert's mindset, I'll hazard a guess that you've experienced it in one form or another.

Often when you're a professional with expertise in any area, you're asked to reflect on something and either make it better or identify all the things that are wrong with it. You have a critical eye. So when I listen to a podcast, for example, I can't help but listen in a way that asks, 'How might this be better?' My husband Darcy is a film director, so when we watch movies, he's mentally critiquing the script or the soundtrack or the casting. Monique can't read the news without rewriting the paragraphs and editing the layout in her head.

The expert's mindset is questioning, sceptical, judgemental. It can sometimes get you into trouble in terms of creativity (you're more rigid because you're used to being in the know) and the relationships you have with other people. The expert's mindset can jump the barriers and wind up running amok in your personal world.

What can end up happening is that you create a standard and then review parts of your life against it. So you might look at your teammates: here's the standard and here's how you are lacking. You might look at your family: here's the standard and here's how you are lacking. Everything is judgement and critique. And that eye turns inward too – 'This is why my job is not good', 'This is why I'm not successful', 'This is why I'm not up to the standard that I want to be'. Nothing ever measures up to the standard. It's quite depressing.

This is why we need to bring more awareness to our mindset and the way we see ourselves, our work and the world. This is where growth mindset, fast fail and applied improv all fit in.

So, let's get stuck in.

Growth mindset

The term 'growth mindset' comes from the groundbreaking work of Stanford psychologist Carol Dweck. She identified that we all hold ideas about our character, intelligence and creative ability, and that these ideas fall into two different mindsets: fixed and growth. These mindsets play a big role in shaping our relationship with success and failure, and how we form ideas about what is possible. They can either propel us forward or prevent us from reaching our potential.

Fixed and growth mindsets are two sides of the same coin; we are all a mixture of each, and that mixture continually evolves over our lives. It's constantly in flux.

Someone with a fixed mindset sees their talents as more or less set in stone – they're either good at something or they're not. They're born with it. Any success is an affirmation of their inherent intelligence and avoiding failure becomes a way of maintaining that sense of being smart and skilled.

Someone with a growth mindset, on the other hand, believes they can learn pretty much anything (within reason — I'll never be an Olympic high jumper, no matter how much I try). They see their talents as something that can be developed with time and effort. Challenges are stepping stones to mastery and failure is a springboard for growth (even if it's painful).

People with growth mindsets tend to be more persistent. They'll keep going even when it's hard, even if they really suck at first. Someone with a fixed mindset will give up more easily because they believe their efforts will ultimately be fruitless.

Those with a growth mindset cultivate a passion for learning; as a result they reach ever-higher levels of achievement. As Carol writes in her book *Mindset*, 'a belief that your qualities can be cultivated leads to a host of different thoughts and actions, taking you down an entirely different road'.[1] Why hide shortcomings when you could be overcoming them? Why fall back on the tried and tested when you can reach for things that will challenge you?

Many of us have a more fixed mindset than we probably realise.

Monique had to grapple with her fixed mindset when she retrained as a forest bathing guide. She was used to being an expert and having the answers and knowing what to do. Being in a space of learning again felt confronting and uneasy. When she wasn't instantly good at it, her first impulse was to exit stage left and never look back.

Maybe you can think of a time you were enjoying doing something — a puzzle, playing a sport, learning a new language — but then it became hard and you got frustrated and felt like giving up ('I'll never be any good at this!'). That's the fixed mindset in action.

Professional musician Deirdre Dowling, who is now doing an MBA, is one of the most open and curious people I know. Like Monique, she was shocked to discover she had a more fixed mindset than she thought. Through her studies, Deirdre realised this had influenced her definition of success. She's the only one in her 'super academic' family who isn't a doctor of some sort, so she felt like a black sheep who had to prove her intelligence in her 'artsy career'.

'I had this funny, outdated definition of what success looks like that was developed many years ago, probably when I was a teenager,' she recalls. 'It revolved around playing with certain orchestras, certain ensembles. I was like, "These are the good groups. Anything less than that is OK, but that's what success is."'

The thing is, Deirdre has been playing with those groups for twenty years; she doesn't need to aim for that anymore. Applying a growth mindset to the idea of success helped her define it in a way that felt unique to her: built around time affluence and the enjoyment of day-to-day life.

We need to be aware of when the fixed mindset is hindering or holding us back. When this happens – like with Monique in her training – we need to switch into a growth mindset. Otherwise we can end up sabotaging ourselves.

The 'power of yet'

There are many ways to develop a growth mindset. The internet is chock-full of tips, from 'replace the word "failing" with the word "learning"' to 'focus on the journey, not the destination'. These tips do help – mining your experiences for valuable learning moments instead of fixating on the outcome is what a growth mindset is all about.

But I find the most useful one is to use the 'power of yet', a phrase coined by Carol in her book *Mindset*. 'Yet' is a tiny word that packs a mighty punch, and it's really simple to unlock its potent power. All you need to do is identify where you're using phrases like 'I can't' or 'I don't' or 'I'm not', and add the word 'yet' on to the end of the sentence.

So fixed mindset self-talk like ...

- ▸ 'I'm not good at this.'
- ▸ 'I don't get it.'
- ▸ 'This doesn't work.'

Transforms into ...

- ▸ 'I'm not good at this ... yet.'
- ▸ 'I don't get it ... yet.'
- ▸ 'This doesn't work ... yet.'

See what a huge difference those three little letters make? Using 'yet' brings hope. 'Yet' signals that with a bit of hard work, patience and belief in yourself, you'll get there.

All you have to do is keep going.

Fast fail

'Fail fast, fail often' has become a bit of a buzzword (buzzphrase?) in business, used by start-ups and in R&D for creating new products and services.

It involves testing new ideas and concepts quickly and cheaply, and shutting them down just as quickly if they don't fly. Instead of flogging a dead horse or getting pulled into the jaws of the sunk cost fallacy, you cut your losses and move on to the next idea (known as pivoting).

It's important to note that it's not simply about failing over and over and over again. Doing that can waste money, anger customers, damage reputations and destroy team morale. Rather, it's about learning from each failure and using that learning to make the next idea better, making incremental tweaks until you hit the jackpot. Duke University's Sim Sitkin, a management professor, uses the term 'intelligent failure'[2] to describe this process. It's all about applying the learnings iteratively, and getting more and more data points on the path to the right answer.

You can pull out these data points by taking a moment to reflect on what worked and what didn't. If you're working in a team, you might have a debriefing meeting, but you can also do this on your own.

A useful framework for reflection is the 'innovation sprint retrospective'. A sprint is a burst of activity for a short defined period. It usually starts with a hypothesis, which you test during the sprint.

Reflect by asking these four questions:

1. What went well (that we must remember)?
2. What did we learn?
3. What would we do differently?
4. What next?

Those reflections all become valuable data points.

One fast fail from my own career (there are many) involves Vic Lorusso, 'the traffic guy'. In 2003, he was all over radio and TV news, up in a chopper, announcing the traffic reports and telling us which roads to steer clear of.

I was at the tail end of my course at the Australian Film Television and Radio School, where our fearless leader Steve Ahern was setting us up in a very practical way to be 'job ready'. I was learning how to program music, how to interview, how to panel, how to produce, how to write copy for advertising, and I was also meeting leaders in the industry to learn directly from them.

Sometimes they offered us the opportunity to have a go. Enter Vic and his megawatt smile.

When he came to present, his energy lit up the room, and I got really curious about traffic reporting. Maybe I could be the next Vic Lorusso! I talked to him at the end and he offered to listen to my 'traffic tapes'. I made some, but oh boy, they were awful. I couldn't think of enough ways to say 'the traffic is bad today'. It is so much harder than it sounds to make something that's both conversational and informative. I listened to some radio and borrowed phrases I heard: 'foot on the brakes at the intersection', 'bumper to bumper on the highway'.

I sent my tapes through to Vic for his assessment. He said they were rough and awkward, but encouraged me to keep trying. Did I want to come and see the traffic centre? Of course I did! We talked about his job in more detail. But as the date got closer, I felt anxiety building. If I (retrospectively) apply the innovation sprint retrospective to this experience, it would look something like this:

1. **What went well (that I must remember)?** I love learning new things and connecting with people, and I'm excited about a career in radio.
2. **What did I learn?** My tapes weren't getting any less awful with time and effort. In the lab of life, it was a 'no' for my career as a traffic reporter.
3. **What would I do differently?** Not a lot – it was a valuable experience. But one lesson was to think about how I fit with the job. I am scared of heights and have no sense of direction, so why would I want to be up in the air, naming all the roads?
4. **What next?** I had to call it for what it was: a fast fail. It didn't mean I was a failure or that I'd never make it in radio, but I had to pivot to something else.

So I moved away from my short-lived dream of being the next Vic Lorusso, and a new dream quickly replaced that one.

In this way, the fast fail mindset actually strips failure of some of its stigma, because each attempt gives you more knowledge and increases your chance of eventual success.

Applied improv

Another great way to reshape your relationship with failure is through an approach called applied improv. I learned it from Dan Klein, an all-round legend who lectures at Stanford in both theatre studies and business management. They sound like strange bedfellows – until you hear him talk.

Improvisation is a form of live theatre in which the plot, characters and dialogue of a game, scene or story are made up in the moment. It's mostly used in comedy, but Dan has some big business names (think Google, Uber and Netflix) taking it very seriously. Why? Because he takes the skills underpinning improv and applies them to the workplace, where they are highly relevant (and highly valuable). Hence the name: applied improv.

It can help with creative collaboration, working under pressure, resilience and team cohesion. For example:

- paying attention and listening to each other
- building on ideas rather than cutting them down
- supporting your partner and making them look good
- being agile, curious and imaginative
- feeling safe to experiment and explore ideas
- not being afraid to look silly or say the wrong thing.

Dan says improv training often starts with changing how you react to failure. Everything is happening on the fly and when you mess up, bolting towards the nearest exit isn't an option. You have to learn to roll with it. When you make a mistake, you learn to simply go, 'OK, what's possible now?' And on from there.

In the workplace, this mindset is what we need to drive innovation and creativity. 'We are always trying to get it exactly right, and if we are allowed to mess up more we can make more discoveries; we can learn more, we can learn faster,' says Dan.

Often the fear of failure prevents us from sharing our ideas – and from coming up with them in the first place. But filtering our own ideas is the biggest fail of all. So we need to build more resilience around this.

Applied improv helps you to brush up against failure in a low-stakes way. You learn to love the setbacks or mistakes (that's often the most fun part of improv) and over time become more comfortable with things not always being perfect.

'It's like training people to overcome phobias. You just do a little bit, get a little closer, get a little closer, get a little closer,' Dan says. 'If we put people under pressure, and their career is not at stake, and there's no money involved and there's nothing about their reputation, they can get in that sort of physiological state and realise, "OK, it's going to be fine." And sometimes something interesting or fun can come out of that, and even if it doesn't, it's OK.'

The more OK we are with messing up in a low-stakes situation like an improv game, the more OK we will be with messing up when the stakes feel a bit higher.

Bill Holmes, the head of business development at Netflix, told *This Working Life*[3] how a few simple applied improv exercises helped his global team break down barriers and build trust very quickly. Through celebrating failure together – cheering each other on even as they made mistakes – they built a supportive environment where people could be candid, confident and creative.

'I think that builds a muscle that it's OK to venture into the unknown and be supported by your peers, and then use that as an experience to iterate from,' says Bill.

Sounds great, right?

LAB EXPERIMENT

How do you respond to failure?

How aware are you of how you respond to failure: how it makes you feel, how you internalise it, how you exhibit your reaction to it in the world? Becoming aware of your response to failure is the first step to reshaping it.

To do this, Dan thinks an improv game called '123 Fail' is the way to go.

You'll need a partner for this game, taught to me by Dan, which has two quick rounds.

ROUND 1

In the first round, count to three with your partner, back and forth. So person 1 says 'one', person 2 says 'two', person 1 says 'three', and person 2 says 'one', and so on. All you're doing is seeing how many times you can successfully count to three in fifteen seconds.

There is one rule. If you mess up, if you make a mistake, absolutely nothing happens. Nothing. There's no penalty. You just start over.

OK ... go! Fifteen seconds. (You can set a timer or make a guesstimate – the idea is to do it for a short while.)

When you're done, take a moment to debrief.

How did you respond? Dan says he notices that some people slap themselves on the head, or wince or flinch. One hypothesis is that we're conditioned to look out for punishment or retribution when we make a mistake, so we sometimes punish ourselves before someone else can. And while it's totally normal to be defensive and protective, that reaction isn't the best way to generate creativity and resilience.

ROUND 2

For this next round it's going to get a little harder. You're going to intentionally shift your physiological response to messing up. Instead of closing up or punishing yourself, every time you make a mistake you're going to treat it as a moment of glory. Throw your hands up in the air, feel the metaphorical spotlight on your face and exclaim loudly, 'How fascinating!' This term comes from the work of Benjamin Zander, an author and the conductor and music director of the Boston Philharmonic Youth Orchestra. He has instructed his students to say, 'How fascinating!' at top volume whenever they make a mistake. His point: every setback is an opportunity to learn. (More from him soon.)

In this round, do the same again, but instead of saying 'one', clap your hands one time. So person 1 will clap, person 2 will say 'two', person 1 will say 'three', person 2 will clap, and on from there.

When you make a mistake, throw your hands up in the air and say, 'How fascinating!'

OK ... go! Fifteen seconds.

Then your final debrief. How did it feel to respond to failure in this way? Dan says we spend our lives 'practising not celebrating failure', but there's something very liberating about embracing it.

Maybe there's a lesson here that we can take into our lives. Can we learn to celebrate all failure as a learning opportunity? As a world of possibility? As something we're not ashamed of?

How fascinating!

Psychological safety

I want to acknowledge that it can be difficult to embrace failure at work if you work somewhere that is more likely to punish than celebrate it, even if it brings a valuable learning opportunity.

There are plenty of organisations that embody a fixed mindset – that don't like change, that are averse to anything with even a hint of a misstep or mistake. Thinking outside the box from inside the box is a tricky thing to do, especially when that box is built with steel-reinforced walls that would rival those of a bank vault (or panic room).

It's also worth acknowledging that there are some professions where failure does have dramatic or even life-or-death consequences, such as in medicine. But all humans make mistakes, including doctors. That's what training and internships and supervisors and organisational systems are for. It's safe ground to iron out the kinks before the stakes get really high.

To fully extend the idea of Lab Day to the workplace, we need a company culture with a net of safety around failure. We need a sense of what Amy Edmondson calls 'psychological safety': a workplace climate in which people know their voice is welcome, even if they're speaking an uncomfortable truth.

Amy is a professor of leadership and management at Harvard Business School and the author of many books, including *The Fearless Organisation*. On *This Working Life*,[4] she explains that our natural human tendency is to stick to the status quo. We want to stay in people's good graces and to be seen in a good light by those above us in the hierarchy, so we tend to hold back. This can lead to a culture where we only speak up about successes and stay quiet on problems, have a desire to 'agree with the boss', and don't take risks or ask questions because we are afraid of the consequences.

These tendencies are understandable, but they are also deeply counterproductive in the modern world. From an organisational perspective, they carry two big risks:

▸ the risk that we don't see a failure coming that could have been averted, because someone didn't speak up with their concerns
▸ the risk of a lost opportunity, because someone didn't share an idea that could have improved processes, or led to a great new product or service.

Amy uses the Volkswagen emissions scandal as an example. VW set out to dominate the US marketplace and focused its strategy on the so-called green diesel car.

'Unfortunately, the diesel technology at the time was not able to meet exacting environmental standards,' Amy says. 'And to make a long story short, the engineers, who were told in no uncertain terms by their bosses, who were

told by their bosses all the way up, that this engine had to pass emissions tests, just felt unable to speak up. They felt afraid of the boss, they felt afraid of saying what they knew to be the truth.'

Instead of speaking up about the reality of the situation, the engineers designed a 'defeat device' to cheat the emissions tests. VW deployed the software in about 11 million cars worldwide before it came to light in 2014. 'Dieselgate' has since cost the company more than $33 billion in fines, penalties, financial settlements and buyback costs.

That's a colossal example of where it can go wrong, but Amy says you can point to the same story in different shapes and sizes 'in company after company, in sector after sector … where people are afraid, they've got the message very, very clearly that "This must work", "These targets must be hit" and so on'. People can find themselves in a position where it's somehow better to create an illusion that something is working, rather than speaking up with what they know to be true.

It is difficult to build psychological safety if your organisation doesn't support failure, or if you aren't in a position of leadership. But I believe in the systems thinking approach – you may not be able to change the entire system, but you can change how you show up in it. That can create a ripple effect that will lead to lasting change. And remember, this is about a mindset shift, not rushing out and actively failing.

Amy offers three simple steps[5] that we can take to foster psychological safety at work:

1. **Frame the work as a learning problem, not an execution problem.** Explicitly recognise that there are uncertainty and challenges ahead. Normalise talking about the uncertainty and responding in a positive way. This creates the rationale for speaking up.
2. **Acknowledge your own fallibility.** Say simple things like, 'I may miss something', 'I don't know everything' and 'I need to hear from you'. That creates more safety for speaking up.
3. **Model curiosity and ask lots of questions.** This creates a necessity for people to speak up. Some good questions are: 'Does anyone have a different perspective?', 'What have we missed?' and 'Any ideas on how we can change this?'

I don't believe you need to be in a leadership position to put these steps into action; however, Dan adds that if you are in one, it's worthwhile being mindful of what you're signalling about mistakes and failure. Are you walking the talk? When you make a mistake, is it out there for all to see? Are you down in the arena or watching from the stands?

'If a leader is hard on themselves every time they mess up, or they try to lead by demonstrating how brilliant they are and how hard they work, that puts an unproductive, unsustainable pressure on others,' Dan says. 'They have to be the example where it's OK to make mistakes.'

It also helps to follow Rule Number 6.

Rule Number 6

I'm not the biggest fan of rules, but Rule Number 6 is one I can live by. It comes from *The Art of Possibility*, a brilliant book by Benjamin Zander and his wife Rosamund. They explain the rule with a story about two prime ministers sitting in a room discussing affairs of state, but for our purposes I prefer to think of two high-ranking executives. The story goes something like this.

A CEO is visiting the office of another CEO. They're gathered around a large desk, talking all things strategy, when a man suddenly bursts in, red with anger, and starts banging his fist on the desk. The resident CEO reminds him: 'Kindly remember Rule Number 6.' The red drains from the man's face as he calmly apologises and leaves the room. The CEOs return to their conversation, only to be interrupted shortly later by a woman, urgently demanding attention. Again the CEO says: 'Please remember Rule Number 6.' She also leaves the room with an apology.

When the scene is repeated for a third time, the visiting CEO turns to her counterpart: 'I've seen a lot, but never anything quite like this. Would you be willing to share with me the secret of Rule Number 6?'

'Very simple,' replies the resident CEO. 'Rule Number 6 is "Don't take yourself so seriously".'

After a moment of pondering, the visiting CEO enquires: 'And what are the other rules?'

'There aren't any.'

Rule Number 6 is the only rule. It is one rule to rule them all: don't take yourself so seriously!

When we take ourselves too seriously, everything becomes this mountain, this Everest of expectations that towers over us. Failure becomes this horrible, embarrassing, shameful thing. And when you are scared to fail, when you can't laugh at yourself, you stop trying new things. You get stuck.

According to the Zanders, the practice of Rule Number 6 'is to light up, which may well light up those around you'. By not taking yourself so seriously, you can light up. You open yourself to joy and lean into the adventure that can be found in things that feel a bit daunting or risky or uncomfortable.

Rule Number 6 feels so wonderfully aligned to the idea of thinking like a scientist. It's not about lumping more pressure on ourselves. It's about giving ourselves permission to let some of that pressure fall away, to loosen our grip and approach it all with more self-compassion.

At the end of the day, if the experiment fails – the *experiment* fails. But *you* don't fail. *You* are not a failure.

With every experiment, we gain something, regardless of the result: another data point, another opportunity to learn. Sometimes we learn what not to do and that's OK. Sometimes what seems like a failure at first ends up being the best thing that could have happened. But you'll never know unless you start experimenting.

So go on, have a crack. Every day is Lab Day.

SIT SPOT

A stream can wear down rock – not with power, but with persistence.

What would it mean, in this moment, to let yourself go with the flow?

02

TIME TO TINKER

Look ahead. Can you see them?

Three paths stretching out before you, soaking in sunshine as they weave through the forest towards the horizon.

Light and shadow dance across three signposts, one pointing down each trail. Tweak. Pivot. Reinvent.

Listen closely. Can you hear them calling to you?

We will answer their call in the next few chapters as we begin our walk towards a future of our own design.

Along the path of **Tweak**, we'll learn how job crafting can help us unearth more meaning and satisfaction at work, without any drastic changes. We'll also get some advice on how to ensure our skills don't float away from us in this rapidly changing world.

Along **Pivot**, we'll discover the value of having multiple strings in your career bow — a little bit of everything you want. We'll pinpoint your transferable skills (trust me, you have many) and set you up with a framework for building a portfolio career.

In **Reinvent**, we'll explore how to approach a big career change — the Career 180. This is all about getting over your fears, putting yourself in the right position, and knowing that you're making the change for the right reasons.

These three paths crisscross along the way; they build on one another. So even if you're ready to charge down the direction of Reinvent, there are concepts in Tweak and Pivot that will help you navigate that path. And the ideas in Reinvent will help you Tweak or Pivot, and so on.

They all work together. They blend back into one path in Chapter 11, where we look at how to leave a job, whether by choice or otherwise, without leaving your identity as well.

You'll notice a shift in the practical activities in each chapter. Where we've previously gone deep with personal reflections, now we're turning our focus to our work. We're running active experiments and explorations, tinkering with little things as we go.

Are you ready?

Let's walk these paths, together.

CHAPTER 8

Tweak: Job-craft your way to more meaning

This is the moment. The moment a wildly underappreciated superstar of the working world has been waiting for. The moment it struts out from behind the curtain, steps into the light and proclaims to a breathless audience: 'I am here to help you turn the job you have into the job you want!'

Job crafting has officially taken centrestage.

No matter where you're at in your career – whether you're pretty content or leaning more in the direction of a monumental change – it's worth considering job crafting.

Why? Because no matter how great a job is, it could always be greater. It could always have more meaning. No job is absolutely, unreservedly, 100 per cent perfect, unless you've managed to lasso a unicorn, in which case 1) I don't believe you; and 2) I want to know everything. Immediately. Tell me how to find mine!

No job is perfect. When it comes to our work, we can't afford to wait for someone else to magically swoop in and hand us the change we want.

We have to tap ourselves on the shoulder. This is where job crafting comes in.

Job crafting involves taking proactive steps and actions to redesign what we do at work and how we think about that work. It can help us:

- change how we value and connect to our work
- shape our work so it is more meaningful and engaging
- feel empowered to learn new skills and truly grow in a role
- better align our jobs to who we truly are
- think about the larger purpose of our work and who it benefits – be it a client, team, organisation, industry or community.

The idea of job crafting is a very useful one, regardless of the type of work you do. Full-time? You can job-craft! Part-time? You can job-craft! Focused on one career? You can job-craft! Have a portfolio career (more on this in the next chapter)? You can job-craft! (Have you ever seen that clip of an exhilarated Oprah giving away a free car to every single person in her audience? 'You get a car! You get a car! You get a car! Everybody gets a car!' Well, I'm like that, but with job crafting.)

To job-craft, you first need to see your job as being alterable. You don't need to make radical changes or completely overhaul your job description. But is there some malleability within the framework of your role? Can you stretch the boundaries, even by a fraction? A lot of people scrunch up their faces at this point and shake their heads. 'Not really, my job is an immovable beast! My tasks are an unstoppable force!'

That's when a cheeky smile creeps onto my face.

'I reckon I can change your mind,' I say.

Job crafting 101

Let's backtrack a little and find out exactly what job crafting involves.

The term was coined by organisational psychologists Amy Wrzesniewski and Jane Dutton in 2001 in a study on hospital cleaners.[1] They discovered that the people who were the most fulfilled had found a way to add something to their work, beyond what was required in their job description. One cleaner reported rearranging the pictures on the walls in the rooms of coma patients, in the hope the change of scenery might have some positive effect. Others reframed how they saw themselves: not as part of a janitorial team doing unglamorous and low-value work, but as a vital part of the healing profession: creating clean and supportive spaces in which people could safely recover.

Amy and Jane started looking at other professions – everybody from engineers to cooks – and found the same thing across the whole gambit of work: people altering the boundaries of their job descriptions to make more meaning.

Job crafting can take three different forms, which involve reflecting on different aspects of your work:

1. **Task crafting: changing up responsibilities.** This can involve adding to or dropping the responsibilities set out in your official job description, changing the nature of certain responsibilities, or dedicating different amounts of time and energy to particular tasks. (While at Radio National, Monique used her digital expertise to help podcasters fine-tune their approach to reaching audiences online, not because it was part of her day job, but because she was interested in the podcast space.)

2. **Relationship crafting: changing up interactions.** This can involve changing the nature of the relationships you have at work, or who you interact with on a regular basis, in a way that changes how you think about the meaning of your work. This could extend as far as a mobility placement or secondment. (Monique had an interest in innovative storytelling on social media so she sought out collaborations with teams in that area.)

3. **Cognitive crafting: changing up your mindset.** This is perhaps the most useful and powerful form. It involves changing your perception of the tasks you do – seeing beyond your technical job title in a way that enables you to find or create more meaning. (Monique wasn't sub-editing articles, she was providing a valuable source of information and entertainment for people, and helping uphold people's trust in the ABC by ensuring copy errors didn't slip through.)

No matter what job you have, you can absolutely shift your mindset, even if you don't have much autonomy over your role.

To guide your crafting efforts, researchers have found it useful to reflect on three aspects of yourself.[2]

1. **Your motives**. Can you craft your job in ways that align with your key motives or drive you to put in persistent effort because it moves you closer to a specific goal? This could include things like enjoyment, meaningful relationships, personal growth, career progression, achieving recognition or job mastery.
2. **Your superpowers.** Can you craft your job in ways that enable you to leverage your strengths or productively apply your talents at work? Perhaps you're great at problem-solving, have high attention to detail, are a fabulous public speaker or possess incredible interpersonal skills.
3. **Your passions.** Can you craft your job in ways that create opportunities for you to pursue your passions, or the activities and topics that spark deep interest? This could be things like learning new skills (or utilising neglected ones), mentoring or teaching others, creative collaboration or using technology in different ways.

Your motives, superpowers and passions are a great starting point for job crafting. Looking at your Life Flow Exercise can also provide insight.

Consider how you might craft a better fit between these characteristics and your job through tasks, relationships or cognition.

What job crafting looks like for me

I've been an unconscious job-crafter to some extent, because my strengths and weaknesses are quite polarised and obvious. But within the frameworks of my various jobs I have used task, relationship and cognitive crafting to make them better suit me.

MY TASK CRAFTING

When I started as a lawyer, I was able to adapt my roles. As a people person, I was drawn to spending as much time with clients as possible, even at the beginning of my career (as a junior lawyer you usually spend less time with clients). I increased the number of client presentations and workshops I did, gravitating towards the marketing aspects of a lawyer's role. And I put my hand up for roles that involved strategy, such as leading an internal merger of two large corporate sections, because it meant interviewing people about their values and hopes for the future. Another example of my task crafting is that I'd often do my presentations by way of song!

MY RELATIONSHIP CRAFTING

One of my most rewarding and impactful roles was in a newly formed position in Melbourne. After I recovered from shingles, I knew I needed to move back to Melbourne from Hong Kong. The fast pace didn't work for me or my family.

I spoke with the leaders of our division, who supported me 100 per cent, and agreed to move me home. They helped me to craft a role which focused on client relationships that were not as deep as they could be. This role played to my strength of listening to clients.

I also love creative collaborations so I did a bit of relationship crafting. I gravitated to other people in different areas to see if we could join forces to create a new offering. This led to a movement towards a broader area of 'legal innovation'. Building on this, I formed strategic partnerships with people outside the organisation, from areas that traditionally didn't collaborate with lawyers, such as designers.

A special alchemy emerged from this relationship crafting. Our law firm and client innovation ended up winning awards and Harvard Law School even wrote a case study about this innovative approach.

MY COGNITIVE CRAFTING

One example of cognitive crafting is in relation to my role as a facilitator. I loved doing presentations and performances, but the role of facilitator left me cold. I felt exposed and uncomfortable. I realised I liked it better when no one talked back!

Underneath this roadblock was a belief that I wasn't a facilitator at heart. I feared I'd be found out when people asked me questions. My co-facilitator Tristan Forrester suggested a way of reframing it. Could I view facilitation as 'applied interviewing'? Could I imagine that all the participants in the workshop were my interviewees – like one massive panel? This mindset shift helped me to move away from myself and my fear, and utilise my natural curiosity. I later did the amazing Skilled Facilitator Program with Roger Schwarz, which fully unleashed my inner facilitator.

I find cognitive crafting one of the most powerful tools to employ on a day-to-day basis. Sometimes I catch myself viewing work as a burden. I see back-to-back meetings in my calendar and feel stressed out. When I catch that feeling, a bit of cognitive crafting helps me reframe it. Instead of a bunch of meetings, I have valuable moments where people have set time aside to connect, to share their story, to seek my help and advice, to share their expertise. That simple check-in helps me feel better about my work on the days I'm not feeling too crash hot.

Craft the role you want

Dominic Price crafted himself an entirely new role at software company Atlassian.

He started his career as a chartered accountant, but he didn't enjoy it — he jokes that he was begging to be fired the whole time. After eight years he took some time off, but found it difficult to get a new job when he was ready to return to work. He ended up taking a job he hated, knowing it came with the chance to pick up the skills he needed to transition to an industry that wasn't accounting.

'I made myself a promise that I would do it for three years. Every morning I'd say to myself, "I know you hate it. I know it's toxic and you hate the products, and the people, but you're learning."'

After three years he moved into software development. He got drunk with a mate one night and they 'found wisdom at the bottom of the seventh bottle of wine'.

'My mate said to me, "Don't apply for a job, because you're not looking for a job. I think you're looking for a place. I think you'll pretty much do any job, if the place is right."'

Dominic applied to Atlassian, and it felt like home. He spent four years as a program manager, then sat down for an honest conversation with his boss. He said he wasn't that great at being a program manager. He didn't have the passion to take the team to the next stage, but he really loved the other part of his job that involved evangelism and learning and exploring ways of working. Was there any way his role could be split into two?

The answer was yes. It was meant to be a three-month experiment, but it never ended.

'The funny part was we had to pick a name for the role. Atlassian CEO Scott Farquhar said, "He can call himself anything, but he can't call himself a futurist. I am never, ever introducing him on stage if he's called a work futurist."'

But within weeks, an article had come out describing Dominic with that title, and it stuck.

'The ironic thing is that the role of the time was just evangelism,' says Dominic. 'We didn't even realise it was a thing to ask questions around "What does the future world look like and how can we take action today, to live into it?"'

Now, of course, it seems silly not to ask those questions.

LAB EXPERIMENT

Release the hounds!

This experiment is all about unleashing the crafting hounds on to your job. (I like to picture fluffy golden retriever puppies clumsily bounding through a meadow of wildflowers rather than a pack of snarling mongrels with an insatiable thirst for blood.)

The first step to job crafting is to bring some more awareness to what your work involves, how you feel about it, and how you're allocating your time and energy.

Keep a running list of your tasks throughout the day, big and small. Do this for a week. That's a useful amount of time to get a holistic overview of everything that goes into your job. We do so many little things every day without thinking about them. (There are apps that can help you log how much time you spend on particular tasks – check out RescueTime, Toggl Track or HourStack.)

At the end of the week, check in with yourself. Dominic has four great questions to reflect on.

1. What do I love?
2. What do I long for?
3. What do I loathe?
4. What have I learned?

This gives you an idea of your work as it is now. Then ask yourself:

- How does your time break down? Are you spending lots of time on the tasks you like the most – or the opposite, because those are the tasks you struggle with?
- How do you feel about the people you're connecting with? Do certain interactions give you energy, while others feel more draining?
- What meaning would you like your job to have? What would you like your impact to be?

The next step is to make a small adjustment that will help you to move closer to a more ideal job. Pick out one of the tasks you have identified.

- If it's something you loathe, how could you move it closer to something you love?
- If it's something you love, how could you do more of it?
- If it's something you long for, how might you make it a reality?
- If it's something you have learned, do you want to do more or less of that?

What action can you take to craft this task and what crafting tool will you use? Remember, you've got task, relationship and cognitive crafting up your sleeve.

Take that action as a little experiment (an experiment within an experiment within an experiment) and see what happens. Did it work? If it did, can you incorporate more of that into your job? Then pick a new task to adjust, and onwards from there.

Let the crafting hounds run rampant until you've got a job that feels more meaningful and satisfying.

A few things to be wary of

Job crafting is exciting and empowering, but it's important to be aware that it isn't a silver bullet for every work woe. Some jobs are more craftable than others. If your role is closely interdependent with another role, for example, it may be hard to change yours in a way that isn't disruptive to the other person.

When job crafting, we also risk:

- overworking ourselves
- doing work we aren't recognised for
- crafting ourselves out of a job.

I have experienced limitations to job crafting, which meant I needed to leave jobs or roles to continue my exploration of my highest potential. When I was in London in the airless, windowless room, I had a sense that no job crafting could help me. The tap on the shoulder for me that time was making the choice to leave.

We craft within the framework of the job we have and if the framework is wrong, then crafting isn't going to help in the long term. We need to be aware of that so we can recognise when a bigger change is needed.

We also need to be mindful not to take too much on. Studies show that we are at a high risk of exhaustion if we load ourselves with too many new tasks – and stress, unhappiness and burnout can follow soon after. Can something be taken off your plate if a new task is being added as part of your crafting efforts?

Monique fell into this trap of overwork at one point. She picked up more things she loved but didn't let go of any of the other things that were part of her role. 'In hindsight I should have delegated more. I developed a bit of a complex around it. I was surrounded by incredibly capable people but still felt like I had to do everything myself.' Sound familiar?

Dominic's advice is to prioritise ruthlessly. 'I'm not allowed to add things until I remove something I loathe, because I'm full. There's no capacity. There's no point sprinkling in a new thing without actively removing stuff, otherwise you're pouring water into a full bucket – stuff just spills out.'

He also tries to focus most of his energy on tasks with big-picture impact and meaning. 'There's been stages in my career where I'm like, "I'm busy, but I don't know that I'm effective" because I'm moving fifty things a little bit, instead of a few things a lot.'

As part of any task crafting, I suggest looking at your work day and asking:

- Is there any way you could claw back some time? (A great routine might help here – hang tight because there's a chapter on that coming up.)
- Are there low-value or low-impact tasks that could be delegated?
- Could any tasks be dropped entirely?

As with so many things in life, baby steps are key. Get some small wins under your belt and build on it from there.

Getting your manager involved in your crafting initiatives can be useful in avoiding overwork. It can also help to avoid another pitfall of job crafting: gaining extra skills and investing time and energy without this being recognised and rewarded.

Bring it up with your manager in a setting that feels right, in a meeting or even a performance evaluation, and get them excited about it. It can be intimidating to have this conversation with your boss, but ask yourself: 'What's the worst that can happen?'

Dominic says, 'If all you find out is that you work for a monolithic, archaic, backward organisation, that's a good learning. At least you know and you can invest in your growth somewhere else.'

Your desire to job-craft is evidence that you care about a job – it's just that you want to care about it even more.

Involving a manager can help you cultivate something that is more meaningful and engaging for you, but also more helpful for your organisation. Research shows job crafting is associated with job satisfaction, and higher levels of commitment and attachment to an organisation. It also boosts happiness, drives up performance and facilitates mobility to new roles. Make sure your crafted role still aligns to your organisation's goals. If you change your role beyond recognition, you risk crafting yourself out of a job.

I was able to job-craft because I was acutely aware of my weaknesses and teamed up with others with complementary skills. I enjoyed bringing them in and helping them identify and utilise their superpowers. This enabled our manager to see that our teaming was ultimately beneficial to the whole, rather than viewing my changing job role as a flight of my own fancy, with no benefit to the greater good.

As I became more experienced, I was able to craft more of my role. This was due in part to seniority, but also because I became more aware of my superpowers and how I needed to align the values of the organisation with my own in order to do my best work.

The L word

If you've reached this point and you're still scrunching up your face and feeling like your job is an immovable beast – never fear. I've still got a cheeky grin on my face because job crafting has one more trick up its sleeve. It's also for the people who are totally on board with the concept of crafting and champing at the bit to get started. Like Oprah's car giveaway, this trick has something for everyone.

It's all about learning, because that's a form of crafting too. It's a matter of being curious and empowering ourselves, and making sure we're picking up the skills we need to stay relevant into the future. If we're not learning, it can feel like our jobs are floating away from us as we watch helplessly from the shore. We can worry that in the not-too-distant future, they'll have moved so far away that we won't know how to do them anymore. It's a very real concern in this era of disruption. There are massive changes happening that we need to keep pace with.

So you'd think we'd all be learning heaps at work, right? Nope. I was astounded to hear some pretty dismal statistics from Sean Gallagher, the director of the Centre for the New Workforce at Swinburne University. He came on to *This Working Life*[3] to talk about the centre's *Peak Human Workplace* report into unlocking innovation in Australia, which found that three in five Australian workers worry that their current skill set won't see them out five years.[4] That's the sense of your job floating away. Sean described that as a 'pretty extraordinary statistic', and he's right. Five years is far too close.

According to the report findings:

- ▶ 53 per cent of workers had undertaken no formal training in the past twelve months
- ▶ only 37 per cent of workers are encouraged to share their knowledge and expertise with colleagues
- ▶ 51 per cent of workers spend less than an hour a week on any form of learning.

On that last point, even more concerning is that the survey defined learning 'as broadly as possible'. It included 'any activity that advanced your skills, your capability, your experience, your expertise, it could be doing a new task, it could be watching an online video, it could be talking to a colleague'. So just over half of Australian workers don't feel they're doing any of that learning. It's no wonder people worry their skills and capabilities are eroding.

The survey also found 78 per cent of workers want to learn new skills in the next twelve months but aren't sure where to turn. So there's an increasing desire to learn, along with the need to learn – but we're not doing that learning.

Knowing what you don't know

I wonder how many other people out there are oblivious to the fact that their skills are floating away.

When Adam Grant, an organisational psychologist and bestselling author, came on to *This Working Life*,[5] he told me about something psychologists call 'cognitive entrenchment'. This is when you have so much knowledge in an area that you 'start to take for granted assumptions that need to be

questioned'. Basically, you stubbornly stick to old ideas and opinions instead of changing with the world around you.

Adam says there's evidence, for example, that when you change the rules of bridge, expert players will play worse than less experienced players, 'because they're stuck to the strategies that have worked for them in the old version of the game, and they don't even realise they need to rethink those'. There's also evidence that experienced accountants are slower to adapt to new tax laws than novices because they've internalised a certain way of doing things. But just because we've always done something one way doesn't mean it's the best way to do it.

We're all vulnerable to cognitive entrenchment, especially as we age. The danger? 'You can become an expert for a world that doesn't exist anymore,' says Adam.

If the world around you changes and you effectively stand still, the world will leave you behind.

Adam says it is useful to 'know what you don't know'. If knowledge is power, then that is wisdom. Saying that you don't know something or haven't figured it out yet isn't an admission of weakness. It's a source of strength and a reflection on your drive to learn and continue to grow. 'Too many of us work in organisations that reward people for knowing,' Adam says. 'And yet the best route to learning is asking.'

We need to embrace the value of curiosity and ask more questions. We need to deliberately and proactively bring more learning into our labs.

Two ways to take charge

As well as being more curious, perhaps we need to change our mindset about what learning is. Traditionally we've seen it as a structured delivery of content, but perhaps a more useful approach is to look at learning as something we have agency over, something we can do in the flow of our work.

Sean Gallagher suggested a couple of great approaches to this:

1. Work more collaboratively, share knowledge and do more problem-solving with colleagues. Learn from others and let them learn from you, too. This is a form of relationship crafting.
2. Take charge of your learning as the need arises, in order to solve problems or advance your work.

Taking charge of our learning is something we can all do. Why hang back and wait for your employer to serve that opportunity up? Summon your curiosity and courage and throw yourself into something new, in any way you can.

Life is a lab and we are here to learn. This is where developing microcredentials can be incredibly useful.

Developing microcredentials

Microcredentials are exactly what they sound like: bite-sized qualifications that demonstrate your skills, knowledge or experience in a particular subject area or capability. Unlike traditional qualifications like a degree, they tend to focus on one niche skill and hone your proficiency over a short time. They're usually completed online and tend to be fairly cheap, or even free. It feels consistent with how some of the younger generations are learning — by watching tutorials on YouTube, for example.

There are a wide range of learning activities under the microcredentials umbrella: they can be as short as a few hours in length, or as long as a few months. They include industry-based certificates, short courses and 'digital badges'. (There are a list of providers and platforms to explore in the resources section.) The Australian Government is also keen on shorter forms of postgraduate qualifications. In 2020 it announced a new $4.3 million 'marketplace for online microcredentials' as part of its Higher Education Relief Package.[6]

Some of these qualifications are more reputable than others, and they're not valued in the same way as a degree. But employers do value skills, and they value initiative — and microcredentials are evidence of both. They are a fast and practical way to build a portfolio of learning beyond your degree, to show evidence of upskilling, to personalise your career development and to expand your options.

Sarah is a 'microcredentials addict' who works in digital media. She gave us a rundown of the courses she's done of her own accord on *This Working Life*: learning Mailchimp, Google AdWords, prioritising tasks, developing a career plan, tips for writing business emails, Excel for marketing, advertising on Facebook, writing a media plan, cultivating a growth mindset.[7] Sarah had something like forty-eight courses in progress. 'My boss actually asked me one time if it was only me using the account because I had so many different courses that I was doing,' she laughs.

So Sarah is accumulating microcredentials while still doing her job and obtaining skills she can use as stepping stones in her career. But they don't always have to be related to work – you can do microcredentials just because you're interested in something. I've done African drumming, Flemish and fencing. Monique's done conversational Japanese and repotting plants. (She unwittingly inflicted a grim death on anything green she touched during lockdown. The poor *Monstera deliciosa* never stood a chance, nor did the fiddle-leaf fig.)

A rolling experiment

Think of job crafting as a rolling experiment. It might involve small tests at first, but you can build up to the mixing-unstable-chemicals-in-a-beaker-just-to-see-what-happens type. There's no pressure. If the experiment fails, try a new one. It's all useful data.

Your job is your guinea pig now, and it's more malleable than you might think. The first step is to harness your creativity and your courage, and to tap yourself on the shoulder.

Release the hounds!

SIT SPOT

Komorebi is a Japanese word that captures the effect of sunlight gently filtering through trees – the interplay between the light and the leaves.

What would it mean, in this moment, to reach towards the light in the forest of your career?

CHAPTER 9

Pivot: Curate a portfolio career

My current career germinated from an experiment, a husky yet heartfelt rendition of a song I wrote to the tune of John Lennon's 'Imagine', and a few healthy dollops of serendipity.

It wasn't something I consciously grew. I didn't even know there was a term to describe it when the seeds were being planted. It seemed to rise up around me over the course of a few years as I followed my curiosity and accepted different offers to collaborate with people.

In the early days, there was tension between my business consultancy and my ABC work, which I jokingly called my 'side hustle'. The line between working and overworking wasn't clear. Despite this tension and without me having any real endgame in sight, my mishmash of a career blossomed. Today I have several strings to my bow and I'm earning from multiple streams. I play across different sectors and all my jobs add up to a full working week.

This is the definition of a portfolio career. Mine has helped me align to my values and bring my whole self to work.

Not just a side hustle

It was Dorie Clark who first gave me the terminology to describe the way I was working. As a bestselling author, consultant, communication coach, keynote speaker, blogger, lecturer and the producer of a Grammy Award–winning jazz album, she certainly walks the talk of a portfolio career.

When she came on *This Working Life*,[1] she explained that a portfolio career isn't necessarily about doing a huge number of totally different things (she gave the example of a swim instructor/horse breeder/lawyer, which actually sounds like so much fun). Instead, it's about finding the things you're already good at and working out new ways to offer those skills. It's a useful way to pivot without leaving your existing skills in the dust. 'It gives you optionality, which I would argue in the modern business world is the most important thing we can have,' says Dorie.

The concept resonated with me immediately. That framing dissolved the tension that had been skulking around between all my different hats. My mindset shifted. I'm not a full-time consultant with a side hustle of broadcasting – I'm a consultant *and* a broadcaster. I am allocating different time to each role, but they are both valid parts of my career.

It's important to differentiate this from the pursuit of multiple jobs out of necessity because your main job simply isn't paying you enough to make ends meet. The working poor experience the darker side of the gig economy, and there is no intention here to glamorise or promote work that is precarious, insecure and unprotected.

Building in job security

Security is a key element of a portfolio career. The pandemic helped shine a light on this for me.

During COVID, my consultancy work had a little hiatus (which I didn't know was a 'hiatus' at the time). It became clear to me that I couldn't rely on anything lasting forever. Career-wise, it is prudent to make sure you aren't putting all your eggs in one basket. This is why lifelong learning and stoking many fires is a useful thing to do. It mitigates risk. This applies even if you are currently in a full-time job. There's no guarantee that you won't be sideswiped.

In fact, Dorie believes a portfolio career is 'the only way to really build in true security in a world where we can't predict what's going to happen next'. She told me about when she was unceremoniously sacked from her full-time journalism job, which she thought she'd have forever. She was chucked into the deep end with a week's severance pay and very quickly had to figure out how to swim.

'It was September 10, 2001. Keen observers will note that the next day, we had the biggest terrorist attack ever on US soil. So it was a really bad time to be looking for a job and unemployed,' Dorie recalls.

It seared into her the importance of having options. If you only have one job and you lose it, you go to zero jobs. That's a precarious position to be in. The more income streams you have, the less you have to be afraid of if you lose one of them.

Dorie started building her portfolio career around 2014. She was doing speaking tours and travelling for work when she caught a horrible flu. It made her realise that if she ever got sick in a more substantial way and wasn't able to travel, her income would be imperilled. So, little by little, she started investing time and energy into creating and offering online learning courses.

In 2020, life on the road came to a grinding halt due to COVID and hundreds of thousands of dollars in income dried up almost overnight. But her online courses cushioned her against the financial impact. 'My income actually dramatically increased in 2020, as a result of those small investments I've been making since 2014.'

Five other upsides

Beyond job security, having a portfolio career also brings the following benefits:

- **Adaptability.** You can utilise your skills and superpowers, and develop different areas of interest.
- **Independence.** You can curate your career on your own terms in line with your values.
- **Freedom.** You can choose to do work you want to do and when you want to do it.
- **Opportunity.** You can pursue different things without the risk of putting everything on the line. Plus, in some job markets, part-time, freelance or contract roles may be more available than their full-time equivalents.
- **Variety.** You can follow your interests. Your day-to-day work may feel less monotonous as a result of doing a few different things.

Later in the chapter, we'll meet other owners of portfolio careers and hear how these benefits play out in their lives – along with the downsides, because there are a few to be mindful of. I'll also spill the beans on how my own portfolio career unintentionally came alive.

But given a portfolio career is all about finding new ways to offer skills you already have, it is helpful to first get a clearer idea of what those skills are.

Your transferable skills

Take a moment to think about your field of expertise. Ask yourself these questions:

- What are you great at?
- What do people come to you for help with?
- What would you like to do more?

Basically, what do you have to offer that someone else would pay for? What is the thing that makes people go, 'Oh you just have to ask [insert your name here] about that, it's like they were born to do it.'

Don't sell yourself short. Your skills *are* valuable.

If you've been in one job for a large amount of time, you might be thinking, 'But Lisa, I don't have any transferable skills. My experience is so specific to this particular role.' Trust me – each and every one of us has transferable skills waiting to be unearthed. Rather than getting lost in the weeds of your responsibilities, step back and ask yourself two questions about your role(s):

- What problems do I solve?
- What skills do I use to solve those problems?

Your transferable skills should emerge from that.

Let's use one of the hardest and most demanding jobs in the world as an example: parenting. Think about the types of challenges you need to overcome in this role and then think about the skills you utilise to tackle those challenges. They're skills like:

- creative problem-solving
- time management

- planning and prioritisation
- multitasking and coordination
- managing difficult situations and staying calm under pressure
- adapting to different kinds of learning
- effective communication, listening and negotiation
- being a persuasive influencer
- mentoring, coaching and counselling
- being highly organised
- financial management.

All of these skills are highly transferable (and highly attractive to employers).

Many businesses are pivoting to digital channels – this trend only sped up during COVID – and you may feel that your skills don't translate to a technological world. My advice is to think again.

Digital business models still need very human capabilities such as problem-solving and critical thinking, empathy and creativity. So if you've developed great problem-solving skills in a retail management job, you could apply those skills in a digital marketing job. They're two different arenas but the challenge is the same: unpacking issues that impact end users or end customers.

Collaborations, new connections and a Beatle

OK, let me share how my own portfolio career came to be. It feels like one of those cases where you can only see the dots connecting with hindsight, but boy oh boy, do they connect! Like Dorie's portfolio career, it grew over the course of a few years – I was just less intentional about it.

The groundwork for me was laid in 2016 when I went on that health retreat in the Gold Coast hinterland and felt an urge to exist without my job title – just as Lisa. When I returned to work, I felt a little more confident and conscious about exploring the parts of the world that I was curious about. I wanted to see how the connection to my work and career might emerge from that.

One thread I decided to pull on was design thinking, which is a human-centred approach to creative problem-solving, anchored in understanding a person's needs and desires. I read some books (there are many listed in the resources section), saved up money and funded myself to attend the

Customer Focused Innovation program run by Stanford Business School and Stanford d.school.

When I returned, I started to bring this perspective to my work. My hypothesis was that design thinking could help lawyers better connect with the core needs of their clients, and so I worked with my organisation to job-craft my role to test the hypothesis.

I brought my whole self to work, and instead of compartmentalising certain parts of my personality, I was just me. I allowed myself to be led by curiosity and connection, and followed the momentum it built. I said yes to a bunch of different things and I did them my way, as Ol' Blue Eyes would say.

I love karaoke so I decided to work a song into the finale of a big presentation where I'd be talking about my work. But the day before my performance, I lost my voice. It was completely gone. I fretted and cried. My fellow presenters gave me advice: stay in your room, drink honey and lemon. Do. Not. Talk. I was scared; imagine me, not even so much as whispering.

I woke up the next morning with about 10 per cent of my voice. By lunchtime, I had about 40 per cent capacity. It was barely listenable.

But I bit the bullet and decided that the show must go on. I got through my presentation – but then, the song! I had put the words on a groovy interactive slide and I implored the audience: 'I have written a song, but my voice is nearly gone. Will you help me sing?' As the music began, the whole room came together, singing about empathy, experimenting and being open to new ideas, to the tune of 'Imagine'. (*Re Imagine Legal, it isn't hard to do. Human-centred law firms. Yes. Lawyers are people toooooo!*')

It was an incredible and heartwarming experience. We all felt connected. One person even joked on Twitter that I should release a charity single for Christmas, with proceeds going to struggling law firms.

By rolling with ideas that resonated with my whole self and aligned with my values, I found myself on the right path with the right people. One of the other speakers, Erika Concetta Pagano, introduced me to Michele DeStefano, David Wilkins, Scott Westfahl and Nathan Cisneros at Harvard Law School, and we collaborated to bring a Harvard case study to life.

In 2017 I did my TEDx Talk on whether robots can make us more human. It was another collaborative affair, which ended with me circling back to my old friends at the ABC.

The first shoots of my portfolio career had sprouted.

Shoes off! A new way of working emerges

After stretching my job crafting as far as it could go, I started thinking about what might happen if I did something new. This led me out of the law firm and into consulting work.

As the consultancy grew, I was also doing fill-in work for the ABC, which I loved. Because I had a full-time job, I held the radio gigs lightly. I did a lot of prep, but I also felt free to 'be myself' on air because I wasn't stressing about any particular outcome. I remember a moment while I was filling in and interviewing Rinske Ginsberg, a lecturer in acting at the Victorian College of the Arts, who conducts workshops on effective communication. She said, 'When I get a new team to work with, the first thing I do is get them to take their shoes off.'

'Hang on,' I said into the microphone. Off mic I shouted, 'I am taking off my shoes!' I leaned down under the broadcast desk, kicked off my shoes and peeled off my socks. Rinske and my other guests looked surprised – and started laughing and taking off their shoes and socks too! We all felt the effect it had on our energy. It was empowering and it helped us connect with vulnerability. Try it for yourself. Notice the feeling of standing barefoot, especially with others – and especially with strangers. The show went out and even though I sound rusty as a presenter when I listen back now (it had been ten years between radio gigs, after all), something magical happened in that episode: I brought my whole self to work as a broadcaster.

The ABC picked up on this and asked me to host a new show called *This Working Life* in the new year. It was a dream come true for me and I was able to do it in conjunction with my existing consultancy. At first, that was something I had to work through, but over time, I started to feel a rhythm emerging.

Without putting all that much thought into it, and without realising, I'd started building a portfolio career that is now flourishing. Some three years later, Dorie gave me the words to describe it.

A few different takes

While this concept is fairly new to me, portfolio careers are old news for others in the world of business. Economist and management writer Charles Handy popularised the idea in the '90s, calling it 'a way of describing how the different bits of work in our life fit together to form a balanced whole'.[2]

Basically, one job doesn't have to fill all of our needs; we can get different things from different bits. You can choose your own adventure.

Portfolio careers come in packages as unique and varied as all of us, and each one is a veritable treasure trove of insights and inspiration. Let's explore two examples.

ENTREPRENEUR/FOUNDER/CEO/INVESTOR

Madeleine Grummet started out in journalism before moving to embrace a portfolio career.

She's now an award-winning education technology entrepreneur – the co-founder of career education and skills platform Future Amp, and the co-founder and CEO of girledworld, which connects the next generation of female leaders with real-world mentors. She's also a board director and does some investment and mentoring across the early-stage start-up ecosystem. Oh, and she's a keynote speaker, podcaster and media commentator as well.

All of these roles draw on her expertise; they're all part of the same ecosystem. 'I have curated a portfolio that is quite complementary. It's about transferring or growing skill sets across all the different buckets,' she explains.

Madeleine is a mother of four and says the nine-to-five life has never suited her. She prefers a value-based metric, rather than something based around time and presenteeism, and loves the flexibility her portfolio career brings.

'I've been a long-time convert because I want to make my work work for me, and I want to work my way, where I know I get the best out of myself,' she says.

The different ports in her folio allow Madeleine to work to both her interest areas and her skill set, and feel like her work has a true impact. 'My portfolio is deliberately designed. I usually move towards people or projects that light me up. I've got a good gut feel for what's a yes and what's a no.' Her portfolio evolves based on where the returns on her time are driving the highest rewards – financially, professionally or personally. 'I'm able to dial things up or down as I need to.'

This approach helped her to respond with agility when 2020 threw a spanner in the works. She redesigned her work to capitalise on the opportunities the pandemic catalysed for the education technology sector. Into 2021, her portfolio career was deliberately dominated by her work at Future Amp.

This is one of the things I love about curating your career in this way: you can change how much you focus on different slices of your portfolio pie according to your needs and what's in demand. It's completely adaptable. You're completely in charge.

JOURNALIST/PODCASTER/PRESENTER

Marc Fennell is often referred to as the busiest man in journalism, and that feels about right. He is on our TVs hosting *Mastermind*, co-hosting *The Feed*, and in regular slots on *Dateline* and *The Project*. He is on ABC Radio, with *Download This Show*. He has produced several podcasts for Audible and he makes a podcast about mental health for Beyond Blue. He also champions cultural diversity in the media, as creative director of not-for-profit Media Diversity Australia. He's a busy guy and a fantastic example of someone finding many different ways to offer their skills.

Marc says his early career was unplanned: when he was eighteen he was plucked out of community radio and suddenly put on TV, replacing beloved national icons Margaret Pomeranz and David Stratton as one of the hosts of *The Movie Show* on SBS.

'My first thought was "Who's going to watch *The Movie Show* without David and Margaret?"' he jokes. He was right. The show was axed before he turned twenty-one.

At a young age, he'd had a taste of the unreliability and unpredictability of the media industry and, like Dorie, learned a hard lesson about job security. 'I made a decision that I was always, always going to have at least two, if not three jobs at any one time. And that's how it's been ever since.'

Marc says a lot of his career has come down to luck. But I think it's more about his strong work ethic, which he thanks his parents for. 'I've always worked my ass off. I've often worked for free when I shouldn't have, but it has paid off largely. The other thing is that I chuck a lot of shit at the wall. I try a lot of different things.'

Talking to Marc, it is clear he's frequently on the go: he doesn't get to sleep until well after midnight most days. He is quick to thank the people whose support he says make his workload possible – his colleagues, family members who help look after the kids, and his wife, who has her own career as a journalist and producer. As in all relationships, there is give and take involved.

'There's a notion out there that work is extractive, and it is to some degree,' he says. 'But if you do it well, if you pick the roles well, the work also gives something back.'

Wait, what's the catch?

While a portfolio career can be inviting and exciting, it's not all easy sailing. Curating your career in this way takes discipline and grit.

It can be hard to manage different roles, involvements, time commitments and income sources, and if you're not careful in your approach, it can wind up creating more stress or completely burning you out.

Here are a few lessons I've learned along the way.

YOU CAN'T DO EVERYTHING

I've found my portfolio career exhausting at times. The main struggle I have is juggling all the different parts. I sometimes feel like I am letting one area down when I'm spending time on another. The upside is that I have to be constantly diligent (and vigilant) around my intention – and attention. I have to ask myself, 'Where is my attention and focus right now?'

My development work is around maintaining focus and only doing the things I really need to do. I can't do everything, no matter how much I try. So I need to have a clear idea about what to prioritise, and what is really important.

Marc has also realised this. He says for a long time, his approach was 'bite off more than you can chew, then chew as hard as you can'. This helped him work out what he likes, and also what he doesn't; both are useful. But he's now in a place where he can put a bit more architecture around his career trajectory. He wrote down the idealised version of his life in five years' time (even though it felt 'awkward and presumptuous and a bit obnoxious'). Then he mapped out how he might get there.

So now, when he's throwing shit at the wall to see what sticks, he's clearer on the reason for doing it. And if it sticks, but ultimately won't help him reach his goals, he might just leave it hanging.

YOU ABSOLUTELY HAVE TO TAKE CHARGE OF YOUR TIME

While there is fantastic flexibility and independence in a portfolio career, you do need to be very disciplined. When you're starting out in something new, you can't afford to underestimate the amount of time you will need to spend on unpaid work: things like learning, networking and business development activities.

'You've got to be really accountable to yourself around managing your time, and balancing work with your other commitments, whether that's family or other personal interests,' Madeleine says. 'With a portfolio career, your to-do list is never done.'

BE AWARE OF SWITCHING COSTS

Hmmm, did you feel a tad exhausted just reading about our friends' portfolio careers? Technically, it *is* tiring because of the 'switching costs' – one of the potential pitfall about portfolio careers.

In a portfolio career, we do two types of mental switching:

▶ **task switching:** when you shift your attention from one task to another
▶ **context switching:** when you jump between various unrelated tasks.

Our brains take time to switch gears from one thing to another. So switching comes at a cost to our productivity and focus; the more you switch, the higher the cost. And these costs add up fast, so we can't afford to be chopping and changing all the time.

I asked Marc about his approach to managing switching costs and he gave me some food for thought.

Instead of looking at all of his roles as completely separate, he focuses on the many ways they cross-pollinate. He says the skills he has learned for TV, like how to hook an audience, and how long to hold and release tension in the air, help him make better podcasts. The storytelling lessons he's learned while making podcasts in lockdown, like ensuring there's real emotional connection between two people even though they aren't in the same room, carry across into TV.

So even if the slices of your portfolio pie feel very different, it is useful to think about how they inform each other. Group related or similar tasks together – tasks that draw on the same skills or the same parts of the brain – even if they are across different roles.

Marc also suggests working in different areas of the house for different things. 'There is a weird psychological power in just stepping from one space to another space,' he says. Monique does this too: the kitchen table is for writing, the outside table is for forest bathing work, the office is for her freelance work. 'Your brain starts to associate certain areas with certain ways of thinking and certain types of work,' she explains. 'It can help me get into the zone faster.'

STAYING CONNECTED REQUIRES EFFORT

Depending on the make-up of your portfolio career, you may find yourself working alone a lot more. You're still part of an industry, but not part of an office.

Many freelancers talk about this as a challenge. Monique found she initially felt quite isolated when she started working for herself. She was used to being in constant communication with her colleagues and working as part of a team, but all of a sudden she was her own boss and mostly alone.

The solution is to be proactive and get involved in your professional communities, organisations and groups. Even something as simple as connecting with people on LinkedIn can make a big difference.

LAB EXPERIMENT

Plant the seeds of your portfolio career

Dorie says it's important to pace yourself and start small when planting the seeds for a portfolio career: 'Even if you only have a couple hours a week, you absolutely can do this.' She recommends building a portfolio career incrementally by adding one new revenue stream per year.

Monique's mate Camille Layt manages an editorial team for a day job, but also does a little freelance editing and marketing work each week. Voila! Portfolio career. Maybe you work in recruitment or HR and you see a lot of résumés. Could you help somebody with their CV for an hour or two a week? Voila! Portfolio career. If you're an expert in a particular field, could you extend that to consulting, coaching or advising? Voila! Portfolio career.

Dorie outlines three different waves in the building process.

WAVE ONE: LEARNING

Can you carve out two hours a week for the next three months (even if it's like squeezing blood from a stone) and simply school yourself about what it might take to branch out? This might involve reading books, signing up for microcredentials, talking to other people in the industry about their experiences or seeking out a mentor. Dorie says this will help you make smarter decisions when the time comes to make a move.

Take a moment to jot down how you might immerse yourself in learning.

WAVE TWO: EXPERIMENTING

Once you've done some learning, it's time to experiment. Start putting yourself out there. Tell a few people about your offering, gauge interest in what you're doing and see what happens next.

For example, if you've decided that you might do some coaching, can you get one or two clients and coach them for an hour a week? Do that for a couple of months and see how it goes. If they like it, they could give you a testimonial that will help you get more clients moving forward.

This is also a good opportunity for you to see how *you* like it and whether it's something you want to keep working at. Doing a secondment is another great way to 'try before you buy'. Is that an option for you?

Take a moment to jot down any ideas (or potential clients) that spring to mind.

WAVE THREE: BECOMING A RECOGNISED EXPERT

If you are a recognised expert, people will want to work with you, and you will have more leverage in terms of what you charge. Why? Because people trust that you'll get the result they're after.

There are three factors involved in becoming a recognised expert.

1. **Creating your own content.** This helps people know what your ideas are and will help build up your personal brand, aka your reputation. Find a way to create content around your work and ideas. You might have a blog or do some writing, give speeches or post about your ideas on LinkedIn.
2. **Social proof.** Dorie describes this as your 'marker of external credibility' — something that helps people understand that you are worth paying

attention to. People are busy and often don't have time to do a deep dive into your experience. They need to quickly get a sense that you know what you're doing. Here are four things you can do just on LinkedIn (or any other online platform):

- Align yourself with trusted brand names that people know and respect. (Working at the ABC, for example, gives me more credibility than if I were broadcasting out of my basement. Because of that connection, a busy person could make a safe assumption that I must be all right at what I do.)
- Highlight key clients or brand names you have worked with.
- Include links to publications you have been quoted in.
- Mention your degrees, qualifications and any involvement in professional associations.

3. **Your network.** To extend your reach and impact, you need to build up your network. Why does this matter? Dorie puts it bluntly: you can be the most talented person in the world, but if nobody's heard of you, you're not going to get very far. The good news is that you already have a network – all the people you know – so you don't have to start from scratch.

There's a lot baked into the idea of networking. It sometimes makes us feel uncomfortable and awkward. There's a yuckiness about it, because it feels like you're setting out to exploit others for personal gain – 'How can I use this person to get ahead?'

But networking is about connection. It's about building sincere relationships, not enduring shallow introductions and collecting a stack of business cards. Bring a sense of curiosity to the idea and to the people around you. Think about why you might want to get to know another person. How do they look at the world that could enlighten or challenge you? Where are the places you might play together?

Networking isn't limited to networking events, or even people in your industry. You can use social media as a tool to connect. Participate in conversations online. You might even create your own events and invite people along to them. I also encourage you to just go up and introduce yourself to people.

This can be scary, because you're putting yourself out there into the unknown. Have courage. The possibilities of every new connection are infinite.

SIT SPOT

A single tree can be an ecosystem in and of itself; it is home to many different plants, animals and organisms, each with its own role to play.

What would it mean, in this moment, to know your career can also be home to many different things?

CHAPTER 10

Reinvent: Do a Career 180

I've often felt like my approach to reinventing my career has been a bit haphazard, so I asked Dorie Clark for her advice.

'How do you make a big career leap?'

Her answer surprised me.

'You don't.'

Wait, what? You *don't*?

What Dorie said next made a lot of sense.

'We should reformat things so that nothing actually has to be a big leap. If you are trying to make a transition that feels enormous, and you don't have training, you don't have skills, you don't have the connections, that's stacking the deck against yourself,' she explains.

We need to find ways to stack the deck in our favour. Instead of taking a big run-up and leaping over a steep-sided chasm, hoping we don't tumble down into the abyss, we need a more calculated approach.

We need to build a bridge.

You don't have to find your career soulmate

To build a bridge, you first need to have some idea of where you want it to end up. What do you want to get to on the other side? This isn't always an easy question to answer.

While some people have an incredible vision or dream that they want to chase (if this is you, I am cheering for you), not everyone has that clarity. There are a lot of people who know they want a change, but have absolutely no idea what they want to change to. They're stuck in a kind of purgatory, an in-between. Often the advice around getting unstuck is to 'follow your passion'. But that narrative can start to feel a bit oppressive if you don't know what your passion is. You can start to feel like something is wrong with you.

Dorie agrees the narrative around passions is a 'very loaded thing'. 'It's like "Oh, you're dating someone. Well, is he your soulmate?" "I don't know … he's nice?"'

Let's lower those stakes right now. You don't have to start with a 'passion'. You don't have to find your career soulmate. And you don't have to default to pursuing more money because you don't know where else to start.

In her book *The Long Game*, Dorie suggests a gentler way forward: optimising for interesting.

Think about the things you're interested in. Things you'd like to learn a bit more about. How might you experiment with these things in the lab of your life? Can you let yourself follow your sense of curiosity?

'No big deal if it starts being boring at a certain point – you can pivot,' Dorie says. 'But if you continue to find something interesting, that is actually a pretty good indication that it is a path worth continuing to pursue. I think that if we lower the stakes, a lot more of us could actually find things that we feel like, "Yeah, that seems cool."'

The idea of optimising for interesting resonated with Monique, who realised she had unintentionally used this approach in her own career transition. When she was thinking of where she wanted to build her bridge to, she kept coming back to the dream of spending more time outside, in a way that connected her with her body. She was interested in nature, so she followed the path – experimenting with the idea of becoming a park ranger or tour guide, working in landscaping or getting into bush regeneration – until she stumbled across forest bathing and completely came alive.

Tapping into your interests

What if you don't even know what's interesting to you anymore? I often see this in people who have been doing one profession for a long time. You lose the capacity to visualise a different reality; the energy and motivation to explore dries up.

The Life Flow Exercise can give you a useful steer here. Go back to your childhood and see what was interesting to you back then. The broad brushstrokes of what I loved as a kid tell me a lot about what I find interesting and fulfilling now.

Dorie says it can be illuminating to home in on your 'weird childhood behaviours'; what were you doing that none of the other kids were?

If you're still having trouble discerning your interests, ask yourself:

▸ What do you do that you aren't required to do?
▸ How are you voluntarily spending your time?

How you vote with your feet can be incredibly revealing, even if you feel like you don't have any special interests. It might just be that they aren't something you recognise as hobbies. Dorie gives the examples of eating out at restaurants or listening to music. If that's your thing, run with it.

Go the half hog

Keep in mind that it isn't all or nothing. You can go the whole hog and reinvent your entire career, or you can go the half hog or quarter hog, and portion out some of your career to reinvent and some to keep as it is. There's no one right way to do it.

Dr Daniel Hu is a dentist. Monique is one of his clients and she's got to know him a bit over the years. Recently, before the chair was lowered, he revealed that he also runs group fitness classes. We had to know more.

Becoming a dentist had been a dream for Daniel ever since his shy teenage self got braces — and a massive confidence boost along with them. But he found university stressful and the gym became an outlet for all of the pent-up pressure. He thought about training as a group fitness instructor but a friend talked him out of it, saying: 'There's a difference between liking something as a hobby and doing it as a job.'

Several years into his career, however, the idea was still on his radar. He mustered the courage to take the plunge and train as an instructor. These days he does a little of column A and a little of column B – plus a little of column C, teaching and supervising dentistry students. Each slice is a valid part of his career whole; none are seen as 'side hustles'.

Daniel's 'slasher career' seems to involve very different things, but there is a thread of connection between dentistry and group fitness: both are about helping people with their health, in places where showing up is often the hardest part. Many people avoid the dentist because they're afraid, and Daniel says that same fear often surrounds going to the gym. 'I think it takes a lot for someone to come up to me before a body pump class to tell me, "Oh, I've never done this", or "I just had a baby".'

Does being a fitness instructor make Daniel a better dentist, and vice versa? 'Most people don't believe it, but it does,' he says. Group fitness helps him deal with the stress of dentistry, which means he can bring more energy into the room and be more attentive to his clients. In turn, that helps him fine-tune his attentiveness skills, so he can more effectively apply them in a gym environment, 'where you have to take care of lots of moving parts and lots of people'.

Group fitness gives Daniel a feeling he doesn't often get with dentistry: the feeling that he's made someone happy and is appreciated. 'As a dentist, I get people telling me that they hate coming to me, all the time, like three times a day,' he says. In fitness, on the other hand, people will often come up and say, 'Wow, that was a great class!'

Daniel didn't have to leave dentistry completely behind to do a Career 180. Working across different roles works beautifully for him and he adjusts the balance as needed. 'In each, I feel like I'm helping people make a small difference in their life.'

Building the bridge

Once you know where you want to end up, you can start building the bridge. It's important that this process isn't rushed. Big changes often feel impossible because it feels like you have to achieve them instantly, but they're much more attainable if you approach them slowly over time. If you build the bridge bit by bit.

When I resigned from law, many people felt like it had come out of the blue. But it hadn't. I'd been testing my ideas for a while and figuring things out behind the scenes. In hindsight, my approach wasn't as lawless (pun intended) as I once thought. It was actually pretty close to the method Dorie uses, and the way Monique approached her transition too.

Looking at the areas of overlap revealed a useful framework for reinventing your career:

1. Get started in a small way.
2. Absorb as much as you can.
3. Experiment in the field.
4. Put yourself in the right position.
5. Be patient.

There are some similarities here with building a portfolio career in that we aren't jumping in without some learning and experimenting first. But where a portfolio career tends to involve developing different roles in your existing field of expertise, a Career 180 is usually about creating something completely new.

Let's dive in.

GET STARTED IN A SMALL WAY

Big changes whisper big promises into our ears: 'Don't overthink it', 'Fortune favours the brave'.

But fortune also favours the prepared. There are very good reasons to be prudent in your approach: bills to pay, mouths to feed, plans that need space to take shape, safety nets that take a while to weave.

Getting started in a small way helps us stack the deck in our favour.

In my case, I started volunteering at the hospital radio station while still doing my day job in law. Monique started in forest bathing just by reading as much as she could about it. Daniel initially ran a few group fitness classes each week, around the edges of his dentistry work.

Dorie talks about the concept of '20 per cent time': spending a fifth of your time on new ideas and projects. 'If you lose 20 per cent of anything, you "waste" 20 per cent of your time or "waste" 20 per cent of your money. It will be annoying, but it's never going to destroy you,' she says.

It lowers the risk, and 20 per cent is also enough to create something substantial over time.

ABSORB AS MUCH AS YOU CAN

As part of our 20 per cent time, we want to turn ourselves into sponges and soak up anything and everything we can in the seas of our desired new path. The goal is to develop a clear picture of what your new career might look like – the real deal, not the romanticised version – and what it will take to succeed. Basically, you have to understand what you're signing up for.

For me, this meant listening to a lot of radio alongside my volunteering. I analysed radio shows and read books about the art and science of the craft. I practised panelling with pens, pretending they were faders and moving them up and down as I imagined talking to a guest, taking a caller, crossing to someone in the field and then playing a song. I also embraced short courses and said yes to every opportunity to learn more.

As you're absorbing, it's useful to reflect on your Life Flow Exercise and your values. Ask yourself a few key questions:

- Why do I want this new career? (Go deeper than just saying 'because I hate the current one'.)
- What does this new career look like in reality? What's the day-to-day like?
- How will this impact my life? In what ways will it make it better? What might be the downsides?

For Monique, being a sponge meant talking to people who were doing the profession she was aiming for. This helped her realise that forest bathing probably wasn't going to be a full-time career, at least not initially. She didn't speak to one guide who was making a living solely off the practice.

The reality was that she would have to have another source of income if she was going to keep a roof over her head. She wouldn't be able to go the whole hog. That sent her off on a new exploration: what might this look like now? Did she still want to chase this dream if the reality looked a bit different?

These simple check-ins along the way can help ensure you're making the change for all the right reasons and keep you on track to land in a place that aligns with who you truly are.

EXPERIMENT IN THE FIELD

Over time – still with that 20 per cent figure in mind – you can make the switch from absorbing knowledge to getting experience.

Ask yourself how you can test your mettle out in the real world.

- ▶ Can you volunteer somewhere?
- ▶ Can you do work experience, an internship or a secondment?
- ▶ Can you shadow someone working in the job you want?
- ▶ Can you spend time with people in your desired industry?
- ▶ Can you audit a class or course, to see what's involved in making the switch?

Around my law work, I volunteered at as many radio stations as I could, watching, learning and collaborating. I often teamed up with my friend Zoe 'Mackalack' Mack. We got on like a house on fire and sparked off each other with so much energy. I decided to take my 20 per cent in one hit and took a month off work in order to devote myself to an opportunity that had emerged. Mackalack and I were asked to co-present a breakfast show on 87.7 Riverside FM. I felt that the stars had aligned. The gig filled me with exhilaration and energy, and I learned a lot about how to create and air a breakfast show. After the radio show finished, I went back to work as a lawyer, but Zoe and I continued to try to find ways to get on the air.

We loved Christian O'Connell from X FM in London. He was funny, creative and a great team player in terms of his on-air squad. Magician David Blaine was going to be interviewed and Christian wanted objectivity in relation to the magic that was going to happen. He did a call-out for listeners to be on a panel of 'independent observers'. Mackalack had the crazy idea that we should apply together – she thought my being a lawyer would work in our favour. She was spot-on. Christian loved that I was a lawyer and also that I was Australian. Exotic!

So instead of hopping on the train and going to work one day, I got up at 3 am and we made our way to the studio to be on breakfast radio with Christian. It was super nerve-racking and also super exciting. Nerv-citing! After having a lot of early-morning fun, I went to work. One of my colleagues came up to me: 'I woke up this morning and thought you had walked into my bedroom and started talking to me. Were you on the radio with Christian O'Connell?'

I was truly doing everything in my power to get as much real-world experience as I could.

Along the way, I made sure to keep track of how I was improving. This is important so that you can know if you're heading in the right direction. So, as you experiment, remember to check in and ask yourself:

- How am I going?
- What am I intrigued to learn about next?
- Who should I connect with professionally?
- Am I still loving this? Is it everything I expected?

PUT YOURSELF IN THE RIGHT POSITION

The knowledge and experimentation stages are like the load-bearing supports of the bridge. Next, we can build the structure. The aim is to make the transition as smooth as possible when the time comes.

Ask yourself:

- What skills will I need for this new career?
- What transferable skills can I bring across with me? (See the previous chapter for a simple way to pinpoint these.)
- What new skills do I need to obtain?

Putting yourself in the right position might involve doing a short online course or an industry certification, or embarking on a process of extensive retraining. You might get a CV expert to help highlight your transferable skills on your résumé, or do some interviewing coaching so you know how to position yourself in your new industry.

It's not always going to be possible to straddle both sides at once. If you need to go back to uni, for example, you're probably not going to carry on in your current role unchanged, but perhaps there could be a way to keep a toe in the water.

Dorie says it can be useful to think of your current and desired careers like two circles in a Venn diagram. The secret is to find the overlap.

She uses the example of an attorney who wants to be a filmmaker. 'What if you try to get hired as an attorney at a film company, or you start to work in entertainment law? That gives you much more of a sense of who the players are, how the industry works; you start to make contacts, you start to make connections, and eventually you know enough people that someone will give you a chance to make a film, or you'll understand the system so that your work can get seen.'

This is also a chance to get in cahoots with the right people.

Michelle Cheng provides a beautiful example of how to do this. She is an amazing connector and makes a point of reaching out to people when she thinks they've done a great job, or they've inspired her or made her think differently about something. I know this because she sent me a beautiful message after I hosted a TEDx Melbourne event. She wasn't asking for anything; she just sent a note saying that she loved my hosting, 'especially the D-minor chord' – a reference to the one chord on the guitar that I have mastered. She even wrote me a recommendation on LinkedIn.

She says she gets this from her mum, Jenny, who would always tell people if they did a good job – even the cashier at the supermarket – because 'it really makes their day and it costs you nothing'. Michelle's sphere of connection is wide, because she puts genuine effort into growing it.

When Michelle was working as a publicist but wasn't feeling as engaged or energised as she wanted to be, she decided to find a way back to her previous career in media. Not all jobs are widely advertised so instead of relying on job sites like Seek, she began connecting with people in relevant groups on Facebook and LinkedIn. She reached out to people, articulating her dream to find a new role. Whenever someone posted about a job she might be interested in, she researched them and sent them a personal message.

Then an ad was posted for the role of Content Industry Diversity Manager in SBS's Television and Online Content division. Michelle reached out to the woman who shared the ad, who put her in contact with the person who was hiring for the role. 'We had a phone chat for maybe half an hour. I just tried to listen to what he had to say about the role, expressed my interest, shared any relevant points of my background,' she says.

She got the job – a role 'beyond my wildest dreams'. The love you put out will always come back.

BE PATIENT

It's important to give any career transition the time it needs to flourish.

Dorie is a mega fan of long-term planning, as the name of her book suggests. She says if you give something enough time, and are willing to endure the ups and downs along the way, you can achieve almost anything. It just requires patience.

We live in an era of instant gratification and Dorie says a lot of people are too quick to give up on things, especially when it feels like too much work. That's partly why we do all the work to absorb and experiment: so we know at the outset what reinventing our career is actually going to take.

Dorie shares a story taken from Jeff Bezos in his 2018 Amazon shareholder letter.

'A friend of his hired a handstand coach, and the handstand coach revealed that most people who want to do handstands think that about two weeks of consistent practice will get them there. The truth is, it is six months of daily practice,' says Dorie.

'That is literally a twelve-times differential. Imagine if you entered college, and you're like, "Oh yeah, I'm gonna rock it, I'm gonna get my degree" and then part way through, it's like, "It's going to take forty-eight years."'

So what Dorie calls 'a long time horizon' is critical: we can't expect a long-term change in a short-term time frame. If I think about the time that has passed between hospital radio and today, it's a lot. It's twenty years between starting out and getting a gig in my hometown, with years and years of rollercoaster experiences in between.

You need to be patient, and you need to be gentle on yourself as you learn.

Monique found it confronting to be new at something because she was used to being an expert. Being in a space of learning was as uncomfortable as it was exciting. She remembers the first forest bathing walk she guided during her certification. It was just her and her partner. 'I was so nervous and anxious that I vomited in the very public parking area of a botanic garden. Then I just absolutely sobbed because I felt like such a failure – how did I ever think I could do this?'

She says she was holding the experience far too tightly. 'I had outrageous expectations of myself as a beginner guide. In my heart I had already picked this as my next career, so that meant I *had* to be great at it. The fear that I'd choose this but not be good enough to make it work was absolutely crippling.'

But with time, she grew.

Stroll across that bridge

Once you've worked through this process of starting small, absorbing and experimenting, and patiently putting yourself in the right position, you will look up and see that the bridge is there.

Waiting for you.

The change is still nerv-citing, of course, but there's no huge leap required. When you are ready, you can step out onto the bridge you have built.

Getting a radio job is notoriously difficult, and during all of my learning and skills gathering I had unconsciously come up with a rule for myself: I'd only make the change if I had a very good chance of getting an actual job. I needed to see some evidence like 'this program has a 95 per cent success rate in getting graduates their first radio job'.

That's the success rate of the Australian Film Television and Radio School, where I had applied for the prestigious nine-month Commercial Radio Broadcasting program. This program is for radio DJs what NIDA is for actors. I got an exhilarating phone call one morning: I was one of twelve people who had got in. I put down the phone. 'This is it. I am leaving the law and becoming a radio presenter.'

I felt 100 per cent pumped. I felt … free. There was not one atom in my body saying, 'Hold on, you are walking away from six years of university study and five years of practice as a lawyer!'

The door was open and I walked right through it and didn't look back.

It isn't that easy for everyone. Sometimes it is hard to have faith that the bridge you have built is going to hold up. Fear and doubt creep in.

Get out of your own way

Even after her bridge was built, Monique took a while to cross it. One part of her was excited and the other was absolutely terrified. The two sides were locked in a tug of war and she started to worry that fear was ultimately going to win. The fear feasted away on her self-confidence, sucking the bones clean before throwing them to the floor.

But she realised that she was privileged to even be in the position to have a viable chance to change her career. Not everyone is as lucky. How could she waste that by talking herself out of it? She decided not to let her decision be dictated by fear.

A lot of the fears Monique had to overcome were common ones. Let's take a moment to unpack them.

MONEY, MONEY, MONEY

Sometimes a career change involves a hit to the hip pocket: if you're starting from scratch somewhere new, you can't expect to go in on the same salary you pulled in as a seasoned expert. If a pay cut could put you in a precarious position, that fear is absolutely valid. But if it's more that you've become accustomed to a certain type of luxury that can be pared back, there's plenty of room to experiment.

One of my lessons from COVID was about going back to basics and looking at what I actually need as opposed to what I want. What is essential, and what isn't?

These questions make me think of Henry David Thoreau, the naturalist and writer who went to live in a tiny shack in the woods to live a more deliberate life. In *Walden: Life in the Woods*, he describes how he noticed that many people were living unhappily, spending most of their time in work they hated in order to afford things they didn't really need, like Venetian blinds, which were all the rage at the time. His experiment was to see if he could live more fully – 'to suck the marrow out of life' – by embracing simplicity.

You don't need to go full Thoreau and move to a tiny shack in the woods. I like to think of it more in terms of sustainability than scarcity. But it is worth questioning how much money you *really* need to get by. Do you actually need those Venetian blinds? How much are you a slave to the wage at the expense of health and happiness?

IRREPLACEABLE COMPLEX

You've put a lot of time and energy into your job and bring a lot of value to your work, so there can be fear around the idea of leaving it behind. What if the things you've worked so hard to build come crumbling down when you're not there to hold them up?

The key thing to remember is there is a difference between being hard to replace and being irreplaceable. Nobody is irreplaceable. Your workplace will adjust to your absence, even if it takes a while. That world will keep turning.

JUDGEMENT DAY

A fear of judgement can be a biggie, especially for people in jobs with a certain social status. 'How will people label me based on this new job? What will they think about who I am as a result?'

By being conscious of these fears, I think that can help us realise something very important: nobody's thinking about your social status. Nobody's waking up in the morning and going, 'Gee, I hope Lisa has a high-status job today'. Everyone has their own crap to deal with. We can't lead our lives based on other people's opinions, which you can never really know anyway. And we can't use our assumptions of other people's opinions to figure out whether or not we are going to do a job.

We also have to tame our own egos. It's common for people to feel like they won't be 'important' anymore without a high-status job, because they equate their self-worth with that role. This is why it is important to know who you are when the On Air light switches off. To know that what you do matters, but not as much as who you are.

BETTER THE DEVIL YOU KNOW THAN THE DEVIL YOU DON'T

This is the idea that knowing something bad is better than the unknown.

This was a big one for Monique. She had worked at the ABC for her entire professional career, having started there as an intern in her last year of uni. So she had no idea what it was like to work anywhere else. 'That was a big reason to leave, I think, but also a big reason not to,' she says. 'I was really good at my job and I was respected there. What if I wasn't as good at the new one? What if the grass wasn't actually greener?'

But also: what if it is greener? What if it all works out? There's no way of knowing how it will turn out, but for most people I know who've made a leap, the biggest reflection is: 'Why didn't I do this sooner?' It's normal and natural to feel these fears. The trick is to overcome them.

Give your fears a reality check

Monique found an activity called Fear Setting extremely useful as she worked through her fears. It's the brainchild of investor, author and podcaster Tim Ferriss, and we've adapted his approach, adding in extra questions to help you dive in even deeper.

Think of this as the opposite of goal setting: instead of making a list of what you want to do, think of something you're afraid to do and make a list of everything you're afraid could happen so that you can take charge.

This exercise has two parts and you'll need two pieces of paper.

PART 1

On the first piece, make five columns under the heading 'What if I ...?'

Name the columns from left to right: Define, Source, Prevent, Repair, Chance. You should end up with something like this.

WHAT IF I ... ?

Define	Source	Prevent	Repair	Chance

The big question at the top, the 'what if' question, is where you name the action that's causing you fear. What is the thing you are worried about? It could be anything: giving a presentation, asking for a raise, speaking your mind, admitting a mistake, studying something new, moving to a new company ... but given this chapter is all about career changes, let's run with the example of 'What if I ... quit my job?' Then fill out the columns.

1. **Define:** Map out your fears in detail. Start a new line for each new fear, and go from your minor worries all the way through to those nightmarish, worst-case scenarios that keep you up at night.
2. **Source:** Think about what's driving each of the fears you've listed.
3. **Prevent:** Write down what you could do to prevent each of your fears from happening, or even just decrease the likelihood a little bit.
4. **Repair:** If the worst happened, what could you do to repair the damage? Who could you ask for help or support?
5. **Chance:** What's the likelihood of this actually happening – rare, unlikely, possible, likely or certain?

Near the end of 2020, Monique wrote down all of her fears about making her big leap. Her very long list included things like:

▸ My skills aren't as valuable as I think and I can't find any work. (Who quits during a pandemic?) Or I get fired from the new job. Either way, I can't pay my mortgage and I end up on the street.
▸ I am even less happy after leaving. Maybe I just don't realise how good I've got it?
▸ Everything goes to hell without me in my role; my leaving undoes our team's progress. (Or worse, maybe, everything is just fine without me because I wasn't ever that good anyway.)
▸ I lose all of the expertise I've worked so hard to obtain.
▸ My sense of identity dissipates.
▸ I don't have what it takes to start my own business and can't hack it as my own boss.
▸ I lose my maternity leave benefits. What if I change my mind about not having kids?
▸ Forest bathing isn't a viable career path and I end up being a complete failure.

I wonder how Monique's list compares with yours? It's interesting how our biggest fears often overlap because they're burning on the same fuel. Change and uncertainty are scary. We crave a sense of safety and stability. We care what people think.

Some fears are well founded, so filling out the Prevent and Repair columns can help you feel a sense of control. If the worst does happen, you'll know how to handle it.

The Prevent column can also give you an insight into proactive steps that could help your transition. If you're worried about not getting a new job, could practising your interview skills help? If you're worried about finances, could you set up a safety net? Monique, for example, was afraid she didn't have what it takes to start a business so doing a 'small business basics' course gave her the confidence to say, 'OK, yeah, I've got this.' The fear didn't go away entirely, but it shrank to a more manageable size.

There may also be fears on your list that probably aren't that well founded and this process can help you realise that. Monique describes it as putting on 'realism glasses' that enable you to see how far removed from reality some fears actually are. 'So much of my list is really just excuses not to do the Big Scary Thing, even though I wanted to do the Big Scary Thing,' she says.

PART 2

On your second piece of paper, write down the answers to the following questions. Once again, get down and dirty among the finer details.

1. **What is the cost of doing nothing?** What will your life look like in a month, or six months or ten years, if you take no action?
2. **What if it works?** This is one of my favourite questions to ask. It's where you start to feel excited and hopeful. Assume you quit your job and everything goes to plan. What are the upsides? How will you benefit – professionally, financially, emotionally, physically?

Does what you stand to gain outweigh the risk that one of your fears might come true? Is it better to take that risk than to do nothing?

For Monique the answer was yes, every time. 'Ultimately my biggest fear wasn't about trying and failing – it was about *not* trying at all. What if I wake up in ten years and I'm still in the same job? What could I have done instead? How much would I regret wasting my chance to find out?'

Those were scarier thoughts than anything else on her list. So she walked across that bridge.

And like many people who make a career change, her only regret was not doing it sooner.

SIT SPOT

To give birth to a higher version of itself, the caterpillar has to surrender. Inside its cocoon, it literally digests itself, opening itself up to a mysterious and total transformation.

What would it mean, in this moment, to trust in your own metamorphosis?

CHAPTER 11

Leaving your job (not your identity)

When my friend Deirdre Dowling suddenly lost her job during the onset of the pandemic, she was struck by a feeling she likens to grief. The loss came with an unexpected barb in its tail, a few little words saturated in meaning.

Essential and *non-essential*.

Deirdre, a classical music performer based in Paris, was placed in the latter category of work. You might reflect that they're just words, but words matter, and this one penetrated her to the core.

But then a friend of Deirdre's told her about a nurse whose work had become a hellscape. This nurse was having to make decisions she never thought she would have to make: about who gets a machine and who doesn't, who lives and who dies.

'The only thing, she said, that got her through was coming home each night and listening to Mozart symphonies,' Deirdre says. It helped her see that 'essential is not about "survive versus perish". It's the stuff that makes us thrive, that feeds us and gives us energy and meaning'.

The grief Deirdre felt was because she felt devalued: as a professional, and as a person. She felt like all the choices she had made in her life, to get to where she was, were being held up for judgement, and falling short of some invisible standard.

And perhaps this feeling of *lesser than*, of feeling *not enough*, will resonate with those who have experienced job loss or redundancy.

Our sense of self is so wrapped up in what we do for a living that when we leave a job, we can feel like our identity stays with it.

A crisis of the existential kind

There are myriad reasons why you may leave your job — and you are not always the one making the call.

You might be sacked or your position may be made redundant. You may choose to quit, to pursue a new direction, or focus your energy on other things, like raising kids. You may be forced to leave for reasons that aren't necessarily your choice, like injury, mental health or to care for a loved one.

When you lose your job, often your first thoughts will turn towards money and the need to keep the financial stream flowing. This can be a very real and urgent hurdle, particularly if you have dependants.

But it's not the one that comes up again and again when I talk to people about job loss and redundancy. What seems to hit hardest — and what we are going to focus on in this chapter — is the blow it can land on your identity. This is a storm that hits deep. It leaves you feeling completely unmoored.

This is because work is a major organising principle of our lives. It is where we meet our friends. It gives structure to our days. It gives meaning and purpose to our lives. It's the anchor for our goals. It makes us feel useful.

So many of us define who we are by the work we do; we equate our identity with our résumé. We don't have a strong enough sense of who we are when the On Air light switches off. So when we lose our job, we lose our way of navigating the world. We lose all of these things we maybe didn't even realise were important to us.

Cue a major existential crisis.

This crisis can take hold even if you didn't particularly like your old job, and even if you made the decision to leave.

The pandemic has led to a global trend that has been dubbed the Great Resignation: a mass, voluntary exodus from the workforce as professionals rethink their careers, work conditions and long-term goals. Monique was part of this trend, resigning at the end of 2020 with a new sense of perspective on what really mattered to her.

'I was working really hard for things that weren't essential to me at all. I was grinding it out to get more money to buy more things. The pandemic helped me realise that what really matters to me is a sense of space about my life; I don't want to spend my days rushing from one thing to the next thing until I keel over.'

But just because leaving is the right thing to do, it doesn't mean it isn't hard.

After Monique left, she entered a period she describes as 'the great in-between'. She didn't feel like herself anymore, but she didn't quite know why. 'I felt a sense of loss because I was no longer able to identify myself by my work. I had felt like I had a strong sense of myself and that it didn't revolve around my work, but I was way off,' she says. 'I think my ego took a bit of a hit, and I was also really worried how people would perceive me. People respected me as a journo, but what would they think when I introduced myself as a forest bathing guide?'

She talked this out with a friend who had just had a baby and realised they were both feeling similar things: a sense of grief for who they were, and an uncertainty about who they might become. They were both feeling a sense of being *not enough*, or being *lesser than*.

Those feelings surfaced again for Monique's friend when she returned to the workforce. It can be challenging when you have that year-long (or more) gap in your CV, whether you're returning to your old company or searching for a new job. You can feel like you have to 'prove' you're still serious about your job, even though you might now be part-time and a parent. You can lose confidence or find you overcompensate at work.

I have also heard this from people who have faced redundancy. When they get a new job, they overwork, don't push back on unreasonable requests or don't properly log overtime, because they're scared of being made redundant again. Other people might go the opposite way: putting in less effort at work because they feel a lack of control or agency over what might happen in the future.

So not only can leaving a job affect your sense of identity, but it can also fundamentally shape the way you work.

Trust the big picture, even when you can't see it

Job loss is a struggle; there is no denying that. I'm not going to be one of those annoying people who scoots over to your side and tells you to just stay positive.

But I do believe that you will eventually find some meaning in your situation, even if it takes a while to emerge. Inside every struggle is a gift. You don't have to go looking for it while you're in the depths of despair, but let yourself trust, even a little, that it is out there.

Silvia Regos made a major transition in her career a few years ago, leaving her work at one of the Big Four consulting companies. Like Monique, she made the choice but still entered what she calls a 'period of quiet uncertainty'.

'Sometimes I call it the dark night of the soul, where you lose your previous identity,' she says. 'It is a very unsettling period that can spark quite deep emotions and anxiety.'[1]

Silvia found that after sitting in that space of difficult uncertainty for a few months, she started to feel a spark again. She felt curious about what might come next and was able to take stock of what she wanted to leave behind and what she wanted to take with her, creating a vision for her future. She moved into 'a very exciting period of exploration' and is now working in a job she loves, as a business growth adviser.

Her advice is to give yourself the space to work through what you want your future to look like, as much as you can. There is some privilege involved in being able to do this. If you're financially stressed, you might have to get a new job ASAP to keep income coming in. But maybe while you're doing what you *need* to do now, you can also think about what you *want* to do next.

For those of us with some kind of financial buffer or support, job loss can be seen as a chance to recalibrate. Think about everything you have learned about yourself so far in this book, and consider:

▸ What do you want your next job to look like? (The flip side can be just as useful too: what *don't* you want your next job to look like?)
▸ What transferable skills do you have?
▸ How might you pivot to something new, or reinvent your career?
▸ What excites you about the next stage of your career?

Leave some space for the unimaginable

Don't lose hope, because you never know what might happen.

When Janna Koretz, a clinical psychologist who specialises in the mental health challenges associated with high-pressure careers, came on to *This Working Life*, she told me a great story about a client who was in the start-up business and only had about two weeks' worth of money left.[2]

He'd had stacks of interviews with venture capitalists and investors, but they'd come to nothing: nobody was willing to fund his start-up for the next round. He was upset and talking the problem through with everyone he knew. He happened to tell his mailman about it, and his mailman just happened to deliver mail to an angel investor – who went on to fund the project!

'These are the crazy things that happen in life. Sometimes really interesting things can come out of situations that feel excessively hard and impossible to navigate. So not to negate how difficult it is, but this could be a great opportunity for something kind of unusual and unexpected to happen that might actually be great,' says Janna.

Allow some room in among all the fear for a little bit of wild hope.

Deirdre initially lost gigs when concerts were cancelled due to the pandemic, but was able to return to work part way through 2020. However, a month in, she injured her finger on her left hand and was unable to play. She had to cancel everything. 'That's when it really hit. Not only can the world kind of cancel your career for a while, but something could happen at any time that means from one moment to the next, you might not be doing what you're doing,' she says.

She was privileged enough to have a bit of time to weigh up her options; the French Government gave musicians a stipend so they could get paid through COVID even though they couldn't perform. She had been thinking about taking time off to complete some form of further study, but this wasn't what she had envisaged because she hadn't been given a choice around the timing.

'This kind of inner tantrum hit me. "This was not my choice!" I'd been thinking about taking a sabbatical for so long, and then suddenly a sabbatical arrived on my doorstep and I hated it.'

The impact of that lack of choice feels so relatable to me as I write during another lockdown. I have talked to many people who are stuck at home and going, 'Yeah, I probably would have stayed at home all week anyway. But I would have stayed at home by choice.'

Deirdre had time to consider forms of further study, and there was a heightened sense of urgency to act because of her finger injury. She landed on the MBA.

'At first it felt very much outcome-focused. I wanted to find a solution in case I couldn't play the viola anymore, and this seemed like a logical way to formalise my tacit skills and get a salaried job,' Deirdre reflects.

'The MBA isn't a contradiction to music. I'm really enjoying doing it, and at the same time I have no idea where it's going, so it's become process-focused, subject by subject. I don't need to try to control the outcome – nothing ever really goes to plan in life anyway. I've realised that if I'm happy doing the process, the outcome will take care of itself.'

Deirdre has come to believe that we need a bit of chaos sometimes; that is where the fertile ground for growth is. You can see things from the edge that you can't see from the safety of the centre.

There is some excitement in the uncertainty of what comes next.

Reach for the stars

Sometimes a little push can be exactly what we need.

A decade ago, Kim Ellis was working as a research chemist for BHP Billiton when her position was made redundant. She was thirty-nine; she'd only been back at work for a few years after going on maternity leave.

She knew it was coming but that didn't prepare her for the reality of it. She kept wondering if maybe there was something she could have done to prevent it, as if it was somehow in her control. Once she was able to let go of that idea, it was easier to face. 'I remember thinking it was really personal. But it wasn't. Redundancies never are,' she says.

Her employer handled the redundancies pretty well, giving people three months of training on everything involved with finding a new role, from résumés to job searching. As part of that, Kim did an interview designed to draw out the type of role she wanted to do. Nothing felt inspiring to her. Finally, the interviewer asked: 'If you could do any job at all in the world, what would you do?'

'I laughed and I said, "I'd be a rocket scientist!"' Kim recalls on *This Working Life*.[3] It was a throwaway comment but when she said it out loud, it released something she had held inside for a long time. 'I really was a closet space nerd.'

The conversation catalysed a major change for Kim, who ran full speed in the direction of her passion. She is now a space lawyer and scientist, and the founder of consultancy International Earth and Space Technology. She is also in training to become Australia's first female astronaut, after being selected as a PoSSUM (Polar Suborbital Science in the Upper Mesosphere) Scientist-Astronaut candidate and global ambassador for 2021.

'I would never have imagined the type of roles that I've been able to land and the amazing experiences that I've had. I'm so grateful for the redundancy because it completely changed my world for the better, even though it was really painful at the time.'

Add an 'and clause'

When we go through a challenging time, we tend to turn inward and focus on the problems we are facing. This is where the 'and clause' comes in. Janna says using the 'and clause' can help us see beyond the difficulties to where the opportunities are. Try adding an 'and' statement to things that might feel scary:

- You're facing mega difficulties AND you know you're a mega resilient person.
- You don't know what your next job is going to be AND you know you can get creative and figure it out.
- It's going to be very hard AND you know you have the strength to get through it.

These three little letters pack a mighty big punch.

Monique found them useful in helping her carve a new sense of identity that didn't revolve around her work. She grabbed a piece of paper and wrote down, 'I am Monique, and I am ...' She added as many descriptors as she could think of without mentioning work.

'I am Monique, and I am loving and kind and determined and passionate and creative and queer and strong and vulnerable and anxious and sarcastic and full of laughter and a bit of a hippy and often barefoot and a good cook and a cat mum and a daughter and a sister and a friend and a mentor and someone surrounded by incredible people and ...'

She did it until she filled up the page.

'It helped me see that even though I wasn't the same person in a work sense, I was still the same old me,' she says. 'And that same old me is actually pretty awesome.'

Why not give this a go now? List out some of your concerns AND how you will face them. Then list out everything that makes you, you – but leave work out of it.

You are enough.

Choose your narrative

Words matter, and they can help you take back some of your power moving forward.

Executive coach Amy Poynton has experience in delivering redundancies to her employees and in coaching people who've been made redundant into a new job or new career. She came on to *This Working Life* to unpack the stigma of job loss.[4]

Amy reflects that being unemployed or made redundant has traditionally been associated with negative characteristics, such as being lazy or unmotivated, but this has changed as workplace restructures have become commonplace. COVID has accelerated this exponentially.

Job loss can happen to anyone, at any time, regardless of skill or ability or commitment. It's common, but it can still feel embarrassing and shameful.

What will you tell people? What if you run into a former colleague who asks, 'What are you doing now?' What if the person at the supermarket checkout asks, 'How was work today?'

Amy says it helps to have an answer ready. You might say you're on a holiday or on a hiatus. This can effectively function as a shield around you; you're protecting yourself because you have the story. You are in control of the narrative that surrounds you. It's not about inventing BS stories about yourself, but reframing how you think and talk about your new circumstances, and how you think and talk about your new identity. This is also a useful mindset to take into the job hunt going forward.

I asked Amy how people can best position themselves as they look for a new job, beyond giving a dusty old CV a revamp. She gave me some great advice: think about the narrative you want to tell, and remember that it isn't personal.

Think about the difference between these two phrases.

- 'I was made redundant.'
- 'My position was made redundant.'

See what a huge difference that slight tweak makes?

The *position* was made redundant, not the *person*. It's not personal.

Amy uses the example of someone in the mining industry going for a new job following a redundancy. They might say: 'Mining is going through changes because there's less production and less sales. So as an industry, we've had to readjust. That means I'm doing this other thing.'

Amy says, in her experience, employers don't care that much about a gap in your work unless they get a sense that it was a result of poor performance.

'I worked with someone who did not want to be made redundant. He wasn't happy about it and wanted to stay with the company. He built that into his narrative,' she says. In job interviews, the man would talk about how sad he was to leave his old position. It became quite a powerful way to showcase his loyalty and dedication to potential employers.

Parents returning to work may also benefit from putting a structure around their narrative. You haven't been doing nothing – you've been working hard! Could you highlight all the incredible skills you've been nurturing that transfer directly back into the workplace? (Chapter 9, page 129, has some fantastic examples to get you started.)

Amy says it is also helpful for parents to have a strategy for building and maintaining their confidence in being back in the workforce. 'There is often a real dip in self-confidence combined with mixed emotions about not being with your child 24/7 that can really mess with a parent's mindset,' she says.

Parenting interest groups, either through work or outside of work, can be powerful as they help parents see that many others have had similar challenges and they are not alone.

Everything matters, and also nothing matters

Deirdre gave me a beautiful philosophical lens through which to look at job loss, and at life and its struggles in general.

For her, the pandemic has been a time of prodigious paradox. Of grief and loss and difficulty, and incredible gratitude. Of being terrified of the unknown ahead, and excited by it. Of somehow finding a way for these seemingly contradictory things to exist together.

The biggest and most wonderful paradox, she has realised, is that everything matters, and also nothing matters.

'I mean, it really, really matters, who we feel we are, and our identity, and what we do, but from the perspective of the whole big universe, it also doesn't matter at all; no one is going to remember who we are. It's like, every moment matters, every note I play matters, how I pass from one note to the next note matters – but none of it matters. This is nothing.'

It's messy and hard to define, but it's like standing on top of a mountain, and feeling huge and small all at once. It's like staring up at the vastness of the night sky, and feeling significant in your insignificance. Everything and nothing, at the same time. This is a wonderful paradox to hold within our every experience. What a beautiful perspective to carry through the world. How freeing it is.

What you do matters, but not as much as *who* you are. They both matter. But also, not at all.

SIT SPOT

A new dawn follows even the darkest of nights. The rainbow is never far behind the storm. Rain can come to rinse things clean.

What would it mean, in this moment, to trust that after an ending is a new beginning?

03

LET'S PLAY OUTSIDE

Take a moment to pause.

How far we have come, together.

Look around, and take it all in.

Sometimes as we walk, we get so focused on where we are going that we forget to notice where we are.

We don't see the tiny wildflowers carving out a life at the edge of the path. We don't hear the music the wind is playing with the leaves. We don't smell the scent carried on the breeze, or feel the soft crunch of the earth beneath our feet.

This section is all about the moments along the way.

It's about bringing some intention to how we're walking, as well as where we're going and why.

For the next few chapters, we're going to explore what our day-to-day work looks like, and how we might make it better.

We're going to bring the lens of curiosity to the concept of work–life balance.

We'll explore the extraordinary power of routines and rituals to help you turn on and switch off, and how your innate connection with nature can help you unleash your full potential.

We'll look at the light, and also the dark. Imposter thoughts, stress and burnout – the shadow sides of our working lives. We can never outrun them, but perhaps we can befriend them.

This section is all about the here and now of this journey.

Often when you look back, you realise that the little things were really the big things. More than the view from the summit, the moments along the way are what make the walk feel worthwhile.

So, let's enjoy them.

Let's play, together.

CHAPTER 12

Work–life coherence

What is your relationship with the concept of work–life balance? I think it's difficult to separate 'work' from 'life', and that by trying to balance two things in a dualistic fashion we are setting ourselves up for failure.

What does 'balance' even mean? Do both sides have to be equal, all the time? When does this mythical state occur? Even if it is real, surely it is fleeting at best.

Instead of feeling useful, the idea of achieving balance has felt like an added stressor to an already crowded list. And now that many of us have experienced working from home, I wonder if a new concept might emerge …

The concept of work–life coherence.

Wait, coherence?

If you look up coherence in the dictionary, you'll read something like 'the quality of forming a unified whole'.

Think about someone who is speaking coherently. They're putting individual words together in a way that conveys meaning. There's a wholeness to it; what they say is more than the sum of the individual words. When someone is speaking incoherently (say, after a night on the booze), you lose that sense of wholeness. It's just words.

In many branches of science, coherence is used to describe a harmonious connectedness between the parts in a system. When a system is coherent, it's operating at an optimal level. Our body is a system – a very complex one.

Dr Rollin McCraty is the director of research at the HeartMath Institute, which researches the communication pathways between the heart and the brain. Rollin says that while most people have been taught that the heart is constantly responding to 'orders' sent by the brain in the form of neural signals, we now know that the heart is also sending signals to the brain. It's a two-way relationship. The brain interprets the rhythms of the heart to determine how we feel. When we have heart–brain coherence, our mind, body and emotions are aligned. We feel better, and we perform better. The whole is greater than the sum of its parts.

Heart coherence is reflected in heart rate variability (HRV), a measure of the variation in time between each heartbeat. We used to think a sign of good health was a regular and steady heart rate, as if the heart was a metronome. But according to Rollin, that's 'completely wrong – it's actually the opposite'. The rhythm of a healthy heart is surprisingly irregular, even under resting conditions. Rollin says to 'think of it as a measure of flexibility, which underlies our ability to adapt to changing circumstances, whether at home or work, and adapt to stress'.

LAB EXPERIMENT

Cultivate heart coherence

Cultivating a deeper connection between your heart and your brain can be incredibly powerful. To maintain optimum heart rate variability (HRV) – the higher HRV, the better – I do a practice called HRV meditation.

If you want to dip in and give it a try, HeartMath has a simple exercise: the Quick Coherence Technique.

STEP 1: FOCUS YOUR ATTENTION IN THE AREA OF YOUR HEART
Imagine your breath is flowing in and out of your chest area, rather than through your mouth or nose. Find an easy rhythm that's a little slower and

deeper than your normal breath, perhaps breathing in to a count of five, and out to a count of five.

STEP 2: TRY TO EXPERIENCE A GENUINE POSITIVE FEELING

As you continue the breathing, start to focus on feelings of love, care or appreciation. Think about someone or something that makes your life great – a person, a pet, a place, an experience, a memory. (If nothing comes to mind, focus on feeling calm and at ease.)

Keep the breath going for a few minutes.

Do you feel more connected to your heart, and to your body?

A measure of flexibility

I wondered if we could apply this concept of coherence to our lives, and find a harmonious connectedness between work and all the other stuff. What might we learn from playing with this concept in our labs?

If work–life balance is about drawing a dividing line between work and life, then the idea of work–life coherence is to unify the two sides. Like the heart and the brain, work and life are in a two-way relationship – they are interconnected – so everything works better when they're in flow. When there's some flexibility.

In its most literal sense, work–life coherence means we can work in a way that suits our life. We don't have to colour in the lines because that's how it's always been done; now we have the whole page. It means we're not stuck in one way of operating. We can shift around and move up and down as needed, and work in a way that is optimal for us as individuals. Perhaps, like the heart, our lives are healthier for this.

A more flexible way of working became the norm for many of us during the pandemic when we started working from home, aka living at work. We found we could do life admin during the work day: getting the groceries out of the way in between meetings, knocking out a gym class during lunch, walking the dog when the weather was too good to be stuck inside.

But work also crept into our homes. Maybe you started answering calls after hours, thinking through work issues while watching TV or clearing out the email inbox after dinner. A lot of commentary labelled all this as a negative – and for some people, it was. Work was an unwelcome home intruder. But others found this new way of working quite useful; they were able to function at an optimal level.

If that's you, this is an example of work–life coherence. Instead of focusing on what's 'work time' and what's 'life time', you focus on the best time to do things. You work the hours that suit you and your life, not just during 'work hours'.

For Monique, work–life coherence means working every day, but don't label her a workaholic just yet. She spreads her work time across the whole week instead of grinding through long weekdays and only resting on the weekends. So she works about five hours each day: usually a chunk in the early mornings, when she feels most effective, and then an hour or so after dinner.

It's what works best for her, and her business. 'It means I can manage my business presence on social media in the evenings and on weekends, when it gets the most traction, without feeling like work is taking over my entire life,' she explains. 'I'm not working any more than I used to, or not much more. It just looks different.'

How much flexibility you have in how and when you work will depend on your job (and your boss). Monique's approach wouldn't be possible everywhere, but it's not impossible either.

The idea of working every day would be a mega no-no under the umbrella of work–life balance, but it fits beautifully with the notion of coherence. By working in this way, Monique is functioning at her optimal level – both at work and in life.

'I do still feel a bit guilty when I clock off after lunch and enjoy the afternoon free of work, even though I've done my time at work,' she says. 'That's what my development work is around now. A state of true coherence, for me, has no guilt about the "life" side.'

Work–life coherence will look different for everyone. It may mean choosing to get up from your desk every two hours to take a three-minute break in the fresh air. It may mean logging on earlier or later to attend some meetings if you work with people in different time zones. It may mean turning down some social events so you can focus on a big work project or presentation. For me, it means that every morning I do one thing to support my health – one of my top priorities in life. That may be booking a doctor's appointment, going for a walk or saying no to something.

With work–life coherence, nothing is set in stone. Sometimes work may take priority, and sometimes life stuff will. Your needs will change over time and you can make tweaks as often as you need to.

The key is to be kind to yourself. Remember, this is about taking the pressure off.

Getting over the guilt

The guilt Monique mentions is something so many of us have felt while working from home. It can feel wrong to take any time off during the day, even if it's entirely legitimate.

I know many people who are stuck in a 'presenteeism' mode: feeling like they have to be online for every split second of the work day and beyond. I know people who have really struggled with transitions. When it's time to stop work and clock off, they keep squeezing in 'just one more thing'. And then one more thing. And on and on. If anything, working from home has meant more work, not less.

So work–life coherence is also about realising and accepting that you have limited time, and you can't do everything. We have some great ideas on building routines, managing time and reinforcing boundaries coming up in Chapter 15, page 211.

The guilt can run both ways, too. Sometimes I feel guilty for doing work stuff when I feel like I'm meant to be focusing on life stuff. When this happens, a quick mindset shift can help me achieve coherence.

I often spend Sunday afternoons reading books in preparation for my interviews with guests on *This Working Life*. I could interpret this as a burden, but I don't have to see it that way. I intentionally reframe it as something enjoyable, because I do enjoy reading and learning, even if it falls under the category of work.

Flexible work: A two-way exchange

There's some overlap here with the concept of work–life integration, which also focuses on bringing the two sides closer together.

We did a live show on work–life integration at Pause Fest,[1] and one of the things that came up was, 'OK, this is all well and good, but how do I get my employer on board?'

This is a really big question and one that is going to play out in the next few years. I think the answer has probably got something to do with hybrid work, where you split your time between the office and working at home.

Natalie Feehan, the chief customer and commercial officer at EstimateOne, says whatever the form, it's important to remember that flexible work is a two-way exchange. It needs to be mutually beneficial. It's not only about the best outcome for you, but also about the best outcome for your company and your team.

People often talk about the importance of trust, but James Law, chief people officer at EstimateOne, says that's not the best thing to focus on because trust can be betrayed. James says transparency is more important: transparency around what you're working on and how it's going and how you're tracking. 'Rather than constantly thinking, "Is that person working hard enough?", you can see it,' he explains.

To be transparent is to be see-through; in a business sense it relates to the open and honest sharing of information. It's what Atlassian describes as 'open company, no bullshit' in a list of its core values.[2] It might feel daunting at first, but clear communication of your results, wins, losses, challenges and endeavours helps to build trust. People respect honesty more than they do perfection.

It can also be a way to stave off some of that guilt we feel while working from home. By keeping track of what you're working on and what you've achieved over the course of a day or a week, and then logging it or feeding that back to your manager, you can foster transparency.

This might not work in every situation, of course, but it's good to keep in mind as you start experimenting with work–life coherence in your lab.

Know what wholeness feels like

Work–life coherence needs to be approached with awareness and intention. Because you can work whenever you want to, there is some risk that work ends up overrunning everything else. You can start to feel like you always have to be 'on'. This is where a set point is useful: the point at which a variable state stabilises. In biology, this is called homeostasis.

'Homeostasis means that the system is able to self-regulate around the set point,' Rollin McCraty explains. It isn't static, but it moves around a point of stability. 'You always bring it back to stability, like a thermostat in your car. You set the temperature, it goes up and down and around it a little bit, but we're always trying to bring it back to that.'

Work–life coherence acknowledges that sometimes one area of your life will take priority. There will be times when you need to put your work first, and times when you need to prioritise family, health or rest. But you need to know what that set point is in your life.

Think of the set point as that sense of wholeness that springs forth when your life and your work reach a harmonious connectedness, when you feel aligned. When you start feeling stressed or out of whack, what are you bringing yourself back to? That's your set point.

It can be useful here to get rooted. Return to your values, and how you are prioritising them. Rollin says, 'I think it really gets down to how aligned we are with who we really are at our deeper levels.'

Natalie realised she was in work mode too often around her kids. 'Their normal was me with a device in my hand. My one-year-old constantly wanted to be holding a phone,' she says. 'The example that I'm setting for my kids is that it's possible to be a loving, great mum, and also to have a successful career, but I want to make sure they get the loving mum part.'

So she brought more intention to how she was working. She was mindful about how much she used her phone around her kids, making sure she was intentional about when and why she picked it up. It wasn't in her hand while her attention was focused on time with them.

As you experiment, keep checking in on how well you're self-regulating and make little tweaks to move towards a state of homeostasis. It's useful to have an idea of what a state of incoherence feels like so you know how to recognise it and bring yourself back to the set point.

For Monique, it's when she feels stressed and anxious, starts ruminating on work issues, or feels guilty about taking any time away from work. When this happens, she takes a look at everything on her plate and asks herself: 'Is this going to expand my life, or contract it?'

If the answer is the latter, she weighs it up carefully. Is it something she has to do? Can she push it back, or say no? Is it worth stretching for?

A quick coherence check

Every morning, I do a quick work–life coherence check.

Who am I as a human? Do I feel joy, love and energy towards my family, my friends, my work? Or does something feel 'out'?

If it's the latter, I dial up or dial down certain elements to see if things feel better, like you would do to improve your HRV score. It's not static. It's shifting around all the time, growing and changing.

When I have heart–brain coherence, my mind, body and emotions are aligned in harmonious connectedness.

When I have work–life coherence, it's the same feeling. Harmonious connectedness. I feel better, and I perform better.

The whole is greater than the sum of its parts.

SIT SPOT

The air takes many forms: a light breeze, a howling wind, a violent gust. It whispers and whooshes and dances and slaps and roars, rising and falling around a set point of calm.

What would it mean, in this moment, to open up your work and life to natural fluctuations?

CHAPTER 13

Tame and reframe your imposter thoughts

'I don't have an idea worth spreading!' 'I don't deserve to stand up on that stage!' 'They're going to sack me any moment now!'

In my diary, on Friday 12 August 2017, I had written: 'DEPTHS OF DESPAIR'.

It was one month before I was due to stand up in front of 2000 people at the Melbourne Convention Centre and deliver my TEDx Talk.[1]

Voices of doubt were eating away at me. They had risen from a whisper through to a giant crescendo, and now they were screaming.

'I can't do this!'

I had no choice. I would have to call Jon Yeo, the TEDx curator, who had so far read and coached me through fifty drafts of my talk, and tell him that I didn't have it in me. I couldn't deliver a talk.

Pull the plug.

You may know the feeling I am talking about. You may have your own panic voices that get stuck in a loop inside your head, telling you that you don't deserve your success; that people are about to wake up to the fact that you don't know what you're doing; that you've only got this far because of dumb luck or good timing; that you're about to be exposed as a fraud.

Often these voices are referred to as imposter syndrome, but for some unknown reason I've never used that term. It never joined my personal lexicon. My take is that these voices are just a natural part of being human; they're not a defect. Whenever we stretch at something or take on the challenge of something new, we will have a feeling of 'Uh oh, have I gone a little too far this time?'

It's the opposite of feeling in control. It's the opposite of feeling safe. But perhaps this can be a good thing. Perhaps these voices are a sign that we're onto something.

Imposter ~~syndrome~~ thoughts

When we did an episode on imposter syndrome for *This Working Life*,[2] I learned a more helpful term for these voices: imposter thoughts. Really, that's all they are: thoughts. So let's use that term here.

If you have imposter thoughts, welcome to the club. It's not very exclusive.

Around 70 per cent of people experience them at some time in their lives[3] – and I reckon the other 30 per cent are fibbing. All those smart, successful people that you look at and think, 'wow, they really have their shit together', they're probably members too. These thoughts affect both men and women, though women are slightly more represented (perhaps because they're more willing to talk about it).

The good news is that you have some power to tame these thoughts, and can even turn them into a force for good as you navigate your career. The bad news is that you're probably not ever going to banish these voices entirely. You're going to hear them over and over again.

The irony is that the further you go in your career, and the more you stretch yourself, the more opportunities there are for imposter thoughts to strike.

The danger zone

If we let our imposter thoughts run wild, they can seriously hold us back. Often they manifest as little everyday doubts. What if I'm not fully prepared today? What if this is outside my skill set? What if I don't know my stuff?

The danger is when they become debilitating. Left unchecked, they can completely crush your confidence and leave crippling self-doubt in its place. They can stir up a lot of fear and can leave you paralysed.

Hugh Kearns, a productivity researcher who wrote a book on imposter thoughts, says our brains can spiral quickly out of control. This can mean we:

- get stuck catastrophising, instead of getting on with whatever we're meant to be doing
- work way too hard, trying to avoid being 'caught out'
- miss out on opportunities because we avoid them out of fear.

My imposter thoughts were getting in the way of me trying something new, convincing me to pull the plug on my TEDx Talk.

But I wanted to do it. So I needed a plan. I needed a way to tune into my 'hope' voice, which was only just audible above the anxious buzz of imposter thoughts. I had to strain to hear it, but it was there. It was saying, 'Don't give up yet. It might not be that you don't have something deep down to share, it might be that the way you are trying to communicate it isn't coming across for this forum.' It was asking me, 'What is missing? What haven't you tried?'

LAB EXPERIMENT

Turn the volume down

It's critical to know what to do when imposter thoughts arise. If we do nothing, they'll just keep getting louder and louder. We need to take control of the volume and dial those voices right down so we can hear the hope instead.

Here are five simple exercises you can play around with in your lab.

CREATE A BRAG FILE

Make a note of your accomplishments and successes, the compliments and nice feedback you've received. Include times you've helped someone or made a difference to others.

Keep it all together somewhere – in a list near your workspace or in a folder in your email inbox. You've now got what Hugh calls a Brag File. Executive coach Amanda Blesing came on to *This Working Life* and called her version a 'Bragalog'!

When imposter thoughts strike, Hugh says you often can't remember the good stuff because you home in on everything bad (even if it happened that one time, all those years ago). Your Brag File is a way to go back and look at the evidence, and psych yourself back up.

Sometimes all it takes is a little reminder that you are, in fact, awesome. You are in a Category of One.

SEPARATE FEELINGS FROM FACTS

Write down your imposter thoughts and then use evidence to call them out for what they are: absolute BS. So you might write: 'I'm not qualified for this', then objectively list all of your skills and training and expertise. This will help you separate feelings from facts. This is important because we can feel things really strongly, but that doesn't make them true.

Journalist and author Ginger Gorman has a great example of this. When her book *Troll Hunting* came out, she was invited to speak in various countries around the world. When she was mic'd up and about to step onto a stage in Norway, the imposter thoughts struck. 'I had this moment of thinking, "I'm just a fat mum in a headband – what am I even doing here? I just wear bad trackpants and have my coffee spilled on them, and try to get to school pick-up on time!"' she says.[4] But then a tiny voice came through with facts: you are an expert, that's why you've been invited. You wrote the book on this!

Use facts to realise that what you're feeling isn't actually true.

GIVE THAT MEAN LITTLE VOICE A NAME

This tip comes from entrepreneur Kate Morris, the founder of Adore Beauty and Glow Capital Partners. She has found it useful to name the voice of her imposter thoughts, so she can separate it from her 'inner voice of truth'. When imposter thoughts arise, she can then call them out: 'Oh that's just Kevin. You can zip it, Kevin!'

This is a technique psychologists call cognitive defusion. By giving the voice a name, we externalise the issue. Then, we can step back and observe it for what it is. Monique has used it to change her relationship with her anxiety (named Ursula, after the seductive and deceptive sea witch).

Rather than *being* an imposter, we can recognise that we *have* imposter thoughts. It's a powerful distinction.

EMBRACE A GROWTH MINDSET

Zubin Pratap is a former corporate lawyer who taught himself to code at thirty-seven. He's now a software engineer at Google, but there was a time when he didn't think he had it in him to learn how to code. He compares his imposter thoughts to his shadow: he couldn't run away from them.

Zubin was able to reframe those thoughts by embracing a growth mindset and truly believing that he could learn anything. 'The best antidote to self-doubt is the acknowledgement that you can learn what you need to. How you are today is not an indicator of what's possible for you tomorrow,' he says.[5]

Embrace this growth mindset by changing up the negative talk inside your head. Changing what you say to yourself can change how you see yourself.[6]

- 'I don't know much about this ...' → 'Here is what I know about this.'
- 'I don't have the answer.' → 'I'm smart enough to work this out.'
- 'I can never get it right.' → ' I don't know how to get this right ... yet.'
- 'I'm going to fail.' → 'If I succeed, that's great. If I fail, I learn.'
- 'Everyone here is brilliant and I'm not.' → 'Everyone here is brilliant, and I get to learn from them.'

It's not about pretending you know it all, or feeding yourself false positivity or puffing yourself up with illusions about your capabilities; rather, it's about thinking in growth terms instead of fixed, static terms that take away your power. Sometimes just altering a single word can help. Instead of saying, 'I am just a lab assistant', say, 'I am a lab assistant'. Notice the difference?

Zubin says when you have a growth mindset, you'll eventually get to the place you want to be, because you won't give up. Then you stretch into a new role and start to feel like a bit of an imposter all over again because the gap between your current skills and the required skills has widened again — but you now know how to work on closing that gap. He says this can be a wonderful cycle of growth, if you're able to embrace the uncomfortable parts.

BREAK THE SILENCE

Imposter thoughts feed on secrecy and silence. We feel ashamed of them, even though they're normal. Almost everyone wants to know that they're good enough, and almost everyone worries that they're not.

But a problem shared is a problem halved, and you don't have to face imposter thoughts alone. Talking it out with a colleague, family member, friend, coach or counsellor can be freeing. They can describe how they see you as a professional and remind you of your strengths. Let yourself accept that what they're saying is true. You might find they experience the same thoughts too, and have their own tips for overcoming them.

Remember, membership to the imposter club isn't exactly exclusive.

A TEDx emergency

Breaking the silence is what helped me harness my imposter thoughts and turn my 'hope' voice up to max. I realised that somehow my TEDx Talk had become all stats and data. It was missing stories. It was missing me!

I needed help.

Earlier that week, I'd mentioned to a new friend, Amanda Derham, that I was struggling through the 51st draft of my talk, and she mentioned a magic storytelling lady, Yamini Naidu. I sent Yamini an email, and half an hour later, she responded. Answering emails late on a Friday night wasn't her norm, but 'this is a TEDx emergency'.

She had a plan and we set to work on Monday. It was wonderful to share the burden with someone else. But more than that, I loved the creative collaborative process (I know, how many times do I need to learn this?). Yamini also called in her friend and collaborator Sandy McDonald, who knew the feeling of standing on the TEDx stage, and she brought her superpowers to the process.

From that moment, I loved it. I was less anxious and defensive when it came to the dress rehearsals. I was able to absorb the expert coaching of Jon Yeo, the curator of TEDx, who had been trying to get me out of my deep knowledge of lawyers and the law.

Once I was able to bring my imposter thoughts into line, they gave me an advantage. They pushed me down a path I might not have gone down otherwise. They made me turn towards others, and I was all the better for it.

Turn imposter thoughts to your advantage

When we did our episode on imposter thoughts, I was really curious about how people have reframed those voices as a positive force.

While we can't forget how incredibly difficult imposter thoughts can be to grapple with, they can also help us in our careers. This was certainly my experience with my TEDx Talk and I'm far from alone.

Here are three ways people have flipped the script on their imposter thoughts.

A MOMENT OF GROWTH

Leticia Mooney, the founder of communications consultancy Brutal Pixie, describes her imposter thoughts as an insane level of anxiety paired with a running doubt that she doesn't deserve to 'be there' or 'be doing' what she's doing. But she says once she has worked through all the second-guessing (and third-guessing), she discovers a new level of confidence.

This is why she reframes her imposter thoughts as a turning point; 'a moment of growth'. Yes, it's uncomfortable, because you're stretching to something new. You're not in your comfort zone. But just on the other side, confidence is waiting.

THE DRIVE TO LEARN MORE

Jennifer Kent, a senior research fellow at the University of Sydney, jokes that having imposter thoughts is almost a prerequisite for being an academic. She says they push her to keep seeking new knowledge and encourage her to question herself – two vital traits in the world of academia.

She says it's important to put some scaffolding around the questioning: she will question her approach and her work, but will never question herself. That's the boundary. Harnessing imposter thoughts in this way can give us the courage to ask questions instead of feeling like we have to pretend to have all the answers (which makes no sense because nobody has all the answers).

This reminds me of Adam Grant's book *Think Again*. In it, he talks about the importance of knowing what you don't know. Adam says we live in a world that rewards certainty and confidence and conviction, but we're much better off full of curiosity and doubt and flexibility, because that's how we keep learning.

On an episode of *This Working Life*,[7] Adam brought up the research of Basima Tewfik, a former doctoral student at Wharton who is now an assistant professor at the MIT Sloan School of Management. Basima studied investment and medical professionals and found those who experienced imposter thoughts often felt spurred to prove themselves on an interpersonal level. They put extra effort into communication and were more likely to collaborate with and encourage their colleagues. They arguably ended up performing better because of those imposter thoughts.[8] So while having imposter thoughts does elicit fear and doubt, it can also lead you to seek out new knowledge and be more open to learning.

It's somewhat reassuring to know that even if we can't completely eliminate imposter thoughts, they don't actually stop us from doing our jobs and doing them well.

EMBRACE YOUR DIFFERENCE

Remember Monique's dentist, Dr Daniel Hu? The feeling of being an imposter helped him see that he's in a Category of One and to embrace the things that make him unique.

Daniel says feeling like a capital-I imposter was the biggest hurdle he faced when entering the fitness world. 'I'm not a typical bodybuilder guy with big muscles so I felt like people were thinking, "Who is this kid? What's this skinny Asian guy doing here?"'

During a period of 'fake it till you make it', Daniel realised that it didn't matter if he couldn't lift the same as the next person – it's all relative. At the end of the class, everyone has struggled together, whether they're lifting one kilo or twenty kilos.

He also realised he didn't need to be exactly like the other instructors because he brings something unique to the table. He represents a different type of body. He's maybe less intimidating for people who are just starting out. And he brings a sense of fun to the class that others may lack. He isn't like everyone else and that's a good thing.

Be afraid. Do it anyway.

You can tame and reframe your imposter thoughts, but at some point, you may reach the stage where you have to make a choice to just be brave. To run with it, fear and doubt and all.

Give your 'hope' voice a moment to be heard against the noise of your imposter thoughts. Let it ask: but what if it works?

In my first meeting with Yamini the storyteller, she asked, 'So you said you were a little bit different as a lawyer. In what way?'

I said, 'Well, instead of speaking my presentation notes, I sing or rap them to backing music.'

Yamini laughed. Then she looked me dead in the eyes and said, 'Don't say, do. Do a rap.'

I felt an enormous burden lift off my shoulders. I felt elated. The negative voices were replaced with 'Yes, I am going to rap in my TEDx Talk!'

And I did. When I was on stage, with MC Hammer filling the auditorium and 2000 people bopping their heads, I was so grateful that I pushed through.

Imposter thoughts? They can't touch this.

SIT SPOT

A droplet of water doesn't doubt its place in the vast ocean. To borrow from Rumi, it knows it is not a drop in the ocean — it is the ocean in a drop.

What would it mean, in this moment, to let go of doubt, and know you belong where you are?

CHAPTER 14

Stress: The good, the bad and the burnt out

'I need more time.' 'Argh! My work colleague is driving me bonkers.' 'I'm exhausted. I feel pulled from all directions. I just want some sleep.'

We've met and made friends (kind of) with our imposter thoughts (aka Kevin), and now it is time to examine our stress.

We often refer to situations as 'causing us stress', but it might be helpful to see if, like imposter thoughts, we can separate the cause (the stressful situation) from the effect (the stress response). Perhaps there's a better way to carry our stress (because boy, can it get heavy), or even put down some of that weight for good.

Once we understand a bit more about stress, we'll ratchet up to look at uncertainty fatigue – that extra layer of tension and strain that has emerged with the pandemic – and the dangers of burnout.

Trigger or response?

Let's do a quick exercise. In the middle of a piece of paper, write the word 'STRESS'. (Give it all capitals because that's often how it feels.)

Set a timer for two minutes. Now write down any associations you have with the word 'stress'. See you back here in two minutes ...

Monique and I asked our friends to do this exercise and they came back with answers like:

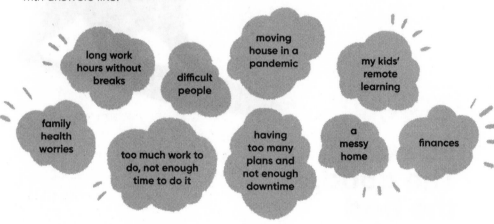

long work hours without breaks

difficult people

moving house in a pandemic

my kids' remote learning

family health worries

too much work to do, not enough time to do it

having too many plans and not enough downtime

a messy home

finances

We often talk about stress as challenging, demanding and taxing situations we face. But actually, these are all *causes* of stress. They're the stimulus. They are more accurately labelled as *stressors*.

Stress is the *response*.

Stress is our physical and mental reaction to the demands of the world. It's what happens in our bodies and in our minds when we're up against it. We're designed to experience stress and react to it. Think of it like a natural defence system: when the situation changes or a challenge arises, the body's 'fight or flight' mechanism kicks in. Our heart races, our breath quickens and our muscles ready for action. Stress is normal and it might not be useful dumping it into the 'bad' bucket. Some stress is good because it is motivating.

Take going to the gym. During a great workout, the body is placed under physical stress. The muscle tissue undergoes microscopic amounts of damage, and then the magic happens. The body is forced to repair itself and the muscles get a bit stronger as a result. This cycle of damage and repair is how we grow. Because our bodies have adapted to everyday activities, we need this little bit of stress to stimulate new growth.

Our minds can be the same. Being put under stress can power us forward. But we have to know our limits. We weren't made to be in 'fight or flight' mode 24/7. When the stress response keeps firing, day after day, it can put our health at serious risk. It can also lead to burnout (more on this soon).

Eustress vs distress

In talking about stress, it's useful to know that it comes in different forms.

Hans Selye, one of the pioneers of stress research, splits the concept into two distinct categories.

- **Eustress** has a positive effect on you. It feels like a *challenge* to overcome for the better. It energises and motivates you, and increases your focus and performance. It only lasts in the short term.
- **Distress** has a negative effect on you. It feels like a *threat* that you can't cope with. It triggers anxiety and concern, decreases focus and performance, and contributes to health problems. It lasts in the short and the long term.

Take a moment to reflect on a time you've experienced eustress.

Monique brought up the example of travelling overseas. That moment when you step off the plane in a bustling new city where you don't speak the language, and you're a bit nervous but also super excited as you push through the crowds and try to find your accommodation? (Aah, remember travelling?) That is eustress; it's a challenge you can deal with. It's nerv-citing.

Starting a new hobby, doing a presentation at work or cooking a complicated recipe for a group of people are other examples — as is the rush to finish a book on time!

Now reflect on a time you've experienced distress. This is what we tend to think of when we talk about stress. It's the form that impairs our functioning and thinking, and leaves us feeling overwhelmed.

We might feel this after experiencing the death of a loved one, serious illness, a job loss, filing for divorce or, say, a devastating global pandemic that upends life as we know it.

Your perspective matters

Stress is subjective. What feels like a slice of delicious eustress pie to me might taste more like deep distress to you. We all bring different perspectives and experiences to the table, and our responses can look different at different times.

I remember talking to Monique about appearing on stage for a live taping of an episode of *This Working Life* (which was later cancelled – thanks for nothing, COVID). She told me how stressed she was about speaking in front of a crowd and I asked her to describe how she physically felt.

'Well, my heart is pounding in my chest. I've got a stomach full of butterflies. My mind is racing, I feel clammy, I have to do about ten nervous wees.'

Aah, the stress response.

Monique put this feeling in the distress category. Speaking on stage felt like a *threat* that she didn't have the skills to cope with.

Interestingly, I felt the same physical symptoms, but I described my feeling as eustress (I called it an 'excited wee', not a nervous one). I interpreted that heart-pounding, mind-racing energy as a positive *challenge* that I could harness as a fuel.

So the same stressor triggered similar physical responses in us, but the stress we felt was completely different.

Uncertainty fatigue

There's a lot out of our control at the moment, and for many people it's fuelling something called uncertainty fatigue.

Uncertainty fatigue is exactly what it sounds like: the deep exhaustion that comes with long stretches of uncertainty and ambiguity (such as during a global pandemic).

'There are lots of questions that we just don't know the answer to,' says leadership expert and coach Julia Steel.[1] 'All of those questions like to consciously or subconsciously work away in our brain, which is mentally taxing.'

Julia suggests that it is helpful to recognise what is in and out of our control. Can we be OK with the idea that we can't control everything and shift our focus to what we can control?

'Control is important but at the same time, it's fictitious,' Julia says. 'I often see people putting a lot of energy into trying to control things that are actually out of their control. The more that we focus on what is within our control, the better off we'll be.'

This fits with the reductionist philosophy of solving problems, which states that narrowing your focus to one part of a complex issue, and working on solving or controlling that, can provide insight into how to understand the bigger issue.

How we react in stressful and uncertain situations can make all the difference. We have more power over our minds than we realise, so maybe we can make a choice about how we respond.

The Circles of Control, Influence and Concern

How do we shift our focus to what we can control? Monique has come across a model developed by management expert Steven Covey that is useful for working through situations she finds stress-inducing. It's called the Circles of Control, Influence and Concern.

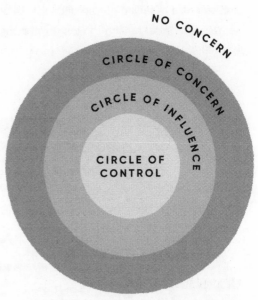

The **Circle of Concern** encompasses a range of things: your past, your future, attitudes in society, the organisation you work for, how your colleagues act and behave, how people drive their cars, global warming, government policy, the economy, the threat of nuclear war ... It's the biggest circle because there are so many things we are concerned about but can't change.

The **Circle of Influence** includes those things you can't directly control but can impact or influence through your actions and choices: your commitments, your reputation, whether you get a promotion, your children's future, your family's health.

The **Circle of Control**, the inner circle, includes those things you do have control over: where you work, who you vote for, who you follow on social media, how much news you consume, how you think and behave and react to certain things. You can't control being stuck in a traffic jam, for example, but you can control your response: you can choose to use the time to listen to a podcast rather than sit in anger.

One way to identify things you can influence or control is to ask yourself: 'Can I make a decision about what I can do?' The things you *can* make a decision about are things you can influence or control.

You can use the Circle of Control for life in general, or a single stressor. Below is an example of what it might look like for someone who is stressed about being in lockdown.

Often, even within something that feels completely out of your control (and stressful as a result), there are little things you can take charge of. You may not be able to control having to work from home, but you can influence what that looks like.

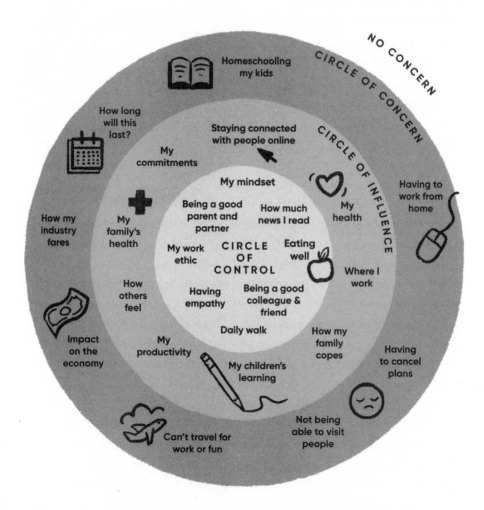

And if you can't control it, why stress about it? Why carry around all this weight when you lose nothing by leaving it behind? Can you relinquish the focus on what you can't control and instead feel empowered that there are some things you can grab control of?

This requires a mindset shift, and I know it's easier said than done, but I have found it useful. Give it a go by focusing on something you're feeling stressed about.

Monique finds it useful to write it down on paper rather than just thinking it through in your head. It makes it more concrete and helps with processing. When you start stressing about things you can't control, you can pick up the piece of paper with the three circles and focus back on what's within your spheres of influence and control.

Burnout: A different state of mind

When stress goes unmanaged, or is sustained for extended periods of time, it can become chronic. It can lead you down the potholed road to burnout.

Burnout is a state of emotional, physical and mental exhaustion, caused by excessive and prolonged stress.

What's the difference between the two?

We can usually link our stress to a particular stressor. For example, 'I've got a big presentation coming up', 'my team is short-staffed', 'my manager doesn't get what I'm trying to do'. We can identify one or two issues and understand that this is probably why we're feeling stressed. We still do our best to cope with the pressure. We can still imagine feeling better once everything is back under control. We still have hope.

Burnout is a totally different state of mind. That sense of hope is gone.

The World Health Organization[2] defines the occupational phenomenon as having three dimensions:

1. feelings of energy depletion or exhaustion
2. increased mental distance from your job, or feelings of negativism or cynicism related to your job
3. reduced professional efficacy.

It's feeling exhausted before the day even begins. It's feeling like the old you has disappeared, and this new version can't handle anything and doesn't even want to try, because what's the point of this damn job anyway?

UX designer Marie-Cécile Godwin has twice experienced burnout. 'I woke up and nothing was possible anymore. I was literally stuck in my bed, and the only thing I could do was cry,' she says. 'We think that only the weak burn out ... but even the people who thought that they were very strong and very resistant to stress somehow find themselves burning out.'[3]

Monique, who was quite burnt out by the end of 2020, describes it as insidious. 'It creeps up on you and takes hold so quietly that sometimes you don't even know it's there at first. It gets worse gradually, which can make it really hard to detect,' she says.

She remembers being in strategy meetings where her colleagues enthusiastically shared their dreams for the next five years. Everyone else had a vibrant vision for what they wanted to achieve, but she was completely blank. She barely made it through some meetings without bursting into tears.

Part of the issue for her was that by the time she noticed the red flags waving within, she was already shoulder-deep into the murky swamp of burnout. She was increasingly emotional and tense and, at the same time, detached. But even though she knew she was in a danger zone and that something needed to change, she was too exhausted to break the cycle. So she just kept wading further in, because she didn't have the strength to turn around. It isn't pretty.

Risk factors on the road to burnout

Absolutely anyone can become burnt out.

Some of it comes down to how well you manage stress. If you manage it well, even a very high-stress job doesn't have to lead to burnout (stay tuned for suggestions on dealing with your stress). But as we've seen during the pandemic, stress can compound on itself: the cumulative impact of many little stressors can be great.

You might be at higher risk of burnout if you:

▸ have a demanding workload and work long hours
▸ struggle with work–life coherence, or feel pressure to be 'always on'

- feel you have little or no control over the work you do, or the environment you work in
- lack clarity around your role or what is expected
- see yourself as a high achiever and have demanding expectations of yourself
- feel a lack of support from your manager
- feel like you are being treated unfairly at work (e.g. experiencing things like favouritism, unfair compensation, conflict or bullying).

Some industries are more at risk than others. People in helping professions, like social workers, healthcare professionals, emergency service workers or veterinarians, tend to be more at risk of burnout, along with workers who deal a lot with people, such as teachers, care workers or retail staff. There are also high rates of burnout in the legal industry, where people have heavy and complex workloads.

And this is all before COVID hit, bringing some industries to their knees.

The truth is, no matter what you do, or how well you handle stress, if it's too much for too long, you're at risk.

Signs you're already burnt out

Here's a set of questions to ask yourself:

- Do you feel exhausted or overwhelmed, day after day?
- Does it take a Herculean effort to get to work and get started?
- Do you feel despondent about your job and wonder what the point is?
- Have your sleep habits changed?
- Have you become more cynical at work?
- Have you become irritable or impatient with co-workers, customers or clients?
- Do you lack the energy to be consistently productive?
- Do you find it hard to concentrate?
- Have you stopped feeling a sense of satisfaction from your achievements?
- Are you isolating yourself (mentally or physically) from those around you?
- Do you have headaches, muscle pain or stomach pain?
- Are you getting sick more than usual?
- Do you feel anxious or depressed?

These questions are based on the most common signs of burnout. If you answered yes to a bunch of these, you may already be burnt out.

Monique remembers seeing a similar list pop up in her Instagram feed: signs and symptoms juxtaposed against a bright and cheery background. She slowly read each of the bullet points, and then read them again. 'Yes, that's me. Oh yep, I feel that. Oh, and that too.' She then showed her partner – 'I tick every single box on this list!' – and he nodded knowingly. She had been burnt out for months, but this was the first time she had acknowledged it. It was a turning point.

To fix a problem, you first have to acknowledge it exists.

Rekindling the flame

When psychologist Herbert Freudenberger first coined the term in 1974, he described burnout as 'the extinction of motivation or incentive'. Extinction implies a total termination – that what is lost is lost forever. The asteroid wiping out the dinosaurs. No going back.

But we aren't the dinosaurs (even those of us whose cracking joints and aches and smile lines sometimes make us feel like we're from that era). We can find our way back.

How? By finding and implementing some strategies to manage our stress. This might include the following:

▸ **Taking some time off work to rest.** If you're really burnt out, it can take months to fully recover. A big holiday would be great, but all rest, any rest, is good rest. Even microdoses count. (Chapter 17 on rituals, page 239, offers some easy ways to switch off.)
▸ **Establishing routines.** Put up some boundaries to help you return to a state of work–life coherence. (There are loads of ideas in Chapter 15 on routines, page 211.)
▸ **Job crafting.** Injecting more meaning into your work and filling your day with more of what you enjoy doing can be a great way to reduce stress. This is most effective when you catch burnout early. (Flick back to Chapter 8, page 113, to see how you can make it work for you.)
▸ **Prioritising a healthy diet.** This has been shown to boost mood and energy levels.

- **Connecting to your body through movement.** We all know exercise makes us feel better, but it can be hard to muster the motivation to work out when you're burnt out. You have zero energy. I prefer to think of it as 'movement' instead. How can you connect to your body through movement? Marie-Cécile found yoga really helpful; Monique went on gentle walks in nature. You don't have to sweat it out to feel a benefit.
- **Nourishing your creative side.** Can you find a hobby or activity that has nothing to do with your work? This will help activate a different part of your brain and bring more joy back to your life. (Check out the resources section, page 296, for some great microcredentials platforms where you can explore free short courses.)
- **Mindfulness.** You could try forest bathing (Monique will give you some starting points in Chapter 16, page 229). There's also the HeartMath HRV meditations (see Chapter 12, page 179), loads of free mindfulness apps, or even the Jon Kabat-Zinn eight-week mindfulness for stress reduction program, which I did during my recovery from shingles.
- **Getting plenty of sleep.** Meditation before bed can really help, as can limiting your screen time in the hours before you go to sleep. Why not try leaving your phone in another room overnight and using an old-school alarm to wake up?
- **Seeking support.** You are not alone and there is no shame in seeking help. Build up a support squad of people you can talk things out with.

I really want to narrow in on that last one because it is so powerful. This is another moment where we can gain so much by choosing to turn towards others.

Often the advice is to go to your manager and ask them to support you in your recovery from burnout. But I've noticed that this doesn't feel like an option for a lot of people at the moment. What I'm hearing is, 'My manager is burnt out too. They have no capacity to listen to my troubles because they've got their own going on. They can't even help themselves.' Other people are worried about their jobs and afraid of exposing the fact that they're potentially not performing at their best.

My advice is to find a trusted person. If you have the psychological safety to go speak to your manager, that's great. If not, try talking to a family member, friend, colleague or therapist. Many workplaces offer employees free and confidential counselling services. If you are feeling like you're deep in a black hole then make sure your doctor is on the list too, or try calling a support line like Beyond Blue (other counselling and support services are listed in the resources section). Please don't go it alone. There is no shame in asking for help.

I have found that talking about my stress is a great way to release it. Talking it out can help us feel far less helpless, and far less alone.

And I would add two more points to the list of stress-management tips:

Almost everyone is feeling some level of burnout after 2020 (and 2021). One of the best things we can do is acknowledge that we need to be gentle with ourselves and be kind to one another. More than ever, I have been trying to bring my value of connection to my interactions with others. I have been searching for the kindest interpretation of a situation.

So if somebody writes an inflammatory email, or does something that makes me feel like they're conspiring to make my day shit, I pause. What is the kindest interpretation of this situation? Almost always, I realise they're probably not doing this to make my life a misery. They're probably exhausted, or even burnt out. Realising this releases some of the stress I would have felt as a result of their actions and I am able to better turn towards them.

It's not just up to you

When I talked to Marie-Cécile about her experience of burnout, she told me that the main misconception surrounding it is that an individual is solely responsible for their situation, and is thus solely responsible for handling it. Let's bust that myth.

Michael Leiter has extensively studied burnout and sees it as the result of a 'relationship breakdown' between the employee and the employer.

'It's not because the job's all bad, it's not because the person is flawed in some way – it's because the connection between the two of them has gone screwy,' he says.[4]

Because both sides are in the relationship, they both have a role to play in helping when it goes awry. It's not enough for your employer to say: 'You go off and fix yourself and come back when you're ready to be the way I want you to be.' We need to double down on being human – as people, and as organisations.

I saw some examples of organisational empathy in action in mid-2021, when the weight of the pandemic started to take a toll. Some companies, like LinkedIn and Bumble, gave their thousands of staff a collective paid week off to de-stress. The idea was that workers wouldn't feel guilty about taking the leave, because everyone was off at the same time, and because they weren't inundated by emails and project requests piling up in their absence, they could *actually* unplug.

During the pandemic, Sarah Harden knew she had to find a way to show employees 'so much freaking grace'. Sarah is the CEO of Hello Sunshine, Reese Witherspoon's pioneering media company. She's based in LA, and the situation there was extremely grim. Sarah talked about burnout as almost a given in times of such extreme psychological and existential strain.

She approached the problem from a place of collaborative leadership. She started talking to the team, asking for ideas of how they could help each other. One of the suggestions was to all take the same day off, on a regular basis. Sarah calls it a recharge day. So now, at least once a month, there is a long weekend 'where the whole company goes dark'. Everyone knows it's coming up; it's something to push towards during some very bleak times.

In many ways, I think this is less about the leave (though, that's obviously great) and more about what it symbolises: this is a workplace that has your back. This is a workplace that values and supports you. It's saying, 'Hey, we know this is hard. Let's stand and face this together.' One paid day off a month is so much more than one paid day off a month. It is a true expression of empathy.

Once we are on the other side of the pandemic, whenever that may be, we need to take stock of what it has taught us about burnout. And this isn't just on us as individuals. Employers also need to put measures in place to reduce the risk going forward. This might involve:

▶ training managers to spot and respond to signs and symptoms
▶ encouraging job crafting
▶ placing performance expectations and metrics within employees' control
▶ designing jobs to allow for autonomy and flexibility
▶ encouraging open and honest relationships between colleagues.

If you're a manager, Michael Leiter advises avoiding going straight to a question like, 'Are you burnt out?' Instead you might just say, 'Does your workload feel OK?' or 'Are there ways we could do this work differently?' The idea is to open the door, without forcing employees into the room.

Studies show people are far less likely to experience burnout when they feel supported in their work, connected to their team and manager, and when they have meaningful goals that they can realistically attain without having to burn the candle at both ends.

Sitting with stress

Stress is part of life. I'm sorry to say it isn't going anywhere anytime soon. But by bringing a bit more awareness to why we are feeling stressed, and what we can and can't control about the situation, we can choose to respond in a different way.

By knowing what to look for in ourselves, and recognising when our stress levels are reaching boiling point, we can better manage how we're feeling.

We can learn to sit with the stress — not quite comfortably, but without it feeling quite so heavy.

We can put some of the load down, and walk forward a little bit lighter.

SIT SPOT

A green leaf doesn't resist turning red when autumn approaches.

A tree doesn't cling to leaves that long to float free; it simply releases them to the ground.

What would it mean, in this moment, to let go of the things you cannot control?

CHAPTER 15

Supercharge your day with a great routine

When you wake up in the morning, what's the very first thing you do after opening your eyes? And what's the very last thing you do before you shut them and go to sleep at night? A lot of people have the same answer to both of those questions: 'I look at my phone.'

There's no judgement here. Those smart little devices are a huge part of our lives, and they're stunningly seductive. The allure of a quick scroll through the news or social media as we start the day is very real, as is the temptation to shoot off one last work email before we hit the hay. It doesn't take long for it to become a habit, and that habit can spread like wildfire into the rest of our waking hours.

While routines sometimes get a bad rap as being drearily monotonous and limiting for our creativity, I've found the opposite to be true. There is a lot to be gained from bringing more intention to how we spend our time.

In their simplest form, routines are something you do regularly. They can be game changers that connect you to your purpose and help you achieve your goals. In this chapter we'll explore specific ways routines can:

- supercharge your morning
- help you become more effective at work
- help you switch off (*actually* switch off) when the day is done.

The importance of contextual markers

It's useful to put the importance of routines into a big-picture context. Our routines, even small ones, are vital signposts that help us navigate our days.

During the first COVID lockdown in Melbourne at the end of March 2020, I felt like I was wading in treacle. My days took way more effort and they all seemed to meld into one. I was working from home, but it felt more like I was living at work.

When my friend and all-round communication legend Colin James came on to *This Working Life*[1] to help us navigate remote working, he helped me to understand why: I was lacking 'contextual markers'.

Contextual markers are all the little things that help us step through the day, almost like the headings in this book. They help our brain know what to expect and what mode it needs to be in.

In the morning, it's all those things that indicate, 'Hey, switch on, it's time to work'. Putting on a suit, commuting, buying a coffee, standing in the lift waiting to be taken up to your floor. All these little things are contextual markers that prime you to focus on work. In the afternoon, contextual markers also tell us it's time to stop focusing on work. We log off, bid our colleagues farewell and commute back home.

Many of us lost these contextual markers during the pandemic. The antidote to this is to consciously and consistently build your own contextual markers, ones that fit the way you're working now.

Monique, for example, found that when she started working from home, her morning routine evaporated. It became far too easy to hit snooze, scroll on her phone, answer work emails from bed, then roll out from under the covers five minutes before logging on to work at her kitchen-table-turned-office-space. Where had all her time gone? How had she ever fit in a walk and shower and breakfast and getting ready and commute all before 8 am? Similarly, in the afternoon, she struggled to switch modes and found it hard to stop working when the work day was done.

Monique was missing the contextual marker of her commute – that space where she could mentally wind up for work and, later, mentally wind down for home. She brought some awareness to the problem and came up with a novel solution: as part of her morning routine, she now leaves 'home', walks a big loop around the block, and then arrives 'at work'. At the end of the day she does this in reverse: leaving 'work' and walking 'home'.

This sets up a mental boundary between the two spaces and helps her shift between mindsets. It restores a contextual marker that helps her thrive. (Added bonus: it means she actually gets out of her pyjama pants.)

A bespoke design

Before we go any further, there's one point I want to emphasise in a big grab-a-loudspeaker-and-crank-up-the-volume-to-max way: routines are not one-size-fits-all. What works for me or Monique or anyone else may not work for you and that's OK. You should work with whatever you've got. You can take inspiration from others, but really you want to end up with something that is unique to you.

I'm going to load you up with examples of different routines and advice on how to start building yours. See what resonates, and start experimenting.

Take what you love, ditch what you don't, and make changes until you get to a place where it feels right for you.

Jumpstart your day

Let's start with routines for the morning – whatever time your morning begins! I'm not here to take a wrecking ball to your body clock and convince you to drag yourself out of bed at sparrow's fart if that's not your thing.

My own morning routine started with a daily mindfulness practice as I was recovering from shingles. As part of a wider focus on health, I then built it up, little by little, adding in other things that made me feel good. It has changed over the years, and it is still changing.

This is what it looks like at the moment. (I know it may appear a little intense, but I genuinely love it. I don't even need an alarm at this point.)

▶ **5.30 am:** This block is about slowly waking up my body. I get up and say, 'Today is going to be a great day!' (This is inspired by Stanford social scientist B. J. Fogg, who says this tiny habit changed everything for him.) I follow that with lemon water, stretching, and the Five Tibetan Rites, a sequence of five exercises. This was introduced to me by my friend Greg

Marsh, who swears by the routine, especially as you get older. It has been referred to as the fountain of youth. I've been doing it for two years and I definitely feel like it has made a difference. I feel pretty good for my age of 49-going-on-150!

- **5.45 am:** Butter coffee (ghee, coconut [MCT] oil, coffee).
- **6.00 am:** Journalling / HRV meditation / Alexander Technique body scan. I started studying the Alexander Technique with Jeremy Woolhouse to help me with vocal tension as a result of my workshop facilitation, radio presenting and loud storytelling at noisy pubs. It is a wonderful practice that feels like magic sometimes. I have adapted a standing body scan for my morning routine as it helps set me up for the day. It also seems to have helped me ease the 'scrunching' habits I had with my shoulders and neck.
- **6.30 am:** Walk along our local creek track.
- **7.30 am:** 'Zen Kitchen' (I empty the dishwasher). Eat breakfast.
- **8.00 am:** An hour of 'deep work', focused on the main priority for the day.

Over time I've come to feel like I'm on autopilot when I do my routine; it's a few habits stacked on top of each other, not something I have to force myself to do. I just wake up and start doing it.

The key with any routine is to blend structure and flexibility. I try to hold it lightly. It's more about consistency than intensity, and it's never set in stone. During the COVID-19 lockdowns, for example, my stress levels rose and my sleep took a hammering, so I softened my routines a bit.

BIG ROCKS AND PHONE BLACKOUTS

Monique revived her morning routine by bringing back her 'commute', and she kept building from there. She finds that having a routine gives her an understanding of what to expect in her morning, which helps to free up some of her brain space.

Like me, she starts the day by waking up her body.

- **6.30 am:** Yoga in the lounge room (thanks, YouTube!).
- **7.10 am:** Breakfast and coffee (out in the morning sunshine).
- **7.30 am:** Walk 'to work'.
- **7.45 am:** Start work (focusing on Big Rocks).

Big Rocks is a metaphor for prioritisation that you might have heard of before. It was popularised by Stephen Covey in his book *The Seven Habits of Highly Effective People*.

Imagine you're holding a bucket that you want to fill with rocks, pebbles and sand. How do you get everything in the bucket? If you put the sand in first, you leave no room for the pebbles and rocks. If you put the pebbles in first, you have room for the sand but not the rocks. The only way to fit everything in is to put the big rocks in first. Then you can add the smaller pebbles, which will disperse among the larger rocks. Then you can pour the sand in and it will fill all the spaces in between.

The big rocks symbolise the things that are the most important in your workload. The pebbles represent everything of medium importance. And, finally, the sand represents all of the smaller items that are less important in your work. You need to schedule the big, important things first, then fill in the remaining time gaps with less important tasks.

You'll also notice there's no phone time in Monique's morning. She's left the ol' roll-and-scroll behind. She bought an old alarm clock to wake herself up and charges her phone in the kitchen. This removes the temptation to look at her phone first thing, or when she wakes up in the middle of the night.

Monique tries to not look at her phone until around midday. Well, not looking at it at all is a bit of an exaggeration. She does a quick check first thing in the morning, otherwise she gets anxious about missing something important and not looking at her phone becomes an even bigger distraction than looking at it.

But the vast majority of the time, that quick scan reveals nothing of great urgency and she can put it down again. All the texts and emails and notifications can wait until the afternoon. That way, her mind stays clear of distractions while she gets her most important work done, the work that needs the most focus. The Big Rocks.

GIFT YOURSELF AN HOUR

When you boil it down, the thread that connects my morning routine with Monique's, and those of other people I've met, is the sense of purpose driving them. While our routines are different, we all use them as a means to start our day purposefully.

My friend Penny Locaso is a former corporate executive turned 'Happiness Hacker' – and a member of the 5 am Club. This is a concept started by leadership expert Robin Sharma, where you wake up at 5 am, then do twenty minutes of exercise, twenty minutes of planning and twenty minutes of study.

The irony is that Penny has been getting up at 5 am for ages, because she's a morning person like me. She just wasn't spending that time intentionally. She now sees that first hour as a gift she gives to herself. The first hour of her day is not for work, or for anyone else. It sets the tone for her day to be 'truly focused, intentional and joyous'.

As you know, I'm 100 per cent here for making adjustments to have things better suit you. So don't tell Robin, but I reckon this could also be the 11 am Club, the 3 pm Club, or even the 9 pm Club after your kids have gone to bed. Rather than being a way to set up your day, it could become a way to switch off or wind down. It is still a way to gift yourself intentional time.

Hack your work day

A sense of conscious, purposeful design can help you make traction during your work day.

Whether through incorporating the practice of timeboxing or time batching, rethinking meetings or avoiding the email suck, these strategies can help you take charge of your time and prioritise tasks, rather than zigzagging between different things as they demand your attention.

TIMEBOXING

I have been experimenting with timeboxing since I spoke to Nir Eyal on an episode of *This Working Life*.[2] Nir is a behavioural design expert and the author of *Hooked* (about habit-forming tech design) and *Indistractable* (about the hidden psychology driving us to distraction and how to control it).

Timeboxing is the practice of setting a fixed amount of time for every activity in your day, down to the minute, and integrating the resulting time blocks into your schedule. Instead of working on a task until it's done, you proactively decide how much time you'll spend on it and when.

Nir believes this practice beats alternatives like keeping to-do lists. 'The way most people use to-do lists is destroying their productivity,' he says. 'Studies have found that people who wake up in the morning and say, "Oh, what am I going to do next, let me look at my to-do list" statistically get a lot less done than the people who do timeboxing.'

Nir says that's because to-do lists do two things:

- They encourage us to do the easy tasks in our day, as opposed to the important tasks, so we can tick more items off the list.
- They guilt us into feeling like we haven't done enough if we haven't ticked off everything on the list. That guilt leaches into our leisure time.

So even though it may feel like the enemy of spontaneity, timeboxing can be life-changing in terms of productivity. But it doesn't begin and end with work: you also plan time with your friends or family, time for yourself, for exercise or hobbies, whatever it might be. It's all on your calendar.

Nir advises people to think about their values, and about the person they want to be next week. How does that person spend their time, what are their relationships like, and how can timeboxing help achieve that? To help answer those questions, Nir gives people three 'life domains' to focus on: yourself, your relationships and your work. (Nir says most people start with work, when it should actually come last.)

- **Yourself.** This is centred on the idea that you need to take care of yourself before you can take care of others. Do you have time in your day for proper rest and exercise? Do you have a regular bedtime? Does how you spend your time reflect your values?
- **Your relationships.** Nir says we have to make space for the most important people in our lives. 'I used to leave whatever scraps of time were left over for the people I love most, which is terrible. So now I have time in my calendar for my daughter.'
- **Your work.** This includes time for both reactive work and reflective work, as Nir terms it. All our work involves elements of reactive work: answering phone calls, responding to emails and all that jazz. But how much time do we allow for the planning, strategising and thinking? If we don't do that, we're missing out.

When I timebox, I schedule in meetings and blocks of time to do the essential work I need to do. I also make time for things like breaks and transit time. I try to do the Big Rocks scheduling first, then fit the pebbles and sand in around that. My Big Rocks extend to life stuff and include my health and family.

The one downside of this approach is that my calendar looks a bit frightening. It can be stressful to look at, particularly in those times when I'm seeing work as a burden and not a gift. One thing I have done to make it a little better is to colour code: yellow for health stuff (which is a priority for me), blue for breaks, red for this book, orange for the ABC, and so on. So, my week tends to look something like this.

	SUN **26**	MON **27**	TUE **28**	
5AM	**Morning routine** 5:45 – 7:30am	**Morning routine** 5:45 – 7:30am	**Morning routine** 5:45 – 7:30am	
6AM				
7AM		**Breakfast** 7:30–8am	**Breakfast** 7:30–8am	
8AM	**Deep work** 8:00 – 9:00am	**Deep work** 8:00 – 9:00am	**Book writing** 8:00 – 9:30am	
9AM		**TWL huddle** 9:00 – 10:00am		
10AM		**Work prep** 10:00 – 11:15am	**Consulting** 10:00 – 12:00pm	
11AM		**Book meeting with Mon** 11:15 – 12:00pm		
12PM		**Transit** 12:00 – 12:45pm	**Transit** 12:00 – 12:45pm	
1PM		**Lunch** 12:45pm		
		Workshop 1:30 – 3:00pm		
2PM	**Lunch** 2:00pm		**Lunch** 2:00pm	
	TWL prep/reading 2:45 – 4:45pm		**Strategy** 2:30 – 5:00pm	
3PM				
4PM		**Meeting** 4:00 – 4:45pm		
5PM				
6PM	**Dinner** 6:00 – 7:00pm	**Dinner** 6:00 – 7:00pm	**Dinner** 6:00 – 7:00pm	
7PM				
8PM				
9PM				

	WED **29**	THU **30**	FRI **1**	SAT **2**
				Tech Sabbath
	Morning routine 5:45 – 7:30am	Morning routine 5:45 – 7:30am	Morning routine 5:45 – 7:30am	
	Breakfast 7:30–8am	Breakfast 7:30–8am	Breakfast 7:30–8am	Breakfast 7:30–8am
	Book writing 8:00 – 9:30am	TWL recording 8:30 – 12:30am	Deep work 8:00 – 9:00am	
			ABC recording 9:15 – 12:15pm	
	Meeting 10:30 – 11:30am			Doctor 11:00 – 12:00pm
	Meeting 11:30 – 12:15pm			
		Break 12:30 – 1:30pm		
		Live cross 1:30 – 2:00pm	Meeting 1:15 – 2:00pm	
	Lunch 2:00pm		Lunch 2:00pm	Lunch 2:00pm
	Interview TWL 2:30pm			
	Call Mon 3:00 – 4:00pm	Meeting 3:15 – 4:00pm	Pick up Billie (can't move) 3:30 – 5:00pm	
		Meeting 4:00 – 4:45pm		
			Meeting with Mon 5:00 – 6:00pm	
	Dinner 6:00 – 7:00pm	Dinner 6:00 – 7:00pm	Dinner 6:00 – 7:00pm	Dinner 6:00 – 7:00pm
			Tech Sabbath 7:30–3am	

I find it incredibly useful because it makes it clear that I can't do everything. Not everything can fit into my life. I only have so much time and I need to prioritise the things that are most important to me. Period.

The colour coding also helps me find (and hold on to) balance within my portfolio career. A quick glance at my calendar can show me if one part of my work life is taking over my schedule.

BATCH YOUR TIME

Timeboxing has some overlap with the concept of time batching, where you dedicate yourself to one task for a period of time, blocking out all other distractions.

Time management expert Kate Christie, the founder and CEO of Time Stylers, gave *This Working Life* the lowdown on time batching.[3] Kate says it is all about 'curating your time so you can live the life you love'. She uses a timer to build 45-minute periods of concentrated work into her schedule. 'The idea is to work in a really intense way for a period of time, against the clock.'

Kate thinks of her output in terms of high-value and low-value tasks.

- A high-value task is one that requires your skill and expertise, and which is either revenue-generating or cost-reducing.
- A low-value task is something below your skill level, like answering emails or doing administration work, and is generally cost-incurring.

Kate feels most productive in the morning so that's when she does her high-value work. She saves lower-value tasks for the afternoon when she's less energetic. If you're someone who takes a while to wake up and feels sharpest in the afternoons, you might do this in reverse order.

Kate's hot tip for time batching for those working from home is to use an oven timer instead of an alarm; that way when it goes off, you have to physically get up from your desk to turn it off. (Hot tip, get it?) You have a break for fifteen minutes, then come back and reset the timer, ready for your next 45-minute batch of focused work.

This will sound familiar to fans of the popular Pomodoro Technique, which uses a timer to break work down into intervals, traditionally twenty-five minutes in length, separated by short breaks. Every two hours – or four 'pomodoros' – you take a longer fifteen-minute to thirty-minute break.

It's not about working every single second of the day, it's about recognising how and when you work your best and utilising that time. As the saying goes: work smarter, not harder.

RETHINK MEETINGS

Meetings can be a huge time suck in our days. There are necessary ones, of course, but there are also far too many meetings that should have been an email (and far too many Zooms that should have been a phone call).

Monique has two days a week where she isn't available for meetings. On these days, she knows she can get into a deep and focused zone, and stay there. If that's not possible for you, perhaps you could block out a few hours on a couple of days each week.

Kate says another simple way to claw back time is to switch up the length of the meeting. We often have thirty-minute or sixty-minute meetings because those are the time intervals set in the calendar, but could a twenty- or forty-minute meeting be scheduled instead? A clear agenda for the meeting and an effective facilitator can also help streamline the amount of time required.

Another tip? Gently question if you're required at the meeting: does it need your specific ideas, skills and expertise? Looking at the agenda of meetings you are invited to can help you determine this. If you don't think you are needed, find the discipline to gently push back, or at least push that meeting into a low-value time of your day.

ESCAPE THE EMAIL VORTEX

The topic of emails – and how to avoid getting lost in them – comes up again and again when I talk to people about their routines. It's something I struggle with at times, and it can feel like my inbox constantly seeps into the rest of my day. Technology can habituate us inadvertently, so we have to make an effort to put it aside.

Kate doesn't check her email until she's completed the first high-value task of the day. She schedules two to three email batches a day, and in between each batch she turns off her email alerts to avoid being distracted.

Penny checks her email twice a day in pre-scheduled thirty-minute slots. 'That has been a game changer,' she says. 'I fundamentally believe that email is someone else's to-do list. It's just noise. It takes you away from the intentional things you want to do. No one goes, "You know what? Today I intend to spend two hours in email because that's going to set me up for my best day.'"[4]

This won't work for every job, of course.

If you do need to regularly check emails, try setting a specific time to do it, such as the top of each hour, and turn off pop-up notifications that will steal your attention in the in-between time. You can also give people a heads-up to not expect an instant response by setting up an automatic reply – Penny's tells people that she practises deep work in segments of the day and will reply when she can.

We can also do small things to help others feel that their boundaries are OK. Our brilliant publisher Arwen Summers has a great email signature on messages she sends after hours: 'I work flexibly and am sending this message now because it suits me. I don't expect you to read, respond or action it outside of your regular hours.' She tells us she can't take credit; she got it from diversity and inclusion specialist Troy Roderick. There are variations on this wording across industries, but the message is the same: just because I'm online doesn't mean you have to be.

Switch off (*actually* switch off)

Winding down can be difficult for many of us, especially if your home is also your office. In my experience, work just leaches into the rest of the house.

What we need is a closing-down routine, what Kate calls a 'hard stop'. A line drawn in the sand that work cannot cross, try as it might. I find a nice warm bath with Epsom salts does the trick on most days. That's my contextual marker that the work day is done. (I've also built a special ritual for Friday evenings – I'll dish out those details in Chapter 17, page 239.)

Before she leaves 'work' and walks 'home', Monique makes a quick written note of the key things she needs to do the next day. By writing the tasks and any associated thoughts and ideas down, she finds she can release her mental grip on them for the evening. She knows that list will hold those tasks until she is ready to pick them up again the next day (come morning, the list helps shape her Big Rocks for the day). If she has a brainwave during the evening, she'll add it to the list, but she won't progress the work until the next day. Interestingly, I think this would make me fixate on work even more. It goes to show that routines aren't one-size-fits-all.

Kate's hard stop is built around when she needs to pick her daughter up. She starts closing down at 3.45 pm, then stretches and spends fifteen minutes doing a puzzle with music turned up really loud. This switches up how she's using her brain. 'Then the rest of the day is mine,' she explains.

How do you claim the rest of your day if you feel guilty for not working? That's a thing for so many people, who feel guilty about any form of 'me time', even if it's well earned and desperately needed.

Steph Clarke, a facilitator, designer and podcaster (there's another portfolio career), finds it useful to incorporate planned relaxation time into her schedule. 'If I've planned the relaxing, or if I've planned reading a book all morning, or sitting in bed and doing some doodling, or thinking about things or listening to a podcast – and this is going to make me sound like a complete weirdo – then I don't feel bad for doing it,' she says. 'I'm trying to unlearn the idea that relaxation equals being unproductive. It's just not true. I know I'm at my best when I balance my work with the space to imagine, so this is how I design my time to make relaxation happen.'

Monique also uses the 'digital wellbeing' functions on her phone to limit usage of certain apps at certain times. There are no email or social media notifications after 5 pm, and no notifications at all after 8 pm when the phone enters a 'bedtime mode'. 'If I don't know the email is there, I can't feel guilty for not answering it,' she says. Can't beat that logic!

The weight of expectation

It's important that our workday routines fit with the work we do and won't stop us from meeting the expectations of our role (provided that the expectations are sustainable).

My approach to this is that creativity follows constraints. You need to work within the boundaries of your role and know what the expectations of the job are. Then you can start to get creative within those constraints. If your job description requires you to be super responsive to emails after hours, you can't suddenly turn around and go, 'Oh sorry, I'm no longer checking my account after 5 pm. I'm entirely offline every weekend too. Deal with it.' That's not going to get you very far if it's part of the job you signed up for.

Similarly, when Monique tried to follow Penny's lead and only check her email twice a day, she ended up missing an important meeting that'd been slotted in at the last minute. 'I felt incredibly sheepish saying, "I'm sorry, I turned off notifications and I was actively ignoring my email because I'm trying to only check it twice a day,"' says Monique. 'Keeping across my emails during the day was part of my job at the ABC, so it wasn't the most appropriate experiment to try.'

The trick is to identify when the expectations you're feeling are unrealistic or unfounded. A lot of people feel that their work carries an expectation to always be 'on', and if you aren't, there's an implicit penalty. That's definitely true of some jobs, and there's no denying that some work cultures have toxic and unhealthy expectations of employees. But I also wonder if, for many of us, that weight of expectation is something we pile on ourselves? If you question it, does the expectation you feel come from others, or from yourself? I think you'll find a lot of it is mostly self-driven.

That's definitely been Monique's experience. At Radio National she had some flexibility around her hours. She works best in the morning, so she'd start a couple of hours earlier than her colleagues. But when the time came to log off, she often didn't. She felt like she needed to be around for the people who worked a regular 9 to 5. Over time, without realising it, she'd painted herself into a corner – people had a perception of how much work she could get done in a day, but they didn't realise it was because she was working some pretty long days.

During the pandemic it started spilling over into the evenings. Having an email app on her phone made it all too easy to be responsive to after-hour emails or get that extra bit of work done. There was never any explicit command from above for her to do any of that, and Monique knows her bosses would have given her a slap on the wrist (with love) had they known.

But she wanted to be seen as capable – in her own eyes as much as those of others – so she didn't say anything. She got stuck on the hamster wheel of overwork and presenteeism, and didn't know how to get off. She didn't even realise how hard her little legs had been working to keep up until the wheel came to a complete halt.

We need to bring awareness to where the expectations we feel come from. If they're fuelled from within, we need to find the discipline to slow ourselves down. We all have superpowers, but none of us are superhuman.

Overworking ourselves ultimately doesn't serve anyone.

LAB EXPERIMENT

Start building your routine

So all this talk of routines has got you super-duper excited about starting one, right? But where to begin? Just like the routines themselves, there's no standard approach to welcoming one into your life.

Having said that, I do have some pointers that might help.

START SMALL. VERY SMALL.

My biggest piece of advice is to start with one thing. Something easy and satisfying. And small. Very small.

B. J. Fogg talks about developing 'tiny habits' by linking your desired behaviour to something you already do, and taking advantage of the natural momentum. He has a 'recipe' for this, and it has two ingredients.

- **An 'anchor' moment.** This is something you already do. This may be something like sitting down at your desk, filling a kettle with water or starting your lunch break.
- **A new behaviour.** This is the new tiny behaviour you want to develop into a habit. It may be drinking a glass of water, stretching, or identifying a top priority for the day.

To design your tiny habit, you pair the two ingredients together like this: 'After I [anchor moment], I will [behaviour].'

See how your new tiny habit is now linked to something you're already doing?

One executive friend decided that he needed to build some body strengthening into his life, but he was working long hours so he couldn't get to the gym. He used this recipe to build a new habit. The anchor moment he chose was brushing his teeth. His new tiny behaviour was to do at least five push-ups. So now every time he brushes his teeth, he does five push-ups. If the recipe works for you, the tiny habit will naturally start to follow the anchor moment. If it doesn't, you may just need to rework the recipe.

You can stack tiny habits on top of each other, building them into a bigger routine bit by bit.

THINK ABOUT THE PIECES, NOT THE PUZZLE

It is useful to think about your goals – but with a twist.

Instead of focusing on the long-term, big-picture goals, think smaller. Think about the stepping stones. What do you want to achieve in the next week, or two weeks, or month, or two months? Think about the person you want to be at each of those stages.

Then shift your focus to how you're going to get there. If your goal is a big puzzle, what are all the individual pieces that need to click into place? What needs to happen to get you to where you want to go, and what routines can you harness to help?

Tackle it one puzzle piece at a time.

This is also a useful approach for any goals that feel far away. Writing a whole book, for example? Completely unattainable goal. Writing a chapter? Maybe, at a stretch. But writing a small section of a chapter? That I can definitely do.

When we regularly slot these puzzle pieces into place, it's motivating, and it spurs us on. And small acts can turn into big changes.

BE CONSISTENT AND PERSISTENT

Your routines don't have to be rigid, or something you do every single day forever, but you need to do them enough so that they're not completely hypothetical. You need to be 'consistent and persistent', as Penny describes it, and you need to be patient.

The idea that it takes twenty-one days to form a habit is tossed around all the time, but the truth is that there's no magic number: some habits are easier to form than others, and some people may find it easier to develop new behaviours.

It does help to set a specific amount of time to test out a routine. Can you commit to doing it for two weeks or a month? Reflect on how it goes, adjust as needed and continue on.

If you slip, get back on track, but don't be too hard on yourself. We're only human.

KEEP BUILDING (AND HAVE FUN!)

Once you've got a small routine working for you, start building it up. Maybe think about which parts of this chapter most resonated with you or captured your attention. The ones you're excited about are worth a try.

You can add to your routine over time. You can also subtract from it. Keep making small changes until it feels right, until you've got something designed just for you.

Don't be afraid to experiment along the way – that's part of the fun. Remember, every day is Lab Day.

SIT SPOT

Nature moves in predictable cycles: the rise and fall of the sun, the ebb and flow of the ocean tides, the changing of the seasons, the migrations of birds, the hibernations of bears and bumblebees.

What would it mean, in this moment, to embrace a regular rhythm?

CHAPTER 16

Give your brain a boost in nature

Hey, friends – it's Monique here. You're in my hands for this chapter, and before you read any further, I want to ask you to do something for me. If you can, get up and take this book outside for the next little bit. Yes, really. Find a nice spot to plonk yourself down and then read on. If being outside isn't an option, maybe there's a window you can get comfortable near – even just sitting with a few house plants will do. Welcome a bit of nature into your life in any way you can. It'll make you feel great, and it also means you won't have to take my word on what comes next. You'll be able to feel it for yourself.

I've always loved this world, and have always been a loud and proud nature nerd. For as long as I've been working, the great outdoors has been a source of solace and renewal, a reliable partner for stress management. Whenever things started to reach boiling point for me, I'd get out for a hike or go camping, and return refreshed, ready to face the world again. When I started my forest bathing guide training at the end of 2020, I was right on the cusp of leaving the ABC, and I was completely burnt out. I actually felt like I'd been hollowed out by the cult of busy, reduced to a crispy little shell, still smoking at the edges. My weekend trips into nature weren't really slicing through that stress in the same way.

My training involved a lot of time outside, building deep reciprocal relationships with nature, and it was the antidote to the intense exhaustion I'd been feeling. I realised that nature isn't something separate to me, somewhere 'out there' that I visit when I need help — it's something I am a part of. We are nature, and nature is us.

Gaining that perspective has profoundly changed the way I walk through this world. It's also had all these benefits for the other work I do — all those other strings in my bow. I'm more focused. I'm more creative. I'm more productive. So I really believe that nature can help us unleash our full potential, particularly if we can incorporate it into our daily lives, rather than waiting, as I used to, until we're brushing up against breaking point.

It might sound a bit woo woo, but ...

The biophilia hypothesis is that humans are hard-wired to connect with nature; it's in our DNA.[1]

The term was coined in 1984 by biologist Edward O. Wilson, who believed that since we evolved in nature, we have a biological need to connect with it, and we suffer when we become disconnected.

There is a growing body of research into the link between nature and our mental, physical and emotional health. Studies have found intentional time in nature can lower our blood pressure and heart rate, help combat anxiety and depression, suppress the sympathetic 'fight or flight' nervous system, and enhance the parasympathetic 'rest and digest' system. Phytoncides, chemicals produced by trees, have also been reported to stimulate the production of natural killer cells,[2] which promote immune system health and can help fight off infections.

This is a nascent field. Many of these studies involve small sample sizes and need further academic support to move beyond theory. But when you look at the volume of different studies with different methodologies all coming to similar conclusions, it does feel like it adds up to something pretty remarkable. I believe we all innately know that being in nature is good for us.

Think about the last time you spent a good chunk of time outside. How did you feel after it? I'm guessing you have at least one story of nature making you feel healthier in some way.

Beyond being good for your health and wellbeing, some intentional time outside can also be great for your work life. It can help you focus more acutely, think more clearly, be more creative and reduce your stress.

There are a few different concepts that I find helpful in understanding the power nature has to boost our brains, and how we can harness it.

Attention restoration theory

In a nutshell, this theory suggests that our ability to focus is like a muscle, which gets fatigued after a while. Time spent in nature, or even looking at scenes of nature, restores our focus to its full capacity.

Attention restoration theory was proposed by Rachel and Stephen Kaplan,[3] who described four states of attention:

- directed attention
- directed attention fatigue
- effortless attention
- restored attention.

Things that require mental effort (like our work) fall into the category of directed attention. We have to really focus, avoid distractions, and draw on our knowledge and skills to complete the task. The Kaplans theorised that we only have a limited capacity to do this before reaching a state of mental fatigue. In this state we're distracted, depleted and impatient, less flexible, and more likely to check out. We feel too exhausted to put in the mental effort.

The Kaplans asserted that exposure to natural environments encourages more effortless brain function, allowing the mind to recover and replenish its attention capacity. They suggested four cognitive states on the road to restoration:

1. clearer head, or concentration
2. mental fatigue recovery
3. soft fascination, or interest
4. reflection and restoration.

In the first and second stages, we set aside our day-to-day tasks and worries, and allow our minds to freely wander. (On a forest bathing walk, we achieve this

by gently shifting awareness from the mind into the senses and body.) The third state, soft fascination, allows us to be gently distracted and engage different parts of the brain, creating space for relaxation. Listening to the chatter of birds, watching light glisten on the water, smelling the perfume of a flower, feeling the grass beneath your feet: these are all forms of soft fascination.

After the final stage is reached, the brain's capacity to focus on an intellectual task is restored. We can return to a state of directed attention (read: work) with heightened cognitive performance, greater focus, and improved memory and problem-solving skills. We are far more productive as a result.

In short, sitting outside and gazing up at the clouds for five minutes can actually help you concentrate better when you return to work.

Stress reduction theory

Most of us work more effectively when we're not stressed, under immense pressure or trying to find the stamina needed to achieve even more, day after day. While a little bit of stress might drive our productivity up temporarily (just look at me go in the days before a deadline), high or extended stress has the opposite effect.

Beyond productivity loss, it can lead to serious mental and physical health issues, which can have consequences for ourselves, our relationships, our work and the economy. So it's important that we manage our stress, and research shows we de-stress much faster with a helping hand from nature.

Roger Ulrich's stress reduction theory[4] proposes that natural environments promote our recovery from stress, while urban environments tend to hinder the same process. You don't even need to be outside to recalibrate: simply looking at scenes of nature can ward off stress. This theory has been supported by studies conducted on people in hospitals,[5] prisons,[6] offices[7] and schools.[8]

I also came across the research of Mark Ellison, an educator, author and avid hiker. (He's lucky enough to live in the Appalachian Mountains near the Appalachian Trail and Great Smoky Mountains National Park.) Mark did his dissertation[9] on the restorative benefits of hiking in the wilderness and how it relates to job satisfaction – something he investigated from a human resource development perspective. He found that while hiking didn't make people any happier at work, it did help them deal with work they didn't enjoy. It helped them shed some of their stress.

'It was a coping mechanism to be able to get through it, which I think is a lot of people,' says Mark. 'Not everyone is fortunate to have employment that they enjoy, so they need something to help them get through. That's what people who were part of this study were doing. They were able to be more satisfied with their life and balance out the negative of doing work that they didn't really enjoy.'

Not all of us can go hiking out in the wilderness to de-stress – especially on a work day, as wonderful as that would be. But Mark has done work helping companies incorporate nature into their workplaces, and suggests the following:

▸ Green your space by bringing plants to your desk or office.
▸ If you can't have plants at work, put up images of nature scenes around your desk.
▸ Listen to nature sounds while you work.
▸ For meetings, try holding a walking meeting outside – Mark says it's much better than 'just sitting and staring at each other' in a room. (Lisa is a big fan of walking meetings. She'll often give me a call as she walks around her 'hood.)

Biophilic design is also catching on at an organisational level: green is the new black when it comes to creating office spaces. The likes of Facebook, Apple and Amazon are creating veritable greenhouses in their headquarters. I've heard of companies providing gardens for their employees to grow vegetables and herbs.

Mark has even worked in a company that gave employees a couple of paid hours each week that could be used for outdoor exercise during work time. 'There's a very progressive mentality about being able to see the link between being healthy and doing good work,' he says.

This mentality has scientific backing: one study found that employees who work in environments with natural elements report a 15 per cent higher level of wellbeing,[10] as well as higher levels of productivity and creativity (more on that in a mo!). Another study[11] found plants in office spaces produce higher morale and smoother relationships between employees.

When we're less stressed, we're more productive and we do better work. This is often framed in corporate environments as the ultimate goal, but I think it's more like the cherry on top. The cake itself is much bigger and more holistic: when we're less stressed, we are happier, more present, and more connected with ourselves and the people around us. Work benefits, but more importantly, life does.

The value of breaks, and creative incubation

Do you ever feel like you're too busy to even consider taking a break? For a long time, this was me. Without meaning to, I glamorised the grind. 'Look at how productive I am, chained to my desk all day.' But actually, there's loads of research showing that the more we try to do, the less we actually get done. It seems counterintuitive, but taking breaks actually makes you more productive.

The jury isn't unanimous, but many studies suggest your brain can devote itself to one task for somewhere between fifty and ninety minutes before it needs a bit of space to reboot – a fifteen-minute break is often the sweet spot.

I totally get that sometimes it can feel like you're slacking off if you take a break, and there's no denying some people frown at anyone who puts tools down for a while. I've felt that. But I do think it's changing. Employee wellbeing is increasingly important in the corporate world and addressing only physical health is not enough anymore. We need to create a work culture that recognises that we can work hard without overworking ourselves, that we can work hard *and* take a break.

Now, not all breaks are created equal. Aimlessly scrolling social media or checking emails means we're walking headlong into a barrage of new information. This is not the kind of restful break we need – and it's where the great outdoors come in. If you can, take your break outside or into a greener space. It's a much more effective break in terms of sharpening your brain (and improving focus and decreasing stress). You can also boost your creative thought as a by-product.

Research has found that letting your mind rest and wander spurs what neuroscientists call 'creative incubation',[12] a state where you can nurture new ideas and come up with creative solutions to problems.

When you let your mind wander, it can unconsciously make connections you aren't able to when you're actively thinking about things.[13] It's why so many breakthrough ideas and solutions pop into your head in idle times, such as when you're in the shower, or gardening or doing the dishes. So the next time you're stumped on something or feel your motivation levels sliding, try taking a break and see what happens.

Find a different connection

On a forest bathing walk, a guide helps people to slow down, awaken their senses and connect with nature in an intentional way. They offer a series of what we call invitations: simple and open suggestions for ways to explore and engage. It's all about minimising cognitive thinking and emphasising sensory sensations: getting out of the mind and into the body.

For this lab experiment, I want to encourage you to find some time to spend with nature (or even to look at scenes of it, if you live in an urban jungle). I know that finding the time is sometimes the hardest part. When I first started my guide training, I'd struggle to spare twenty minutes a day (even though I *magically* had hours each night for Netflix and doomscrolling). But when you feel like you can't spare the time, that's probably when you need to the most. As the Zen proverb goes, 'If you don't have time to meditate for an hour, you should meditate for two hours.'

We've already been experiencing Sit Spots through this book; here, I have a few other invitations to offer you, based on those I use during my walk sequences at Heartwood. I use the word 'invitations' deliberately. They're not instructions, just suggestions. There's no right or wrong way to do them. If it feels right to you, you're doing it perfectly, and you're very welcome to adapt them.

They're simple enough to be done on your lunch break — about ten or fifteen minutes will give you a taste. But I wonder what would happen if you gave yourself more time? The possibilities, as with so many things in nature, are infinite.

PLEASURES OF PRESENCE

Here, read the prompt for one sense, close your eyes and get an experience of it, then open your eyes to read the prompt for the next sense, and so on. You can either sit or stand, whatever feels right. (You may also like to listen to my Guided Pleasures of Presence invitation — you can find it via the link in the resources section.)

Take a few moments to notice what's around you. Then, if it feels right, close your eyes or lower your gaze. Take a few deep breaths, then awaken your senses, one at a time. If anything feels pleasurable, linger on that sense, on that sensation. Welcome it in.

- What sounds can you **hear**? What directions are they coming from? What sound is closest to your body, and what sound is farthest away? Is there a rhythm, or a melody?

- What sensations and textures can you **feel**? With your hands, feet, on your face? Perhaps notice the difference between the skin that is touching the air, and the skin that is beneath your clothing.

- What can you **smell**? Perhaps tilt your head back and see if you can catch the scent of the breeze. I wonder where that smell might take you?

- What can you **taste**? You could try breathing as if you are sucking the air through a straw. Can you taste the air?

- What can you **see**? When you open your eyes for this last time, do it really slowly, as if you're seeing the world for the very first time. And perhaps just consider that everything you are seeing is also seeing you. What are you noticing?

WHAT'S IN MOTION

I welcome you to go on a slow wander, and use any or all of your senses to notice everything around you that is moving, everything that's in motion.

'Slow' looks different for everyone, so allow your body to set a pace that feels slow to you. It might help to think of yourself as adopting the pace of nature – patient and unhurried.

Allow your curiosity to take the lead. If something catches your attention, feel free to stop and watch it for a while. If you think something isn't moving, perhaps be curious about whether that's actually true; maybe you need to slow down even more, and get even closer. What are you noticing?

MIRROR IMAGE

You can do this one from anywhere, including while looking out the window.

Let your gaze be drawn to a nature being near you. Perhaps it's a tree, a bird, a rock, the clouds, some flowers, or the earth below your feet.

Make a movement with your body that mirrors it in some way. I wonder what it feels like to connect in this way? I wonder if it is also mirroring you?

Everything is one

You do not have to look far to see how deeply we are tied to the world around us.

Picture the similarity between a fingerprint and the lines of a tree stump; human veins and a sprawling river network; our lungs and the branches of a tree; the human placenta and the Tree of Life.

During the pandemic, people around the world started to revalue their connections with the outside world. Something as simple as a (socially distanced) walk around the block, or the feel of the breeze and the sunshine on our face, took on new meaning. It made us happy. It saved us.

I believe, beyond escaping the confines of a locked-down home, this mattered so much because it offered a taste of the connection that so many people are yearning for, deep within. When we connect with the world, we think better and we work better. But more than that: we *are* better.

We don't need to learn *how* to connect with nature. We need to remember that we already *are* connected, simply because we are human.

For the health and happiness of both people and the planet, we need to continue to cultivate this innate and powerful link. Nature is calling us home.

CHAPTER 17

Unlock the power of rituals

Cue loud anthemic music. Now, put your hands in the air and shout 'woot woot!'

Guess what? You've just joined our ritual for celebration! Monique and I have been 'woot woot-ing' throughout the creation of this book, taking the time to mark the small moments along the way instead of holding it all in until the big finale. We could all do with a little more celebration in life, which is where rituals come in.

Usually, we might connect rituals with a religious ceremony or action: saying grace before tucking into dinner, receiving the Eucharist, acts of prayer, periods of fasting or solitude, or making a pilgrimage. But everyday secular rituals exist too, and we can get so much out of them. As well as being mini celebrations, they can help us step into a space of rest and recovery. They can be a powerful part of our routines. What's the difference?

- A routine is something we do regularly.
- A ritual is something we do with intention.

I got really curious about rituals after Casper ter Kuile, a Harvard Divinity School fellow and the author of *The Power of Ritual*, came on to *This Working*

Life.[1] Casper says that creating a ritual really just involves taking something you do and adding an extra layer of meaning to it. Rituals can become anchors that we use to orientate ourselves around what matters to us. They can help us feel connected. They can help us get rooted. They can nourish our soul.

To flourish, a ritual needs three things:

INTENTION / **ATTENTION** / **REPETITION**

In his book, Casper uses the example of reading before bed. If we do it every day it's a routine, but it isn't a ritual unless we bring a specific intention to it. Likewise, taking the dog for a walk isn't a ritual practice if we're also on the phone, because we're not paying attention to the pup or the walk.

For something to reach ritual status, we need to do it with some regularity, bring a clear intention and stay present in the moment. In this way, rituals make the invisible connections that give life meaning.

I love the elevated feeling of a ritual, particularly if it is shared. In university, I lived at Ormond College, and there were many wonderful rituals that made us feel a sense of belonging. One of them was formal hall. We'd all walk into this Harry Potter-esque dining space, wearing our academic gowns, take our place behind our big heavy chairs and, together, we would say the short college grace. Then we'd take our seats. Simple stuff, but it was a great way to create a sense of connection.

Small and mighty

Like routines, rituals don't have to be big to have a powerful impact. And like routines, it's about experimenting with different things until you find something that vibes with you. Casper says when you land on something that feels like it was made just for you, that's a winner.

These are a few ideas to help you get started.

AFFIRMATIONS

When Casper puts on moisturiser in the morning, he'll say to himself: 'Today is going to be a day of joy and suffering, just like any other.'

This little affirmation reminds him that the coming day will have its high and low points, and that everything will pass. By adding that layer of meaning, the routine of putting on moisturiser in the morning becomes a ritual.

Think about a regular part of your day where you could layer on an affirmation. Maybe it's a mantra you could sing to yourself in the shower, or something you say to yourself over a tea or coffee.

Monique brews honey-soaked chai on the stove every single day after lunch. Even if she's so busy that she's had to smash her food down at the desk, she makes sure the chai happens. While she's standing over the steaming saucepan, she slows down her breathing and mentally affirms that she is doing enough. 'I am achieving what I need to', 'I will have a great afternoon', 'This book *will* get finished on time'. Then she drinks it in the sunshine (from the same cup each day; a prized piece of vintage china).

After this pause, she finds she can reconnect with her day with fresh vigour.

JOURNALLING

Journalling is another common practice that can become a ritual if you approach it with intention.

So many of us did this as teenagers, pouring our hearts (and all their aches) out into a spiral-bound notebook emblazoned with bold texta threats for any prying eyes: 'Keep out or else!' As adults, we can benefit from doing this again, albeit with less angst. Journalling can help us de-stress, reflect on our work and crystallise our goals.

I love the idea of maintaining a daily list of things that went well, or things you appreciate. This can help us cultivate more gratitude and happiness. As you know, I keep a daily gratitude journal. But this can also be done as a verbal practice, or as a family. Over dinner each night, for example, you might ask your partner or kids to tell you something they are grateful for.

Monique fills a jar with little 'gratitude notes' throughout the year. This little ritual forms part of a larger one. At the dawn of a new year, she goes back and reads through all the good things that have happened.

Another idea is to allow yourself ten minutes at the end of each day to write in a 'stream of consciousness'. We can spend a lot of time self-censoring our thoughts and trying to say the right thing, especially at work. Perhaps you could close each day by letting yourself free. Don't edit your thoughts or worry about your spelling and grammar. Just let it flow.

ALONE OR TOGETHER

Rituals can be a solo activity, or a group one.

Once, when I filled in on *Life Matters*,[2] I asked the audience to tell us about the rituals that help soothe their souls. They came back with examples such as:

- swimming in open water to feel more connected to nature
- working on a derelict garden to nurture it back to life
- painting and drawing with family members to connect and unwind
- cooking good food to share with others.

Our publisher, Arwen Summers, tunes into community radio with her family. No Saturday night is complete without them hearing the intro music to Steve Cross's Beat Orgy on Triple R. Other family favourites are MzRizk (Boogie Beat Suite) and Rick Howe (Riddim Yard) on PBS 106.7FM. (You can stream the shows back via their website or app if you want to incite your own family disco after dinner.)

These are all rituals because of the intention behind them, the attention and presence given to them, and the space created to repeat them. Alone or together, what matters is the meaning that is layered on top of the action.

Tech Sabbath time

One of Casper's most important rituals unfolds on a Friday afternoon. At the end of the work week, he takes a 24-hour tech Sabbath. When he first told me about this secular interpretation of Shabbat, the Jewish day of rest, I knew I'd have to give it a go as well.

In this frankly exhausting culture where we are always pushing towards more and better and faster, disconnecting for a day sounded very appealing.

Casper told me about the steps he takes when he embarks on his weekly tech Sabbath.

1. He turns off his phone and laptop, and any other devices that represent work.
2. He stashes them away in his bookshelf. (The idea is 'out of sight, out of mind'; hiding them removes some of the temptation to turn them back on.)
3. He lights a candle.
4. He stands in his living room and sings a song he learned in summer camp.

Casper says it's important to add physical elements into the ritual – whether it's listening to music or reading a poem or smelling incense – because they help us mentally shift from one state into another. 'When I'm lighting that candle, it's like crossing a bridge from one way of being into another way of being. It's crossing from work time to Sabbath time. The reason why so many religious traditions have all of these intricate and interesting rituals is that they're ways of helping our mind and body move to that way of being, from one way to another,' he explains.

Whatever little action you take has an added layer of meaning. It's not just lighting a candle; it's lighting it with the intention of putting your work to one side and creating a boundary that it cannot cross. It's a choice you're making, not something you're being forced to do.

Casper says that once you're free of those external distractions and demands, a new space opens up. You can fill it however you like as long as it's not with technology. Casper finds he often has the most creative ideas and interesting thoughts in this time. The candle is kept on for the whole twenty-four hours to help hold himself accountable (aside from when he's sleeping).

And just as Casper has a ritual to enter Sabbath time, he also has a ritual to end it. When the Sabbath is over, he blows the candle out. The boundary comes down. The devices are pulled out of hiding, and turned back on.

Building my own tech Sabbath ritual

I was so intrigued by the idea of a Friday tech Sabbath that I decided to create my own version. It worked really well at first. I followed it to the letter, and felt mentally and emotionally refreshed come Sundays.

But before too long, I started cheating. The devices were like a magnet pulling me near. I'd sneak over to the phone and peek at the notifications. I texted Monique once and the reply came in fast: 'Isn't this your Sabbath time?' I was caught red-handed. I realised that the problem was possibly that I was doing it alone. There wasn't accountability.

I asked my friend Penny Locaso if she was interested in prototyping our own version of tech Sabbath together, and she was keen. The idea dovetailed beautifully with her own work on understanding our relationship with our devices.

We built the following routine together and ran an experiment to see how it would work.

OBJECTIVE

The philosophy is to give yourself a day of rest to celebrate the fact that you have worked hard and deserve it. Equally the intent is to give your brain a rest and the opportunity to recharge by not being constantly connected to a device.

THE RULES

- The Sabbath runs from 5.30 pm on Friday to 5.30 pm on Saturday.
- Set your phone alarm for 5.30 pm on the Friday. When it goes off, devices must be fully powered down.
- Devices include laptops, phones, smart watches and gaming consoles.
- TV and Kindles are allowed; however, YouTube is excluded as it is considered a form of social media. Streaming of movies and TV shows is allowed, but binge watching isn't.

THE RITUAL

1. Light a candle.
2. Choose a song that makes you happy. (Our choice was Katy Perry's 'Last Friday Night'.)
3. As it plays, do a little dance and sing along.
4. Then, move to your devices and say: 'I am enough. That was enough. It's now time for me to rest, and for you too, my beloved laptop and phone. Goodnight my friends, rest well. I'll see you at 5.30 pm tomorrow.'
5. Power down all your devices.
6. Place them in a drawer. They must be completely out of sight for the duration of the Sabbath.

7. Go back to your candle and blow it out.

8. Erupt in tears. (Just kidding – this is the part where you enjoy just 'being'.)

THE RESULTS

We ran the experiment for four weeks at the start of 2021 and committed to journalling about what happened each time. Penny describes the experience as 'amazing, and also very uncomfortable', which captures it pretty darn well.

I became conscious of the link between my body and my devices. My hand had this habit of reaching off into the distance, like the device was an extension of me. Penny became aware of the front-and-centre role phones claimed in many conversations. When she went out with some friends on one of the Saturday afternoons, she noticed that they'd lean on their phones constantly as they spoke, bringing up images to colour the conversation, or searching for relevant information to show her.

'I think because I was so hyper aware of not having my phone, I realised that we couldn't actually participate as human beings in conversations anymore. The phone had become an active participant in conversation,' she reflects.[1]

We both noticed that we had to be prepared to fully switch off: giving people a heads-up that we'd be offline, making plans in advance and looking up anything we might need to know before losing the convenient utility of our devices. It was like going back to the '90s, before we all had pocket computers with us everywhere we went.

The absence of our devices sparked some feelings of anxiety and discomfort at first, but we found that if we sat with that edge for a while, a refreshing sense of space and freedom soon rose up to take their place.

We found a space where we could just 'be'.

SIX MONTHS LATER

I still do a Friday tech Sabbath. It's not quite as structured as when I did it with Penny – the candle isn't always lit, the order is a bit more random – but I still switch off on Friday nights and don't look at my phone on Saturdays.

I occasionally cheat, to send friends a text on their birthdays (although I try to do this from a 'burner' phone, an old Nokia that isn't anywhere near as smart as my everyday device). The need to scan QR codes when out and about during COVID has also meant phone usage is sometimes unavoidable. But the sense of intention that underpins the Sabbath remains. I look forward to it because I know it means having a really good mental and emotional break, which has become very important to me.

I find that when I pick up my phone after the Sabbath, I've reset my relationship with my devices. When I reconnect again, I don't feel like I have to gorge on screen time or catch up on everything I might have missed.

In fact, I don't feel like I've missed anything at all. It's the opposite: I've gained so much.

Soundtrack

My tech Sabbath now starts with a different song. As a special treat (and to surprise Penny and Casper), I commissioned Little Green to write a song that would become the gentle anthem for the ritual.

It is called 'I Am Enough' (scan the QR code to listen) and it goes like this:

Free your mind it's Friday
Close your eyes and say goodbye
To cyber world

Free your mind it's Friday
Goodnight to all devices

Maybe it was a tough week
Maybe it was good
Maybe nothing went
Like you thought it would

But tonight it's Friday
So remember

I am enough
You are enough
We are enough

It's time to rest

Your own 'shut down' ritual

How did you feel after reading about my tech Sabbath ritual?

A lot of the time when I tell people about it, they say something like, 'Oh that sounds incredible, Lisa, but I could never do it.' And look, I know that twenty-four hours without your phone is a pretty hardcore idea. It can be anxiety-inducing for some people because our phones are so woven into the fabric of our lives.

Our working lives are effort-full so anything requiring more effort can be off-putting. But this isn't a case of 'if you can't do everything you may as well do nothing at all'.

When Greg McKeown, author of *Effortless*, came on to *This Working Life*,[3] he introduced me to a concept that really resonated with me: the minimum viable action, or MVA. Greg says we often make things harder than they need to be because we're thinking about the 10th step in the process, or the 100th step in our goal. We overthink it. We overdo it. We overexert ourselves.

But everything starts at the start, doesn't it? Everything begins with a first step. So why not just think about that very first step, the tiniest little thing that will help us make progress. The MVA.

For your own ritual, start with the simplest action you can take.

▸ Can you take a few really deep breaths, letting the week go as you exhale?
▸ Can you light a candle and dance to a song on Friday (or whatever your last day of work is)?
▸ Can you choose an activity that engages your brain in a different way, like a crossword, or playing with your kids or ten minutes of relaxing yoga?
▸ Can you sit with nature for a while, just noticing what you notice? (Monique does a Friday afternoon Sit Spot, for example.)
▸ Can you savour a sweet treat, a cup of tea or a glass of wine?

Remember, it's the intention that matters, not the activity. Anything you do with the intention of creating a bit of space between work and the rest of your day is valid. Make it easeful. Every little thing counts.

If you want to decouple from your phone and devices, and you've never done it before, twenty-four hours can be a shock to the system. Once again, think of the MVA.

Instead of asking yourself, 'How can I work harder to disconnect?', try asking, 'How can I make it easier to disconnect?'

- Can you put your devices in a drawer so they're out of sight, out of mind?
- Can you turn your devices off entirely, even just until after dinner?
- Can you turn notifications off or have the devices in silent mode?
- Can you watch TV, listen to music or read a book without your phone in your hand?
- Can you leave your phone at home on one outing (e.g. going to the supermarket), just to see how it goes? (If you need to take it to check in to venues, put it in flight mode, switch back to data-land to check in, then return to flight mode.)

The more comfortable you get with a little separation, the more you can build it up. We all deserve rest and a moment to be 'off' in an always-on world. By switching off to one part of the world, we can switch on to another part – and to ourselves.

This is a right, not a reward. But we have to claim it.

Rest and recover

My tech Sabbath ritual is one way I build rest and recovery into my working life. I haven't always known the value of rest, or perhaps I have known it, but I've pushed it aside. 'Rack off, rest! I'm too busy!' I began my career in an era where downtime was a mark of being supremely unproductive and lazy. I ran at things super hard, until I fell over.

When I was a young, hungry corporate lawyer in the '90s, I filled out a time sheet. I would account for each moment of my work day, in six-minute increments. While we had some time for non-chargeable activities such as 'marketing', there was nothing for 'rest and recovery' – that was considered 'dead time'.

I liked feeling valued, and since I was valued for my time, I gave all my time to work. I unconsciously practised presenteeism, because back in the day it was a badge of honour to be at your desk after 8 pm. I worked weekends as well. The partners used to laugh about how I prowled around the firm on weekends and joked that they would deactivate my card after hours so I would stop working so hard. But then I got the Monthly Achievement Award, so my hard work and long hours were recognised. I felt great.

I worked and worked and worked, until I burnt out.

Nowadays, I look at work in terms of high performance and impact, like being an elite sportsperson. There's so much training that goes into running a race, but there is also an enormous amount of rest. (And massage. Let's not forget the importance of a good massage.)

I ask myself what conditions I need, acknowledging that I am human and not a machine, in order to produce my best work. And I acknowledge that my best work – which involves strong connections with other human beings – comes from a place of joy and energy, not frustration and burnout.

This is where rest and recovery comes in. It's why simple rituals and downtime can have such a huge impact on our lives.

Tal Ben-Shahar, a renowned Harvard lecturer and author in the fields of happiness and leadership, uses the concept of micro, meso and macro breaks.

- **Micro breaks.** This is a break within a day. I tend to work in 45-minute blocks with fifteen minutes' rest where I go and walk the dog or talk to my family.
- **Meso breaks.** This is a break where you take a day off to rest and recover after an intense period of work. An example is my weekly tech Sabbath, or taking a day off after completing a big project or workshop.
- **Macro breaks.** This is a holiday. I take a week off every three or four months.

Without rest, how productive are we really being? If I circled back to my old time sheet and billing system, I don't think my output would have been optimal.

Resting doesn't make you lazy or unproductive. In fact, I believe the opposite is true.

Rose, Bud, Thorn

Rose, Bud, Thorn is a beautiful ritual to try on for size before you incorporate bigger ones into your life. When I shared the idea with my daughter, she jumped at it (which is rare – normally my ideas are too daggy). As a family we do this ritual at the end of nearly every day.

I suggest trying this experiment every day for a week, and then reflecting on the process and what you've learned.

At the end of each day, take a moment to identify:

- a **Rose**: a highlight, success, small win, or something beautiful that happened.
- a **Bud**: new ideas that blossomed or something you are looking forward to knowing more about or experiencing.
- a **Thorn**: a challenge you experienced, something that was a bit shit, or something you can use more support with.

I love that it's all connected: if you've got a rose, you've got a thorn, and the bud is new.

You might do this experiment by journalling, or even just talking with a loved one over dinner or after putting the kids to bed. Penny shares it with her son and jokes that while he groans when she brings it up, they always end up laughing together.

To take it one step further, you could also:

- identify ways to make the most of the buds
- brainstorm strategies for turning thorns into roses
- reflect on the ways thorns might support your learning and growth.

Remember, for a ritual to flourish it needs repetition, as well as intention and attention. Let yourself be open to where they may take you: even small rituals are mighty.

SIT SPOT

Jellyfish are the most energy-efficient swimmers in the ocean. Muscles in their dome-shaped bodies relax and contract, relax and contract; drawing in water before pushing it out again to propel them forward.

Without the crucial step of relaxing, they wouldn't move at all.

What would it mean, in this moment, to trust that a little rest will help move you forward?

04

LIMINAL SPACE

You stand at the threshold.

In a liminal space — the space between what was and what will be.

A space of transition and quiet transformation.

Here, together, anything is possible.

It is time to hold the world of work in our collective hands and shape it into something new.

We all have seeds of creativity inside us. As kids, we made mud pies and sandcastles, stick forts and pet rocks, and saw magical animals within the soft clouds in the sky. We transformed things, and gave them new life.

Now, as adults, we can transform the big wide world of work. In this liminal space, there are no rules. We are all free to frolic with freedom as we look at the big picture.

We are going to realise that we're not solo operators, but social beings who thrive through collaboration and connection. We're going to turn outward, towards each other.

We'll explore a new way to approach mentoring, which is helpful whether you're a fresh graduate or a C-suite executive, or anywhere in between.

Then, taking hold of our empathy, we might just bring on the dawn of the Second Renaissance. You'll see.

In this liminal space, anything is possible.

We can walk forward from here, into a future of our own design.

Let's create it, together.

CHAPTER 18

It's not all about you

When was the last time a situation at work made you feel like you were banging your head up against a brick wall?

Maybe you were being told 'no' (yet again), even though you had a great idea. Maybe someone couldn't grasp why something mattered to you so much, or you had a request turned down, or you needed support and got none. Did it involve a colleague? Your team? Your manager?

It is incredibly frustrating to feel unheard. It can make you feel like everyone has some kind of vendetta against you, conspiring to hold you back. It can make your goals feel impossible to achieve.

Now, I want to ask you a tough question, but please know it comes wrapped in silky kindness. I like to label this a 'compassionate challenge'.

Think about that same situation at work: was it all about you? Were you focused on your own needs, or what you stood to gain? Is there a chance it could have come across as 'me, me, me'?

Our ego can quickly get in our way at work. We get so worried about our own success, our own stress, our own future – 'I really want this person to like and respect me', 'I need this project to hit my numbers this month', 'I don't have time to be sitting on this call', 'I have so much to do!'

When our ego takes over, we end up locked in eternal competition and comparison with others, worrying about how they perceive us and our work, and whether they are undermining us or edging onto our turf.

The result? We stop focusing on others because we're focusing on ourselves. We forget that our colleagues are human too, with their own stresses, their own hopes and dreams, their own unmet needs and, yes, their own egos.

Our needs matter, but very rarely are they the only needs in the mix. If we truly want something, often the best way to get it is by aligning our needs with those of others.

To unlock our potential and achieve our goals, we need to turn our focus outward. We need to adopt a simple mantra: 'It's not all about me'. Hold it lightly, laugh, say it out loud. 'It's *not* all about me!'

It's not all about any of us.

Bringing connection back

One of the many insights I gained when I went into radio is that what we think is a conversation is not really a conversation at all. Usually they are serial monologues: one person waiting for the other person to finish speaking so they can put their view across. This has been amplified in our world of sound bites and hot takes and tweets; there is not enough space for the graceful dance of conversations.

This is true of many of the conversations we have at work. They are all about us. They lack a critical element: connection. This is why, so often, we don't get the results we're after.

Connection underpins everything we do at work. In any strategy or objective you have, the lever will be the moment of connection. In meetings, client communications, pitching, selling, negotiating, giving or receiving feedback, everyday interactions – the lever is the moment you connect. If you understand the needs of others, you can start to tune in to the same frequency. Then something can emerge which may not have been contemplated individually, but can be shocking and beautiful. I like to call this 'mind jazz'. You're playing your own instrument and adding your own flourishes and vibe, but you're also connected to the band, the rhythm and the beat.

When you think about it, everything we do at work comes down to a human-to-human experience. Even a business-to-business sales effort is better described as a series of human-to-human connections. It's H2H,

not B2B. No matter how big your organisation is, the success of your strategy boils down to those moments of truth where you're with another human being.

By truly understanding the needs and desires of others, you will be better able to connect your needs to theirs, and find a mutually beneficial (and potentially beautifully compounding) outcome.

The deeper the need, the greater the motivation to do something.

Empathy and design thinking

There is a useful framework for diagnosing needs: empathy.

Empathy is our ability to experience the world as another does – to see what they see, feel what they feel and experience things as they do. It is often described as a soft skill, but I think that term diminishes how hard it can be. Empathy is a huge strength, and it requires effort. Thankfully, empathy is like a muscle, and it gets stronger the more you use it.

I use empathy here in the design thinking sense. The starting place is understanding a person's needs and desires. The starting place is empathy.

Empathy allows us to reframe a problem in a human way and uncover needs that can be very deep, or latent. Once you uncover these needs – often described as pain or gain points – you can work to eradicate the pain, or achieve the gains.

Walk a mile in their ... body

Let's think again about that head/brick wall situation you faced at work.

How might you approach it differently from a place of empathy? Can you imagine, for a moment, what the needs of your colleague, team or manager might have been?

Say you wanted to ask your manager about job crafting, and you went in with a (very valid) list of how it would help your career development, only to be quickly shut down. Could you instead approach it with the perspective of how it would help your team, that manager and the company? Maybe your manager is caught up in their own issues because they need to cut the budget by 10 per cent in the next six months. Could you align your need (to craft your role) with the needs of your manager (to cut the budget)? Could your job crafting somehow help ease their budget pain?

One useful way to get in touch with the person behind the persona, and bring their needs into focus, is to walk in their shoes. Not literally, of course ... well, kind of. Perhaps the more accurate description involves walking in their body.

Laban movement helps people embody a particular character. It's used in dance and acting, and it was shared with me by my filmmaker husband. It categorises human movement into four parts, each with two elements:

- ▸ direction: direct or indirect
- ▸ weight: heavy or light
- ▸ speed: quick or slow
- ▸ flow: bound or free.

Think of your character (or colleague) and how they move. If you're looking at Flow and the movement is bound, it's very tight and held in. Most of us can probably picture someone at work like this. Someone who moves freely is the opposite of bound; think of children, or Monique dancing to The Boss in her living room when she has the house to herself.

Think about someone at work you'd like to have more empathy for. Do you think they are direct or indirect, heavy or light, quick or slow, bound or free? You can use any observations or interactions you've had with this person in the past to inform your answers.

Embody that person for a moment; walk around the house for a minute as if you *are* them. Move how they move. If they're heavy and bound, how does that feel? How does it compare to your way of moving through the world?

Then ask yourself:

- ▸ Why might they be this way?
- ▸ What stresses and challenges might they be facing?
- ▸ What might their hopes and dreams and ambitions look like?
- ▸ What unmet needs might they have?

This can give you a flavour of that person and some valuable insight into where they are coming from. It doesn't matter if you get it 'right' or not; we can never know what it is like to live in another's skin.

The point is that you took the time to humanise them. This is the ground for true connection.

The fairest interpretation

Empathy can transform how you lead and how you relate to others. In fact, it can transform everything.

Sophie Moloney, the CEO of Sky TV New Zealand, gives the example of a time she used empathy to better understand a media executive, ahead of a meeting that her colleagues didn't think would be productive.

Putting herself in their shoes required a little background research, which helped Sophie paint a very human picture of the person she was meeting and put a big-picture context around their discussion. When Sophie revealed some common ground in the initial moments of their encounter, it 'signalled that I valued her time and respected her enough to invest in our meeting'. It transformed the nature of their discussion and the start of their relationship.

'Fairness is a core value of mine,' Sophie says. 'I try to look for the fairest interpretation of a situation.'

If someone is acting a particular way, what is the fairest way to interpret their behaviour? Many of us subconsciously overgeneralise or personalise what other people do; we believe everything others do or say is some kind of direct, personal reaction to us. But this thinking pattern – a type of cognitive distortion – isn't always right. Sophie says it's often not clear why someone behaves the way they do, so the fairest interpretation is that it's not about you (there's our mantra again).

It's likely that it's situational, rather than personal. It's not that they have an issue with you, or don't want to make time for you, or are hoping for a confrontation. Maybe they're dealing with some bad press, drama at home or health issues. You never really know unless you put judgement aside and take the time to scratch beyond the surface.

Banish the intellectual piranha within

Empathy can also help in everyday work situations. When was the last time you sat around a table (or a virtual meeting room) with a bunch of colleagues, discussing ideas or dissecting problems? How did it go?

Often these meetings result in a dead end, because instead of the room being full of people, it is full of intellectual piranhas. When one person suggests an idea, everyone takes turns gobbling it up until there's nothing left. That's what intellectual piranhas do. They list all the things that can go wrong with that idea, or why it's not a good idea, until the idea is dead and buried.

Often the meeting ends and *all* the ideas are six feet under. Or, and maybe this is worse, a pretty average idea is settled on just so you can call it a day.

In a way, we have been conditioned to act like this, conditioned to think it is all about us. The structures in which we learn, live and work promote and reward competition, and lead us to think that if we don't win, we lose. If we aren't the person who has The Incredible Idea That Changes Everything, we're nothing. This can change how we behave; we end up losing our humanity so we can 'crush it' at work.

We need to let go of this way of thinking.

When I talked to my friend and improv legend Dan Klein about bringing more empathy to work, he told me about a revelation that hit him when he was first studying theatre improv. He realised that getting up on stage and making up a story for an audience wasn't about his potential to be the star, or achieve glory.

In fact, it wasn't about him at all.

'Every time you have a piece of ego involved, it's going to sabotage the work. You might think you're doing badly, and it'll suffer,' Dan explains. 'Sometimes even worse is thinking that you're doing great. There's something really inauthentic and unlikeable that comes out when that happens, and you miss stuff.'

The secret sauce is focusing on others. That's what improv is all about.

'It's about your partners, and giving them a good time, and inspiring them, and making them look good,' Dan says. 'When you have that focus, everything works better. You end up being inspired. You're connected, you're grounded, and you're doing great work. You're having fun and it feels effortless.'

The same is true of workplaces.

Imagine how differently our work would look and feel if the aim was to come at the problems together, and build on everyone's ideas. Everyone would feel seen, heard and valued. Nobody would be afraid to speak up.

This doesn't mean indulging every harebrained scheme or vanity project that comes up. Rather, it's about opening your mind to how you view the possibilities of your work. If you can break this frame, new ideas can emerge – ideas that might change everything.

LAB EXPERIMENT

Oh good!

Dan taught me this game, which is a really easy way to challenge the intellectual piranha within. The concept is simple: learn to react to ideas in a positive way, and build on them.

You'll need a partner-in-improv to play with, or a few partners-in-improv! It could be your actual partner, kids, friends or colleagues. You can do this in person or virtually.

How does it work?

You start by 'giving' something to another person. It can be anything that springs to mind – an apple, a bicycle, a brand-new Star Wars Lego set, a private performance by Beyoncé. The rules and restraints of reality don't apply, but keep it positive or neutral.

The person you give it to has to reply with 'Oh good!' and then a reason why they needed it. Then that person gives something to someone else.

If you're playing in a group you can go round in a circle, or if it's just the two of you, go back and forth for a minute or so. When Dan, Monique and I played the game, it went like this:

Dan: Hey Monique, here's a pillow!

Monique: Oh good! I am so tired today and I'd love a quick kip. Hey Lisa, here's a crayon set!

Lisa: Oh good! I'm going to draw a big picture with twenty-four colours. Hey Dan, here's a bonsai tree!

Dan: Oh good! It will help me complete my miniature forest.

And then we all erupted in laughter.

Give it a go, and then take a moment to reflect. Can you see how this might help you at work?

When you practise saying 'Oh good!' in response to someone's idea – no matter what it is – you condition your brain to respond this way in all environments, including at work. So instead of saying 'Oh no' (or perhaps thinking 'Oh f*#!') the next time ideas are being raised or problems are being discussed, you may respond with 'Oh good!', and then build on them. In time, your default will be to support ideas rather than cutting them down.

'Oh good!' fosters a sense of genuine collaboration and helps you connect with your colleagues from a place of openness and curiosity. It's about paying attention, listening and being inclusive – all skills that are useful and powerful in the world of business.

How are you, really?

Genuine connections, built around empathy, can have a profound impact on how you work and how effective you are at work, no matter what you do or where you sit on an org chart.

I want to note, however, that connecting at work is not limited to meeting goals or working towards outcomes. There's also a very human element at play. Connecting with the people we work with can be part of what makes work feel satisfying and meaningful. We all share the desire to be truly seen, and truly heard.

Monique has a beautiful and sincere way of taking the philosophy around empathetic connections and applying it in a simplified way. Her awakening to the value of empathy happened after she passed an ABC colleague in the hall and said, 'How are you?'

It was a common question, and usually it followed a fairly routine path.

'How are you?'

'Good, yeah. You?'

'Yeah, good.'

And on they'd walk.

But this time, something unexpected happened. The person stopped, and broke down. Their much-loved family pet had just died, work was really hectic and they were feeling overwhelmed. Monique knew them quite well, but she hadn't expected that answer. In fact, she hadn't expected any answer at all.

It dawned on her that 'How are you?' had become her equivalent of saying 'Hey' – just a way to acknowledge someone, like a smile or a quick nod of the head. It was something she said, not a question she asked. It had become all about her.

It's pretty relatable, right? It's something so many of us do. 'How are you?' has become a quick verbal exchange, but nothing more. It's ironic because the question is centred around empathy, but it's become empty.

Monique decided she didn't want to be that person who asks a question but is too busy and distracted to wait to hear the answer. So the next time she asked someone how they were, she imbued the question with intention, and made a point of stopping to wait for an answer.

'How are you?'

'Good, yeah. You?'

'I'm great. But how are you, *really*?'

'Oh, well, let me tell you about ...'

Over time, people started to really answer. She asked new questions, became more curious and learned new things about people she'd known for years. She built up these connections in microdoses; it became a superpower.

Empathy is a two-way street. It's not enough to just listen. We have to open ourselves up and be vulnerable. So when someone asked Monique how she was, she answered honestly as well; nothing too deep, no tiny violins, just a taste of something real. She'd tell people if she was feeling inspired, or a bit snowed under. How a weekend hike had been incredibly restorative. That she was loving the challenge of learning the bagpipes, or taking Spanish classes. Without being unprofessional or too disruptive, she sprinkled little flashes of her humanity into the mix. And her colleagues did the same.

These simple acts of true engagement revealed threads of connection that might never have been found otherwise. They were the foundation for some really rich, meaningful relationships that made Monique work better, and feel better about work. In time, Monique was able to identify people's pain points in their jobs, and see how she might help them, and vice versa.

This type of empathetic connection isn't about oversharing, or chewing someone's ear off. You can do it on your own terms. If you're flat chat, wait until you have a bit more time to spare, rather than overstretch and end up resenting the whole thing because it's become a time suck. And you can recognise if someone isn't willing or able to meaningfully interact, and gently move on. It's just a couple of minutes here and there, but those minutes add up to so much more. It's an easy investment with a huge reward.

The ripple effect

I love this so much because it reminds me of the systems thinking approach, which recognises that if one part of the system changes, the whole does too. Just by changing her intention, Monique effected a change in the whole system, and people responded in a more empathy-driven way. Real connections grew.

We don't need to set out to overhaul the whole system, just the way we operate in it. Change is still possible within and around structures and systems, no matter how ingrained they may seem.

We may not have the power or influence to change our entire company culture, nor should that responsibility rest on the shoulders of individuals, but we can change how we show up in it. We can show up with a humanist frame of reference, ready to connect with others from a place of empathy. The ripple effect may be slow, but boy, will it come.

Now say it out loud again: 'It's not all about me!'

It's not all about any of us.

SIT SPOT

Clownfish find safe haven within the tentacles of the sea anemone. In return, the sea anemone receives nutrients and protection from predators. They thrive thanks to this mutualistic relationship.

What would it mean, in this moment, to know that helping others is also helping yourself?

CHAPTER 19

Mentoring Moments

There are many brilliant stories about how mentors have helped people build enduring careers, and incredible pairings that have flourished over many years. A mentor is someone who can be a sounding board, help you navigate a challenge or champion your cause. They are in your corner, helping you grow your skills, motivating you, pushing you and sharing perspectives from their own life and career. They can also:

- act as a bridge from where you are to where you want to go next
- hold a mirror up to you, so you can truly see where you're at
- be a source of knowledge to help you navigate forward
- help you believe in yourself and feel more hopeful about your career
- accelerate your learning
- give you a place to test ideas free from judgement
- peel back your layers to reveal your passion and strengths
- connect you to other people in an industry.

Direction. Faith. Confidence. Inspiration. Learning. Advice.

Sounds pretty good, huh?

If you haven't had a mentor, how do you feel reading all this? Perhaps an uneasy FOMO feeling has started to kick in. 'Why don't I have a mentor? Someone who is the Maya Angelou to my Oprah?' (You are Oprah here!)

You might start to wonder: Have I missed out on my chance? Did I leave Maya waiting in the wings?

A date, not a proposal

One of the best pieces of insight I have gleaned is that you should take the pressure off yourself and your potential mentor. Don't spam everyone in your LinkedIn network, pleading with them to light your way 'til death do you part. Instead, pick a distinct challenge or goal, and seek out the right person to ask for help. You can build out from there, connecting with as many different people as you need to, whenever the need arises.

I call this Mentoring Moments – the agile, speed-dating version of mentoring. It's about what you want to learn, as well as who you want to learn from.

At its core, having a mentor is really about having a relationship, one that centres around learning. So even though I've never had a mentor in the traditional sense, by this looser definition – a relationship centred on learning – I've had loads of mentors. How about you? These relationships have often been as informal as a conversation over a cup of coffee, or a quick chat on the phone. The critical thing is that Mentoring Moments are simple. There's no ongoing commitment required, so it doesn't feel as daunting.

On *This Working Life*, Naomi Simson, the founder of online experience gifting business RedBalloon (and one of the sharks on business reality show *Shark Tank Australia*), told me a story about one of her mentors.[1] She took me back about fifteen years, to when RedBalloon was first thinking about going into the gift card business and wondering if it could get them into retail stores.

Naomi reached out to Launa Inman, who was the CEO of Target at the time. Could Launa give her an insight into what it is to be a retailer? 'She didn't just accept my coffee,' Naomi recalls. 'She came to meet with me. I remember being completely blown away by her generosity. I learned so much from her in that one-hour session that we had together. We became friends, so you never quite know where your mentorship journey is going to go. I'm forever grateful for the insight that she gave me.' A lot can happen in an hour.

Dude, where's my Mentoring Moment?

Mentoring Moments are easy by design; the idea is that you can seek out as many of them as you need. This is a good thing, because it's rare that one person is going to be able to teach you everything you want to know. At work, as in life, we can learn from all kinds of people.

When you're looking for a potential connection, cast your net wide. You may look towards people:

- in your existing network, including colleagues you admire
- in a job you aspire to, or whose work or ideas spark something inside you
- with specific knowledge or lived experiences that you could learn from
- who are leaders in your industry (or the industry you want to go into)
- who actively participate in relevant forums or groups.

Keep your eyes peeled and your finger to the wind. The right person will have the strengths and skills to actually help you – and ideally they'll also be someone who you like the vibe of.

Why? We're more likely to learn from someone we admire and respect for who they are, as well as what they do.

How to make a moment happen

You've found someone you'd like to share a Mentoring Moment with ... now what? I got some expert advice from Bobbi Mahlab, the co-founder of the Australian arm of Mentor Walks, an initiative where senior women support emerging female leaders by literally going on a walk together (or, since COVID, meeting up over Zoom).

Her tips? Keep it purposeful, casual and specific.

'Mentors are not for life. You're not talking about marriage,' she says. 'Even if you are lucky enough to find a lifelong mentor, you can also have other people who guide you at different points in your career.'

Exactly! Let's unpack Bobbi's tips in a bit more detail.

KNOW YOUR PURPOSE

Before you approach anyone, get a clear idea of your 'why'. Why do you need this Mentoring Moment? What purpose will it serve?

- Do you have a challenge you'd like help with, or a particular skill you'd like to learn?
- Do you need someone to creatively bounce ideas around with, or someone to bring a more analytical mindset?
- Do you want someone with experience navigating your workplace culture, or someone external who can bring a fresh set of eyes?

If you're working towards a big-picture outcome, break it down into smaller stepping stones, and start with just one.

This made me think of Priya Parker and her book *The Art of Gathering*. In it, she talks about the difference between a category and purpose. Often we think we're talking about a specific purpose, but really we're talking about a broader category.

'I've got a big job interview coming up' is an example of a category.

Can you drill down deeper until you find an articulation of what you really need to achieve, and how this particular person can help?

'I get super nervous speaking in high-pressure situations. I need to learn how to stay more calm and collected so I'm more confident in my job interview.'

That's more like it.

You don't have to have the answers — after all, that's why you're seeking a Mentoring Moment. But the better you can pinpoint what you're looking to achieve, the easier it will be to find the right person to help, and ensure you come together in a useful way.

Bobbi says it's important to remember that no issue is too big or small to bring to a mentor.

'If it's an issue to you, it's an issue,' she says. 'The likelihood is that your big issue is not so big for someone else, and vice versa. The most common comment we get from mentees and mentors is "I thought I was the only person that had this problem and I found out that I'm not alone". The chances are if you're experiencing something, many other people have as well – it's just no one has spoken about it with you yet.'

KEEP IT CASUAL

When you've found the person who may be The One (For A Moment), it's time to make contact.

Time is one of our richest currencies, and your potential mentor is very busy. (We all are.) 'We've got about 370 mentors and I would say at least half, if not three-quarters of them, every week are asked by someone to have a coffee with them,' Bobbi says. 'All of them would like to say yes, but they can't because they simply don't have the capacity or time.'

She suggests sending a message asking for a 'short conversation' instead. Forget marriage – 'you're not even asking for a first date!' One of the upsides of COVID is that we've all become proficient with Zoom, which opens up a whole wide world of potential mentors of the moment. We're now used to being 'face to face' on a screen and this can be used to our advantage.

MAKE IT SPECIFIC

Even though the aim is to have a casual encounter, you need to put some effort into your request.

Tell them about yourself and your work. Be crystal clear about what you want help with. To set yourself apart, do a bit of homework on them and establish some common ground. Why have they piqued your interest? What do you love about their work? Their values? Have you read some of their research or articles? Do you aspire to similar goals?

If we stick with our job interview example, this might look something like: 'I've got a big job interview coming up and I get very nervous speaking in high-pressure situations. I've noticed that when you give speeches, you seem really calm and collected. I'd love to learn a bit more about how you prepare for these events, because I think it could help me become a more confident interviewee.'

Not everyone will say yes, but you'll never know if you don't ask. If they do say no, reply and thank them anyway, leaving the door open for a future relationship.

Make the most of the moment

When it comes to Mentoring Moments, you only get out what you put in. Be proactive about preparing. It is helpful to have a few questions in mind, questions that will help you move towards the answers you need.

But also leave some space for things to unfold naturally. It should feel more like a conversation than an interview.

To get the most out of it:

- be honest and transparent
- bring your curiosity
- really listen to what the other person has to say
- avoid the temptation to check out or be defensive if it gets hard.

The last point is a big one. If you hang out with the same people all the time, you might be used to a bit of groupthink, so it can feel confronting when someone new comes in with a different take. Honest feedback and criticism are crucial to your growth and just as valuable as a cheer squad that supports you no matter what.

Organisational psychologist and author Adam Grant uses the term 'challenge network' to define a group of people you trust to see the flaws in your thinking, and to call you out on them. 'They will tell us the things we don't want to hear, but actually need to hear,' he explains.[2]

Adam's challenge network pushes him to keep striving to make his work better, and to maintain integrity, humility and generosity. It's made up of some of his 'most thoughtful critics' – people who aren't worried about hurting his feelings – but it could also include someone in a Mentoring Moment who isn't afraid to be honest with you. If you do get tough advice, think of the person as being in your challenge network, pushing you to grow. Put your growth mindset to work by channelling their feedback into constructive action.

Respect the other person's time by keeping your promise of a one-hour meeting (or however long they've agreed to). Don't let it run too far over. And if you're meeting in person, pay for their coffee!

SAY THANK YOU IN A MEANINGFUL WAY

The spirit of generosity and reciprocity is really important in Mentoring Moments. After your meeting, it is good to reach out and say thank you.

I try to reflect back to the person what I learned and how they were helpful.

'We all want to know that we're making a difference,' Bobbi says. 'So, if a conversation has actually helped you solve a problem or achieve something you wanted to do, a little note on LinkedIn or an email or a quick phone call just saying, "Look, this is what happened after I spoke to you" – that is always a really wonderful thing to do.'

Bobbi says you can also ask: 'What can I do to reciprocate?'

'Simply being asked that question is a very, very beautiful thing to be a recipient of. It might be that there's nothing you can do, but the grace is in the question.'

The AAA way to grow a moment into something more

If sparks fly over that first moment, you might start thinking about nurturing a deeper relationship, where you meet with a more regular cadence. This is where Mentoring Moments can start to take the shape of a more traditional mentoring relationship.

Madeleine Grummet is a sought-after mentor, as well as being the founder of education technology start-ups Future Amp and girledworld, so I asked her for advice on how to approach this. She says a great long-term mentor will:

- make you feel safe to be honest and vulnerable
- give you good advice and inspire you to achieve your goals
- share their expertise, as well as their mistakes
- connect with your vision and be willing to help you get there
- make you feel better about yourself, or more hopeful about your career.

Does your prospective mentor tick these boxes? If your answer to these questions is a shrug of the shoulders or a shake of the head, that person may not be the best fit for you. But if you answer yes, it's a good match! So, what next?

Madeleine suggests using the AAA approach as a framework to grow a Mentoring Moment into something more. Any good mentoring relationship will be built on these three pillars:

- **Authenticity.** There has to be mutual trust and respect, and an inherent mentor–mentee chemistry. 'That comes from being authentic in terms of understanding who you are, what your values are, and your vision and purpose,' Madeleine explains.

▸ **Action.** You and your mentor should commit to realistic goals with measurable outcomes; perhaps create some small actions and milestones, or objectives and key results. Madeleine says whichever way you slice it up, having these signposts along the way can keep you on track. 'Some mentoring can end up being almost like a psychology session, but if you're focused around your goals, you can see the progress you're making, and see that what you are getting out of the relationship is giving you the fuel to move forward.'

▸ **Autonomy.** A good mentor lights the way, but they don't cut the path. As a mentee, you should be empowered to develop your own path forward. 'A lot of the greatest learning for a mentee is learning by doing,' Madeleine says. 'Even if that means failing a bit and trying a few things that don't work out. It's about daring to step boldly forward with autonomy and self-direction, knowing that you've got a mentor to bounce off when it gets tough.'

Madeleine says it's also important to set a few ground rules early on. This might include the following:

▸ Clearly state that the exchanges are confidential. (What happens in the mentoring meeting *stays* in the mentoring meeting!)
▸ Define what the relationship looks like in practical terms: is it a Zoom call, catching up over lunch or meeting at a networking event?
▸ Set the frequency of contact: is it once a week, or once a month? Is there 'homework' to do in between catch-ups?

It's worth putting the work in to get this relationship right, because having the right mentor in your corner can make you a force to be reckoned with.

I remember tearing up a little during an episode of *This Working Life* when writer and broadcaster Benjamin Law read out a letter he wrote to his mentor – 'the gay Chinese-Australian Barack Obama of the Australian screen world', aka accomplished writer, director and producer Tony Ayres.[3]

'You kept the faith while also steering someone (me) who had no idea what he was doing, with patience and unwavering encouragement. When I lost faith in myself and in my work, all it took was reminding myself that your faith in me had never wavered.'

Someone believing in you is so powerful, as is having someone to believe in.

Maria Antwan, who jumped from the beauty industry into construction, says

that her mentor – a woman in the most male-dominated industry in Australia – absolutely changed her life.[4] Maria had to confront some negativity and misogyny as a result of her career shift, but her mentor taught her resilience.

'The way that she pushed forward in the industry was just so inspiring to me,' Maria says. 'She started at the bottom and worked her way to the top, and I knew that I could do that too.'

Her mentor gave her someone to look up to; after all, you can't be what you can't see.

Sharing what you know

No matter what stage we're at in our careers, we can all benefit from learning from others – and from sharing our knowledge. We all have skills, stories and experiences that someone else could learn from. So as well as seeking out Mentoring Moments, it's worth thinking about how you could offer them to others.

A great way to begin is to just let people know you're open to Mentoring Moments. You could post something on LinkedIn or another social media platform, inviting people to connect with you. Or you could seek out something more formal through your workplace, an industry group or a mentoring organisation.

So, the question now becomes: what makes a great mentor?

The secret sauce has many of the same ingredients as being a great mentee: being open and transparent, staying curious, bringing a positive attitude and asking great questions. I'd add a sense of humility into the pot, too.

Madeleine's advice is to share your lived experiences and let the other person in on your worldview. You might share:

- times you felt you demonstrated good leadership
- what you identify as your strengths
- any skills you'd like to develop
- times you faced a challenge and how you overcame it
- stories of times you took a risk and it paid off, as well as times it didn't.

It's also important to listen – *really* listen. 'Sit back and let that person be who they are and tell their story,' Madeleine advises.

While giving advice is part of being a mentor, you also want to help people come to their own solutions. It's about helping someone become more of who they are, not turning them into a replica of you.

Flip the script: Reverse mentoring

Reverse mentoring flips the traditional mentoring relationship on its head: younger generations provide senior staff with insights and new skills.

Reverse mentoring has also been shown to:

- encourage diversity of thought
- stimulate creativity and the development of new ideas
- encourage teamwork and collaboration
- promote a culture of inclusion
- support personal development goals and skills development.

'We know that diverse companies perform better,' Madeleine says. 'The more we can diversify the people around a table, whichever table that is, the more there is to gain. That includes a younger person's perspective – they can bring in some learning and unique perspectives.'

If the idea of setting out to learn from someone much younger feels a bit strange, it is time to change up your mindset. Instead of focusing on age, try focusing on 'experience age'. Someone younger than you can be much more experienced in particular areas and have a lot to offer.

Technology is a great example of this. Digital natives have grown up in the digiverse and innately have their finger on the pulse of the latest and greatest tech trends. This means they can often help older colleagues grow technical competence in areas like social media and digital strategy – skills that are becoming critical to understand and leverage.

Madeleine employed a sixteen-year-old to help a UX team develop a product. 'In many ways he's teaching us, because he's a pure digital native. He's shepherding us through some of our decision-making around that product development.' She's also had a group of young girls help drive a marketing strategy 'because they are the core audience of the product'.

But the benefits of reverse mentoring don't begin and end with the skill set of digital natives.

Julie Demsey, a coach and hypnotherapist with twenty years of experience working in Silicon Valley, mentors the start-up community in Australia to help young companies grow. When she and her mentee Kietah Martens-Shaw talk about their relationship, it is clear that the support and learning flow in both directions.

Kietah, the founder of B.OKideas, a social enterprise helping businesses and individuals to send wellbeing-inspired gifts, says that Julie has a great ability to bring her back to her purpose. And Julie says her mentee brings a bright and optimistic perspective that inspires her to look at things with a fresh set of eyes.

Freehills credits reverse mentoring[5] with helping it build a successful team culture, focused on disruption and innovation. Other finance organisations such as PwC, KPMG and the Reserve Bank of Australia also have successful reverse mentoring schemes.

So when you're thinking of future Mentoring Moments partners, don't discount generations Y, Z and A. They have a lot to offer, too.

LAB EXPERIMENT

Do one thing today

In the spirit of ease that surrounds the concept of Mentoring Moments, we wanted to make this one really easy – so easy that you can't not do it.

Identify someone you'd like to have a Mentoring Moment with, and reach out to them ... today! Or, if you're interested in mentoring someone, take a moment to show your interest on your social media or research a couple of options online (you will find a few leads in the resources section). For the overachievers among us, do both!

A journey of shared discovery awaits you.

SIT SPOT

The animal kingdom is full of mentors.

Birds encourage their young to test their wings and coax them from the nest. Otters drag their babies through the water to teach them how to swim. Moose learn migration routes from older keepers of knowledge. Dolphin mothers release a fish they've caught and let their young try to catch it.

What would it mean, in this moment, to embrace mentoring as a natural part of your growth and evolution?

CHAPTER 20

The Second Renaissance

The Renaissance is sandwiched in time between the Middle Ages and modern history; it's a bridge, broadly speaking, between then and now. The word 'renaissance' means 'rebirth', and that is exactly what it was: an explosive reawakening of thought, art, science, religion and politics.

It wasn't just a time period – it was a movement. At its essence (and acknowledging the rose-coloured glasses here), I'd describe it as a 'curious, creative collective' of free thinkers, mixed in with technological and educational shifts, and a refocus on humanism and nature, questioning the old structures and 'certainties' to make sense of the world.

A movement of people pushing the boundaries of what they know, of what they can achieve. A movement that changed the world and that, centuries later, is thought of as perhaps the most important period in human development since the fall of Ancient Rome.

During COVID, I have been playing around with the idea that our current state of upheaval could give rise to the Second Renaissance.

I believe a new curious, creative collective may emerge: musicians, businesspeople, painters, sculptors, poets, philanthropists, scientists, philosophers, technologists, lawyers, teachers, financiers, architects, radio presenters – and [insert your career here].

We have an opportunity to redesign our world through a Second Renaissance.

Underpinning it will be the idea of bringing humanity back to the workplace.

But first, 'soft skills' need a makeover

The label of 'soft skills' in the workplace hinders us.

'Soft skills' are generally defined as the 'non-technical skills that relate to how you work and interact with other people'. It's all the human stuff. It's how you communicate with others, work in a group, lead a team, approach problem-solving, negotiate, plan and adapt. It's how motivated you are, how empathetic, how open-minded, how dependable.

This is the stuff that is actually difficult, and critical. You can't execute anything without bringing other people along with you. Even more so in these chaotic times, it's clear these 'soft skills' are our biggest strengths.

So, we need to step away from this unhelpful label. What might we call these skills instead? Atomic skills? That seems to fit.

They're seemingly small, but crazy powerful.

Three human traits to cultivate

For a new world to emerge, we need to let go of the old one. We need to let go of the way things have always been done, and the idea that our humanity somehow makes us lesser at work and needs to be hidden away.

Often at work we are advised to 'strip out the emotion' to be more effective, but that is a furphy. All we are doing is pushing the emotion underground. It seeps beneath the surface and it affects the growth above. To flourish, we need to let our humanity exist above ground.

To foster the Second Renaissance, we need to cultivate three very human traits: empathy, humour and love. Let's explore each in more detail now.

They may not sound like critical skills for the workplace, but remember: we are designing a new world.

EMPATHY

We already started exploring the importance of empathy, and how using it to understand someone's needs can help you achieve your own, and connect at work in a meaningful way. Let's build on that now.

Empathy sometimes feels like it doesn't belong at work, particularly in very corporate environments. In a meeting with lawyers in 2016, I used the word 'compassion' in relation to our clients and there was silence down the conference call line, followed by snickering. 'Compassion! Next you will be asking us to donate goats!' Then came the guffawing.

The capitalist system in which we work has long underpinned some of this. It's inherently competitive; anything that shows vulnerability is rejected because it feels like the opposite of how you 'get ahead' at work. We are constantly reminded that success in this world is about what you have, and how much you have. It requires money, and to get that money you have to compete with those around you. The cycle self-perpetuates.

But viable alternatives are emerging. There is some very good work being done in the Certified B Corporation space, where businesses are working to balance purpose and profit, and show they care about more than just their bottom lines. They are held to a socially responsible standard; they are legally required to consider the impact of their decisions on their workers, customers, suppliers, the community and the environment. A little more humanity is in the mix.

This is a good thing, because we all want others to connect with us on a level that acknowledges our humanity. Though it may be dismissed by those in charge, empathy often tops the list of what employees want most from their managers. When a workplace demonstrates empathy, it correlates to increased happiness, productivity and retention among employees.

Hello Sunshine's Sarah Harden gave me a beautiful example of empathy in action as she talked about leading her LA team through the chaos of COVID. She painted a confronting picture of trying to maintain a semblance of a normal life in a city where nothing was normal; a city where 2000 people were dying a day; a city grappling with the global reckoning catalysed by the Black Lives Matter movement; a city enduring compounding trauma. She came to a realisation very early on: 'We have to be deeply human in all of this.'

Sarah led from a place of curiosity and humility. She peeled back a layer and showed her employees the truth of who she was and what she was feeling. Because yes, she is a leader, but she is also a human. She was worried about the future of her industry, saddened by how the world seemed to be unravelling around her, and exhausted from juggling work with the very foreign demands of homeschooling her kids. It was hard, and she called that out, not as an excuse, but as an acknowledgement.

By showing her vulnerability, she gave her employees permission to do the same. What rose up was a space of authentic collaboration, where everyone stood and looked at the problems together. Team meetings, for example, became a place for people to share their ideas and uncertainties. Spaces opened up in company chat rooms for people to share mental health hacks and tips on getting through.

Through this, Sarah realised that a major source of stress for her team was uncertainty about the future. Hollywood had basically ground to a halt; her team, like so many around the world, didn't know what would come next.

'One of my kids is on the spectrum, he has ADHD, he is neurodiverse. So I've got a lot of really good parenting techniques, and one of them is to give certainty when you can,' says Sarah.

She brought that technique into the workplace, making a commitment very early on to give whatever certainty she could. So when people started working from home, even though nobody knew how long it would last, Sarah said 'it will definitely be for the next sixty days'. Some certainty.

She also did some scenario planning and looked at bottom lines, and was able to promise people that nobody was going to lose their jobs. Nobody would be asked to take a pay cut. Bonuses might not be paid, but everyone would still have a job. More certainty.

You don't need to be a leader to adopt this mindset. Empathy is for everyone: it works top down, bottom up, sideways and along diagonals. But Sarah's empathetic leadership was especially important because it set the tone for an entire company; when leaders make changes like this, it can have an even more powerful influence than we can as individuals in changing structures and systems.

HUMOUR

Humour is another one of those things that might feel like it doesn't belong in the workplace. It can seem like the enemy of the serious – and work is serious, right? (An old boss of Monique's would often mutter that the only place clowns belong is in the circus and 'does this place look like a circus to you lot?')

But humour does have a place at work. I like to think of it as bringing a sense of lightness and levity to what you do, rather than cracking bad jokes or mucking around.

Laughter and humour connects us. One example is when I interviewed famous chef and restaurateur Yotam Ottolenghi[1] in the very early days of *This Working Life*. He was promoting a new book, so by the time he landed at the ABC studios he'd already done about five interviews and a TV appearance.

We had decided it would be funny to showcase my terrible cooking, so I'd woken bright and early to cook my signature dish: Lisa's Lentil Slops.[2] I had forgotten how bad it was. When my daughter remarked on how a 'horrible smell' was following her around, I gave her a reassuring hug and said in a soft voice (in my good parenting style), 'Oh honey, if it is following you around, then it must be you.' She started sobbing. Then Darcy called out: 'Your mum's been cooking. The smell is her lentil slops!'

This dish made its way to the ABC and into my interview with Yotam. I pulled it out and asked him to try it. It was a very funny moment; he was generous and lovely, and his true self shone through. I felt like I'd got beneath the persona, to the person. He revealed some really incredible things in that interview about his life, his work and his values.

I asked him for his expert advice on how to improve the dish and he looked up, with a wry smile, and said softly: 'Ah ... start afresh.' After we finished, he said the interview had made his day because it had energised him. I'm not sure it would have turned out the same had we not had that moment of connection over laughter.

Humour, when deployed elegantly and appropriately, can be a superpower at work, and I'm not the only one who thinks this. Naomi Bagdonas and Jennifer Aaker teach a course at the Stanford Graduate School of Business called Humour: Serious Business.

Naomi says it's about being able to take your work seriously while not taking yourself seriously.[3] Having a balance of gravity and levity gives power to both.

A sense of lightness can:

▸ create a culture of ease that helps people do their best work
▸ cultivate stronger bonds between colleagues
▸ keep people engaged with what you're saying
▸ defuse tension, especially for people working in high-stress environments.

'We talk to emergency room doctors who have been through incredibly difficult times, and afterwards they are finding ways to laugh with each other behind the scenes,' Naomi says. 'It's not because they don't take their work seriously. It's that they take their work so seriously that they need to find ways to cope, ways to help their bodies and their minds be resilient through what they are doing.'

Read the room before deploying humour, and keep cultural considerations and any power imbalances in mind. Keep it appropriate as well. Humour isn't racist or sexist or discriminatory. It isn't about putting yourself or your work down. It doesn't make fun of other people. One coaching tip Naomi gives her clients is: 'Don't ask yourself, "Will this make me sound funny?" Instead ask, "How will this make other people feel?" The goal isn't to get a laugh, it's to make the room feel lighter and more at ease.'

Naomi adds, 'If you're able to pursue really serious missions that you care about deeply and you're able to do so while staying light … then you will be more successful.'

Try not to force it; just allow a little bit of lightness in.

LOVE

I am curious about the role of love in the workplace. Not the 'sexy time' type of love, or the kind that appears in schmaltzy ballads, but an enduring, connecting force. Something that stokes hope and forges a kind of unity.

When I have done the VIA Survey of Character Strengths in the past, love has been somewhere at the bottom of the pile. When Monique and I did the survey again recently, it was at the top of both of our lists.

VIA says love as a character strength is about the way in which you value close relationships with people, and contribute to that closeness in a warm and genuine way. It tends to facilitate tolerance, empathy and forgiveness. Aha! This is the type of love that can underpin the Second Renaissance.

When I have had conflicts, fights and misunderstandings, it is when I have turned my back on this character strength. It is when I have followed ingrained advice and a well-trodden path to 'be professional'. It is when I have tried to strip my humanity away from what is, at its core, a human relationship.

I am just at the curious stage with love. Because my conditioning is so strongly rational, I find even raising it mildly uncomfortable. Others have fully embraced it, among them Chinese business magnate Jack Ma, the founder and chairman of Alibaba Group.

People often talk about the need for IQ (intelligence quotient) and EQ (emotional quotient) at work and in business, but Jack throws LQ, or love quotient, into the mix. He says love is a secret weapon that needs to be leveraged so that a sense of nobility can return to the world of work.

'To gain success a person will need high EQ; if you don't want to lose quickly you will need a high IQ; and if you want to be respected you need high LQ – the IQ of love,' Jack says.[4] 'You can become a money machine, but what's the use of that? If you're not contributing to the rest of the world, there's no LQ.'

For Jack, love is about being principled, and it needs to underpin everything else.

I think he's on to something.

Building the curious, creative collective

We now know the human traits that will create the environment for the Second Renaissance: empathy, humour and love. Next, we need to find our curious, creative collective.

You may be a Category of One, but you are not alone. We need all hands on deck to redesign this world.

As you know, I love a good framework. So what is the framework we should use to guide this critical redesign? What is our blueprint for a rebirth of the way we work? I believe it needs to revolve around three things:

1. creative collaboration
2. making work work for everyone
3. uncovering our authentic selves.

Shall we step through them, together?

CREATIVE COLLABORATION

We can all learn so much from each other. In order to grow, we need to seek out a diversity of perspectives from people who can challenge our thinking and help keep us curious about the world. I am always looking for ways I can bring people with different ideas together, and being on the cusp of the Second Renaissance feels like a good time to ramp it up a notch.

I first came across the idea of a junto on the daily blog[5] of Stanford's Jeremy Utley.

Jeremy had read a biography of Benjamin Franklin, which detailed how he had convened a junto – a group of people who join together for a common purpose – early in his career. Franklin's junto was composed of enterprising tradies and artisans (rather than the social elite) and they gathered to discuss matters of importance and intrigue – everything from the pressing issues of the day to philosophy and self-improvement.

Jeremy couldn't help but wonder how these conversations impacted and stimulated Franklin's thinking over the years – and I wondered the same. How might this help me at work?

Jeremy, as it turns out, also has a junto: a handful of business leaders who gather monthly. Each gathering explores one issue faced by one of the leaders; the next month, the baton is passed to someone else. He describes the vibe as 'somewhere between frivolous and formal'. People take it seriously but are also relaxed, so it doesn't descend into pontification.

'We had one session where one of the leaders said, "Hey, here's a really hard, strategic issue I'm facing, I'd love to get your feedback," and everybody gave feedback. In another session one of the people said, "I feel like recruiting

is our big challenge and I don't know what young talent even want in a company," so I reached into my network and brought in six or seven really amazing students, and they just appeared in the meeting,' says Jeremy.

Everyone is present, and focused, and invested in one another. Everyone is bringing their superpowers into the mix and putting their unique ideas on the table. I want in, don't you?

Jeremy's advice for forming your own junto is to get outside of your company, and even outside of your industry or discipline, to expose yourself to a broader array of experiences and perspectives. Be deliberate about who you include: aim for people who share your purpose of learning and growing.

Even if you don't rush out and convene a junto, the philosophy behind it is useful. To shape this new world, we need to stand and look at problems as a collective.

The more voices, the merrier.

MAKING WORK *WORK* FOR EVERYONE

No redesign of the world of work would be complete without asking serious questions about whether it is fit for purpose, not just for the majority of people, but for *everybody*.

We have started asking questions around the future of our work. Will it be from home, the office, or a hybrid of both? Does it have to be full-time, Monday to Friday, 9 to 5? Flexibility, it seems, is the new luxury.

Work futurist Dominic Price hangs out with C-suite executives of all shapes and sizes, and talks to them about the future of work. He often hears them say something like, 'Yeah, there's been all this change, but ...',

followed by why they're going to switch right back to the way things have always been done.

Dominic then asks a simple question: 'Why?'

'Why do we have to come back to the office? Why do you think productivity is a good measure of team effectiveness or work or outcomes? Why are you so focused on outputs and not outcomes?'

It's not that he thinks one way is right or wrong, he just wants to help leaders understand that they may be holding on to some nostalgia, received wisdoms, frameworks and mindsets that might have helped them get to where they are, but might not help them get to where they want to go.

'I asked one very senior leader recently, "How are you going to earn the commute from your people? Because you've taken it away and you've let them replace the commute with other stuff, with Pilates or walking the dog or having breakfast. If you want them to replace that with the commute, you're going to have to earn that commute. So how are you going to do that?"'

I believe the Second Renaissance will unravel some of our assumptions about how we work. It will take flexibility under its wing, along with inclusivity and accessibility, which have long been crying out for a new approach.

Let's use the open-plan office as an example. Most of us don't question this way of working, but perhaps we need to.

I had a great conversation with author and autism advocate Clem Bastow about the way modern workplaces are designed. She explained that the open plan office is unintentionally designed to create a sensory overload, which can make it an extremely difficult environment for people with sensory issues.

'I would have these experiences where I'd work in an office, or try to work in an office, and then come away feeling like I'd "failed". For a long time that was a real mystery. It was like, "Am I a slacker? Am I just a bludger who can't seem to work in an office?" And so when I learned the reality, which is that I'm autistic, that made a lot of sense,' she says.

She'd love to see work environments redesigned to be more accessible for everyone. This might include adjusting things like the temperature, sound levels, smells or lighting, and not forcing people who feel most comfortable working from home to return to the office.

This, she says, could go some way to addressing the 'absolutely gobsmacking' rates of unemployment in the autistic community.

Clem also tutors university classes and gives a beautiful example of how she has subtly redesigned her approach to guide her students through their work in a way that makes them feel safe. If her neurodiverse students learn better while listening to music, or moving around, or having a video on, she allows that.

'I think some educators would think, "Oh well, all the rules have gone out the window and it must be anarchy", and it's not. I've been a student fairly recently. I have that memory of how difficult it was for me at uni, so I think, "How can I, to the best of my abilities, help my students avoid similar experiences?"'

By treating them as human beings. By showing up with empathy and being committed to helping make work *work* for everybody.

UNCOVERING YOUR AUTHENTIC SELF

It all circles back to the idea of being your whole self – or, at least, more of your whole self – at work.

We value authenticity in others, but so many of us put on a mask when we go to work because we want to seem intelligent, composed and professional. If we have to give a presentation or run a meeting, we tighten the mask and become more like a robot. We pretend that we're only our IQ or our analytical selves, and we become the person we think we need to be to fully own our job title.

Many of us also engage in a phenomenon called 'covering', where we tone down our differences in order to fit into the mainstream. This includes differences in our unique identity, and our thoughts, opinions and feelings. It can also lead us to copy the traits and behaviours of others so we don't stick out.

Have you ever been in a meeting where everyone is asked to stick their hand up if they agree with a course of action or a proposal? If most people vote one way, you're more likely to follow suit, even if you don't agree. That's covering. (It starts early, too; it's why we wanted what the 'cool kids' had in school and hid things that we thought weren't popular, even if we were super passionate about them.)

The concept of covering was formed in 1963 by sociologist Erving Goffman. Many years later, in 2006, New York University legal scholar Kenji Yoshino expanded on the concept and introduced a description of the four ways people cover at work.

1. **Appearance-based.** This is when people alter their self-presentation, including grooming, attire and mannerisms. For example, Monique covers up her vibrant tattoos when she's meeting with people she fears may form a negative opinion of her based on them. Someone with a disability may

forgo using a cane at work. Other people may wear more or less make-up to work, to fit in with what others do.

2. **Affiliation-based.** This is when people engage in or refrain from certain behaviours to avoid being labelled with common stereotypes. For example, a woman might downplay her childcare responsibilities so she isn't perceived as less available or committed. Or a person may not reveal that they grew up poor and were the first in their family to go to university, to fit in with middle-class colleagues.

3. **Advocacy-based.** This relates to how vocal a person is when advocating for a class or group to which they belong. For example, someone who doesn't talk politics during election season because they're backing the 'wrong' candidate. Or a person who won't raise diversity and inclusion issues in case it impacts their career.

4. **Association-based.** This is when people avoid contact with other members of their 'group'. For example, a person who has struggled with depression may refrain from associating with workplace mental health groups.

Take a moment to reflect on these. What parts of yourself might you be covering at work?

It's important to note that not all covering is bad. Look at the example of Monique's appearance-based covering. She says that while her tattoos are zero indication of her aptitude for her job, there's definitely instances when covering them has helped her get a role or ace a presentation, because having them hidden made her feel more confident. She wasn't worried about being judged, so she could just get on with doing a great job, anxiety-free. In that situation, covering is positive and empowering for her.

We don't have to take off the mask entirely, or shout our truths at the top of our lungs and tell anyone who doesn't like it to rack off. We don't have to step over any lines of professionalism at work, or expose ourselves in a way that we're not comfortable with.

But by bringing some awareness to the masks we wear, we can choose to loosen them if they're not serving us. We can choose to let a little more of our humanity shine through.

This is one of the things I have loved the most about working during COVID: jumping on a Zoom call with someone and getting that tiny glimpse into their life. Family photos on a shelf, loads of books, a great piece of art, a guitar in the corner, kids running amok, a dog barking off screen. It's very human, and it doesn't make anyone less professional.

I would love to see more of it shine through.

Who are you practising to be?

Danielle Krettek, the founder of Google's Empathy Lab, shared with me one piece of advice she received that really resonated with her: work, or anything else you do for a long period of time, is actually a practice of being who you are.[6]

If you're not being honest, then who are you practising to be? If you're not being yourself, then who are you practising to become? And does that work for you?

I've thought about that story a bit since then. Who are we practising to be if we're not showing up with our whole selves, with our humanness?

It's our empathy and creativity and the connections we can forge that make us as effective as we are as human workers. It's our atomic skills that are the most powerful.

Amid the upheaval of COVID is an opportunity to redesign our world.

An opportunity to rediscover and revalue what is truly human in our work.

An opportunity to show up with humour, empathy and love ... and give rise to the Second Renaissance.

Let's not waste it.

We ride at dawn.

SIT SPOT

The trembling giant, or Pando, is one of the oldest living organisms in the world. It appears to be an enormous forest of quaking aspen trees, but it is actually one living thing.

Each of the 47,000 golden trees is genetically identical to the next, and they all share a single root system. The one is the many; the many is the one.

What would it mean, in this moment, to walk forward knowing we are all connected?

Conclusion

I've never been very good at endings.

But luckily for all of us, this isn't really an ending at all.

It's a beginning.

We have come so far together, journeying across these pages to this moment.

We have ventured deep inside, to discover what makes us come alive, what makes us tick, what we want to carry forward and what we want to leave behind. We have stirred our sense of who we are when the On Air light switches off – and who we want to be.

We have awakened our curiosity and courage and compassion and creativity, and learned that while we may fumble and stumble as we walk forward, we will not cower in the face of chaos and uncertainty. We will rise to the challenge. We cannot be stopped.

We have explored some ways to curate a career that is bursting with meaning and satisfaction and joy, whether through small tweaks or big shifts. We have played around with our work days and how we might change them for the better, by building routines and rituals and remembering our home in nature.

We have brought empathy back to the workplace, knowing that our ability to connect on a deeply human level is perhaps the most potent superpower of all, and one that is innate to each of us. We have learned to look for the sunshine, even in the darkest caves of life. We have learned to find those rays within ourselves, and each other.

What has emerged for you on this journey, in all these words and all the spaces in between?

What is stirring within you?

What is your heart reaching out towards — at work and in life?

Now is the time to begin, to take everything you have learned and step boldly into a new world of your own design. Now is the time to roll up your sleeves and get your hands dirty. You might begin by going back to any dog-eared pages, back to the chapters and ideas that have most resonated with you. Begin by testing them out for yourself. Trust the process.

I don't know what the future holds for any of us. If I was to have a crack at predicting it, I'd probably, almost definitely, be way off.

But we can dream, and I believe we should all dream big.

Because we may not be able to predict the future, and we sure as hell can't control it, but we aren't subservient to the hands of fate either. We have some agency over what comes next. What we do today shapes our tomorrows. So why not get out there and start creating the tomorrows of your wildest dreams?

Every day is Lab Day, and this working life is ripe for experimentation and evolution.

You are, now and forever, part of my valiant squad of explorers. As you gather your data and test concepts in your lab, feel free to plug me and Monique into it, through our social media pages. We can all keep learning from each other going forward; we can stand and face the challenges together. We're a community now.

It doesn't end here. You're only just getting started.

Flowers bloom at exactly the moment they are meant to.

So, my friend, will you.

Soundtrack 🎵

You didn't think we could wrap up without a song, did you? What kind of finale would that be? Monique and I got together with Little Green to create something special for our squad —

for you. It's our version of a sing-a-long around the campfire as the moon slowly rises up from behind the mountains to take its place in the night sky.

Scan the QR code to listen. Let's sing, together.

BETWEEN SEASONS
Hibernate for the winter then comes spring
Waiting for the joy the flowers bring
I've been hiding away in my cocoon
But I know that I'll be flying soon

I'm in between seasons
But I'll bloom when I'm meant to
I'm in between feelings
But I'll do what I gotta do

Cause I know my time will come to shine
Everything's gonna work out fine
I know my time will come to rise
Let go, let come, my spirit's high

Navigate through the wild stormy seas
Looking for the land that brings me peace
I've been thinking about how far I've come
All the seeds I've sown, the songs I've sung

I'm in between seasons
But I'll bloom when I'm meant to
I'm in between feelings
But I'll do what I gotta do

Cause I know my time will come to shine
Everything's gonna work out fine
I know my time will come to rise
Let go, let come, my spirit's high

Resources

Recommended books

DESIGN THINKING AND INNOVATION
Change by Design by Tim Brown
Crossing the Chasm by Geoffrey A. Moore
Dark Matter and Trojan Horses by Dan Hill
The Design of Business by Roger Martin
The Design of Everyday Things by Don Norman
The Innovator's Dilemma by Clayton M. Christensen
The Lean Startup by Eric Ries
Scaling Up Excellence by Robert I. Sutton and Huggy Rao
Sprint by Jake Knapp with John Zeratsky and Braden Kowitz

LEADERSHIP
Dare to Lead by Brené Brown
The Essentials of Theory U by C. Otto Scharmer
The Fearless Organization by Amy Edmondson
Finding the Space to Lead by Janice Marturano
Improv Wisdom by Patricia Ryan Madson
The Joy of Leadership by Tal Ben-Shahar and Angus Ridgway
The Skilled Facilitator by Roger Schwarz

PERSONAL AND CAREER DEVELOPMENT
The Art of Gathering by Priya Parker
The Art of Possibility by Rosamund Stone Zander and Benjamin Zander
Atomic Habits by James Clear
Indistractable by Nir Eyal with Julie Li
Reinventing You by Dorie Clark

Think Again by Adam Grant

Thinking, Fast and Slow by Daniel Kahneman

Tiny Habits by B. J. Fogg

NATURE AND MINDFULNESS

A Thousand Names for Joy by Byron Katie

Blue Mind by Wallace J. Nichols

Finding the Mother Tree by Suzanne Simard

The Hidden Life of Trees by Peter Wohlleben

Lao Tzu: Tao te Ching translated by Ursula K. Le Guin

The Mindful Therapist by Daniel J. Siegel

Mindsight by Daniel J. Siegel

Peace of Mind by Thich Nhat Hanh

Walden (Life in the Woods) by Henry David Thoreau

Wherever You Go, There You Are by Jon Kabat-Zinn

Your Guide to Forest Bathing by Amos Clifford

OTHER

Belonging by Owen Eastwood

The Courage to Be Disliked by Ichiro Kishimi and Fumitake Koga

The Gift of Struggle by Bobby Herrera

Late Bloomer by Clem Bastow

Phosphorescence by Julia Baird

The Power of Ritual by Casper ter Kuile

Microcredentials sites

FutureLearn

General Assembly

LinkedIn Learning

MOOC.org

Skillshare

Udacity

Udemy

Many universities also offer microcredentials for a fee.

Mentoring platforms

Australian Business Mentors

girledworld

Mentoring Men

Mentor Walks

She Mentors

Many workplaces also offer mentoring programs.

Guided Pleasures of Presence

Visit www.heartwoodnaturebathing.com/thisworkinglife

Counselling and support services

This book contains real and raw accounts of mental health issues and other struggles that can rear their heads as we live life. Some of these stories may bring up feelings of sadness or discomfort, or affect you in ways you may not have anticipated.

If you need someone to talk to:

- **Beyond Blue** will connect you with a trained mental health professional. You can reach them 24/7 on 1300 224 636.
- **Lifeline** provides 24/7 crisis counselling and can be reached at 13 11 14. You can also chat to someone via text from 1 pm to midnight on 0477 13 11 14.
- **Suicide Call Back Service** provides 24/7 help for anyone affected by suicidal thoughts. Call 1300 659 467.
- If someone's life is in danger or there is an immediate risk of harm, call **emergency services** on 000.

Alternatively, reach out to a friend, family member, colleague, therapist, or to anyone you feel comfortable confiding in. Many workplaces also provide employees with access to confidential counselling services.

You are not alone, and there is no shame in seeking support.

Acknowledgements

We both thank ...

Arwen Summers, the force is strong in you. *Merci beaucoup* for having the incredible vision for this book, guiding us through with wisdom, grace and heart, and Yes And-ing all of our wild ideas. 'Hey Arwen, how about a soundtrack for the book!?'

Camha Pham, thanks for the sharp edits – insert many dashes and exclamation marks here!!! Anna Collett, thanks for keeping us on track, even as we threw tricky QR codes into the mix.

Much gratitude to everyone else at Hardie Grant Books, especially Kirstie Grant, Shalini Kunahlan, Cherry Cai, Julia Kumschick, Jane Grant, Nicole Lemmon, Roxy Ryan, Julie Pinkham, Sandy Grant, Fiona Hardie and Jane Willson.

Julia Murray ... just ... wow. We stand in awe. Bring on the beer can!

Amy Nelson, aka Little Green, thank you for your incredible gift. Can't wait for our sing-along-a-book tour. David Morgan from Lemon Tree Music, and producer Garrett Kato, thank you for bringing our EP to life.

We are grateful for the guidance and support of our wonderful ABC *This Working Life* peeps – Cath Dwyer, Julie Browning, Amruta Slee, and senior producers Maria 'Magic' Tickle and Claudette Werden.

A standing ovation for the squad of people who so generously shared their time, wisdom, perspectives and experiences for this book. And we applaud you, our dear reader and explorer. Thanks for opening your mind and heart – and please do let us know how things go!

Lisa thanks ...

Darcy, my gorgeous hubby, for the pep talks, coffees, meals, walks, ideas, belly laughs – and big hugs! And the rest of the fam: Billie and Buttons, Mum, Dad, Andrew, Lisa, Eli, Holly and Darcy's family: John, Bing, Jeremy, Maria, Victoria and House.

Deirdre Dowling, for your wild heart, sharp brain and compassionate challenges of our early manuscript. Tim for the emergency weekend sense-check. Emily Barnes and Cath Mok for takeaway chai walk 'n' talks, and post-lockdown tennis therapy.

Jacinta Parsons, Kate Dinon and Panio Gianopoulos for reading the first pages!

All my awes friends and mentors in my creative collectives: PLC, Ormond College, Science Law Melb Uni, Leuven Uni, Freehills, anz.com, Ashurst, AFTRS, Stanford d.school, Skilled Facilitator, Harvard Law School, Radio Lollipop, TEDx Melb, Tri-Hards, ABC, Presil, SingularityU, Ohten – and my health squad including Dr Sue, Jeremy, Lucinda, Isaac, Celine, Dr Chris B, Sharon, Jordan, Wiki, Louise, Ann, Aroon, Dr Carolyn and Coach David.

To the *This Working Life* broadcast and podcast listeners – your curiosity, compassion and courage brought this whole squad together and gave rise to this book! Thank you!!!

And to you, Monitron, my copilot ...

Monique thanks ...

Lukeshine (the greatest and the best), for everything. I cherish you, the way we love each other and the life we share.

Tricia, Craig, Dylan, Aaron, Kerry, Barry, Brendan and Sarah, you are the best. Big love.

My Dadooshka, Colin – you would have been so chuffed to have these pages on your library shelves. I hope this book finds you at peace, in the place where the sea meets the sky.

Camille, Jemma, Jeff, Mandy, James, Nat, Mike, Joel, Dee, Emar, Keatyn, Kate, Edwina and Em – you are the fiercest, wisest, warmest, kindest, funniest people. Thanks Claudine for your guidance; Simon for getting me organised and keeping me smiling; Bennaby for teaching me so much; and the entire ABC gang, for being your wonderful selves. Bear hugs all 'round.

I honour Nature, for its unconditional support and infinite inspiration.

And last but definitely not least, Lisa. Thank you for bringing me along for this ride! It's been such a joy. Words can't express how glad I am to know you. Love ya! XXXX Monitron

Endnotes

Chapter 2 – Get rooted

1   Ching, G. (2017, December 6). Redefining success – lessons from Arianna Huffington's Thrive. *HuffPost*. www.huffpost.com/entry/redefining-success-lessons-from-arianna-huffington-thrive_b_5222408

2   Leong, L. (Host), & Jokic, V. (Producer). (2019, January 22). The KeepCup and living in one good street. In *This Working Life*. ABC Radio National. www.abc.net.au/radionational/programs/this-working-life/the-keepcup-and-living-in-one-good-street/10731508

Chapter 3 – Who are you when the On Air light switches off?

1   Renton, S., & McCrindle, M. (2021). *The future of education: Insights into today's students and their future expectations*. McCrindle Research Pty Ltd. https://mccrindle.com.au/wp-content/uploads/reports/Education-Future-Report-2021.pdf

2   Jobs, S. (2005, June 12). Commencement address [Speech transcript]. Stanford University. https://news.stanford.edu/2005/06/14/jobs-061505/

3   International Labour Organization. (2021, January 25). *ILO Monitor: COVID-19 and the world of work. Seventh edition. Updated estimates and analysis*. www.ilo.org/wcmsp5/groups/public/@dgreports/@dcomm/documents/briefingnote/wcms_767028.pdf

Chapter 4 – The gift of struggle

1   Leong, L. (Host), & Tickle, M. (Producer). (2020, April 27). Can struggle be a gift? In *This Working Life*. ABC Radio National. www.abc.net.au/radionational/programs/this-working-life/can-struggle-be-a-gift/12181922

2   TED. (2021, May 21). *Dominic Price: What's your happiness score?* TED [Video]. YouTube. www.youtube.com/watch?v=ejQsLQvfnX4

Chapter 5 – Harness your superpowers

1   Steimer, A., & Mata, A. (2016). Motivated implicit theories of personality: My weaknesses will go away, but my strengths are here to stay. *Personality and Social Psychology Bulletin, 42*(4), 415–429.

2   Zenger, J., Sandholtz, K., & Folkman, J. (2017). *Leadership under the microscope – revised version*. https://zengerfolkman.com/wp-content/uploads/2019/06/White-Paper-Leadership-Under-The-Microscope.pdf

3   Niemiec, R. M., & McGrath, R. E. (2019). *The power of character strengths: Appreciate and ignite your positive personality*. VIA Institute on Character.

4   VIA Institute on Character. (n.d.). *VIA survey of character strengths*. www.viacharacter.org

5   Leong, L. (Host), & Tickle, M. (Producer). (2021, June 21). Crafting a personal brand at work might feel contrived but it's crucial to your success. In *This Working Life*. ABC Radio National. www.abc.net.au/radionational/programs/this-working-life/crafting-a-personal-brand-v1/13395880

6   SYPartners. (n.d.). *What's your superpower?* https://madeby.sypartners.com/products/superpowers-card-deck?variant=1098868541

Chapter 6 – Category of One

1   Scheiber, N. (2015, August 17). Work policies may be kinder, but brutal competition isn't. *The New York Times*. www.nytimes.com/2015/08/18/business/work-policies-may-be-kinder-but-brutal-competition-isnt.html?_r=0

Chapter 7 – Fail like a scientist: Every day is Lab Day

1   Dweck, C. S. (2007). *Mindset: The new psychology of success*. Ballantine Books.

2   Sitkin, S. (1992). Learning through failure: The strategy of small losses. *Research in Organizational Behavior, 14*, 231–266.

3   Leong, L. (Host), & Tickle, M. (Producer). (2019, October 22). Netflix staff find freedom in failure through the power of improv at work. In *This Working Life*. ABC Radio National. www.abc.net.au/radionational/programs/this-working-life/the-power-of-improv-at-work/11617178

4   Leong, L. (Host), & Jokic, V. (Producer). (2019, March 26). Good leadership in turbulent times: Amy Edmondson. In *This Working Life*. ABC Radio National. www.abc.net.au/radionational/programs/this-working-life/twl-22-january-2019/10924458

5   TEDx Talks. (2014, May 5). *Building a psychologically safe workplace: Amy Edmondson – TEDxHGSE* [Video]. YouTube. www.youtube.com/watch?v=LhoLuui9gX8&t=549s

Chapter 8 – Tweak: Job-craft your way to more meaning

1   Wrzesniewski, A., & Dutton, J. E. (2001). Crafting a job: Revisioning employees as active crafters of their work. *Academy of Management, 26*(2), 179–201.

2   Berg, J. M., Dutton, J. E., & Wrzesniewski, A. (2013). Job crafting and meaningful work. In B. J. Dik, Z. S. Byrne, & M. F. Steger (Eds.), *Purpose and meaning in the workplace* (pp. 81–104). American Psychological Association.

3   Leong, L. (Host), & Tickle, M. (Producer). (2021, May 3). We aren't learning on the job, are micro-credentials the answer? In *This Working Life*. ABC Radio National. www.abc.net.au/radionational/programs/this-working-life/life-long-learning-on-the-job/13324432

4   Gallagher, S. (2021). *Peak human workplace: Innovation in the unprecedented era.* www.swinburne.edu.au/research/centres-groups-clinics/centre-for-the-new-workforce/our-research/peak-human-workplace/

5   Leong, L. (Host), & Tickle, M. (Producer). (2021, February 22). The power of knowing what you don't know. In *This Working Life*. ABC Radio National. www.abc.net.au/radionational/programs/this-working-life/adam-grant-think-again-v1/13173280

6   Department of Education, Skills and Employment. (2020, June 20). *Marketplace for online microcredentials* [Joint media release]. https://ministers.dese.gov.au/tehan/marketplace-online-microcredentials

7   *ibid*. n 3

Chapter 9 – Pivot: Curate a portfolio career

1   Leong, L. (Host), & Tickle, M. (Producer). (2021, March 15). Why you need a portfolio career, even if you have a good job. In *This Working Life*. ABC Radio National. www.abc.net.au/radionational/programs/this-working-life/portolio-careers/13241604

2   Handy, C. (1995). *The age of unreason*. Random House Business.

Chapter 11 – Leaving your job (not your identity)

1   Leong, L. (Host), & Tickle, M. (Producer). (2020, May 4). If not THAT then WHO? The loss of self worth and identity when jobs evaporate. In *This Working Life*. ABC Radio National. www.abc.net.au/radionational/programs/this-working-life/job-loss-and-identity-and-self-worth-in-covid-times/12205970

2   *ibid*.

3   Leong, L. (Host), & Tickle, M. (Producer). (2019, April 19). Take the money and run, reframing redundancy. In *This Working Life*. ABC Radio National. www.abc.net.au/radionational/programs/this-working-life/take-the-money-and-run/10993720

4   *ibid*.

Chapter 12 – Work–life coherence

1   Leong, L. (Host), & Tickle, M. (Producer). (2020, February 10). Work–life balance is dead, hello integration. In *This Working Life*. ABC Radio National. www.abc.net.au/radionational/programs/this-working-life/work-life-balance-is-dead/11940238

2   Atlassian. (2021). *Company values*. www.atlassian.com/company/values

Chapter 13 – Tame and reframe your imposter thoughts

1   TEDx Talks. (2018, February 17). *Can robots make us more human? Lisa Leong – TEDxMelbourne* [Video]. www.youtube.com/watch?v=eQlcmUJa6Gg

2   Leong, L. (Host), Tickle, M. (Producer), & Jensen-Mackinnon, K. (Researcher). (2021, June 28). Who do you think you are? Reframing imposter syndrome to power, not cripple, your career. In *This Working Life*. ABC Radio National. www.abc.net.au/radionational/programs/this-working-life/taming-imposter-syndrome-at-work-v1/13419630

3   Sakulku, J. (2011). The impostor phenomenon. *The Journal of Behavioral Science, 6*(1), 75–97.
4   *ibid*. n 2
5   *ibid*. n 2
6   Starecheski, L. (2014, October 7). *Why saying is believing – the science of self-talk*. NPR. www.npr.org/sections/health-shots/2014/10/07/353292408/why-saying-is-believing-the-science-of-self-talk
7   Leong, L. (Host), & Tickle, M. (Producer). (2021, February 22). The power of knowing what you don't know. In *This Working Life*. ABC Radio National. www.abc.net.au/radionational/programs/this-working-life/adam-grant-think-again-v1/13173280
8   Tewfik, B. (2019). *Workplace impostor thoughts: Theoretical conceptualization, construct measurement, and relationships with work-related outcomes*. [Doctoral dissertation, University of Pennsylvania]. ScholarlyCommons. https://repository.upenn.edu/edissertations/3603/

Chapter 14 – Stress: The good, the bad and the burnt out

1   Leong, L. (Host), Tickle, M. (Producer), & Jensen-Mackinnon, K. (Researcher). (2021, July 26). Wake me up in 2022: Working through uncertainty fatigue. In *This Working Life*. ABC Radio National. www.abc.net.au/radionational/programs/this-working-life/pandemic-uncertainty-and-lockdown-creating-fatigue-and-burnout/13467478
2   World Health Organization. (2019, May 28). *Burn-out an 'occupational phenomenon': International Classification of Diseases*. www.who.int/news/item/28-05-2019-burn-out-an-occupational-phenomenon-international-classification-of-diseases
3   Leong, L. (Host), & Tickle, M. (Producer). (2020, July 6). 'I was stuck in my bed – all I could do is cry.' Is COVID making you burn out at work? In *This Working Life*. ABC Radio National. www.abc.net.au/radionational/programs/this-working-life/burnout-at-work/12419850
4   *ibid*.

Chapter 15 – Supercharge your day with a great routine

1   Leong, L. (Host), & Tickle, M. (Producer). (2020, March 30). What you're feeling amid the coronavirus crisis is probably grief. In *This Working Life*. ABC Radio National. www.abc.net.au/radionational/programs/this-working-life/what-youre-feeling-amid-the-coronavius-crisis-is-probably-grief/12096212
2   Leong, L. (Host), & Tickle, M. (Producer). (2020, July 27). Nir Eyal on taking control of technology to become 'indistractible'. In *This Working Life*. ABC Radio National. www.abc.net.au/radionational/programs/this-working-life/nir-eyal-on-taking-control-of-technology/12489344
3   ABC Australia. (2020, September 13). *Routines to help you nail the work day – This Working Life. ABC Australia* [Video]. www.youtube.com/watch?v=6pWyYHaIJ-8
4   *ibid*.

Chapter 16 – Give your brain a boost in nature

1   Wilson, E. O. (1986). *Biophilia*. Harvard University Press.
2   Kobayashi, M., Wakayama, Y., Inagaki, H., Katsumata, M., Hirata, Y., Hirata, K., Shimizu, T., Kawada, T., Park, B. J., Ohira, T., Kagawa, T., & Miyazaki, Y. (2009). Effect of phytoncide from trees on human natural killer cell function. *International Journal of Immunopathology and Pharmacology, 22*(4), 951–959.
3   Kaplan, R., & Kaplan, S. (1989). *The experience of nature: A psychological perspective*. Cambridge University Press.
4   Ulrich, R., Simons, R. F., Lositot, B. D., Fioritot, E., Miles, M. A., & Zelson, M. (1991). Stress recovery during exposure to natural and urban environments. *Journal of Environmental Psychology, 11*, 201–230.
5   Ulrich, R. S. (1984). View through a window may influence recovery from surgery. *Science, 224*, 420–421.
6   Moore, E. O. (1982). A prison environment's effect on health care service demands. *Journal of Environmental Systems, 11*, 17–34.
7   Shin, W. S. (2007). The influence of forest view through a window on job satisfaction and job stress. *Scandinavian Journal of Forest Research, 22*, 248–253.
8   Ulrich, R. S. (1979). Visual landscapes and psychological well-being. *Landscape Research, 4*(1), 17–23.
9   Ellison, M. A. (2010). *An exploratory study of the restorative benefits of hiking in wilderness solitude and its relationship to job satisfaction*. [Doctoral dissertation, North Carolina State University]. NC State Repository. https://repository.lib.ncsu.edu/handle/1840.16/6502

10   Cooper, C., & Browning, B. (2015). *Human spaces: The global impact of biophilic design in the workplace.* Interface. https://interfaceinc.scene7.com/is/content/InterfaceInc/Interface/EMEA/eCatalogs/Brochures/Human%20Spaces%20report/English/ec_eu-globalhumanspacesreport-enpdf.pdf

11   Nieuwenhuis, M., Knight, C., Postmes, T., & Haslam, S. A. (2014). The relative benefits of green versus lean office space: Three field experiments. *Journal of Experimental Psychology: Applied, 20*(3), 199–214.

12   Baird, B., Smallwood, J., Mrazek, M. D., Kam, J. W. Y., Franklin, M. S., & Schooler, J. W. (2012). Inspired by distraction: Mind wandering facilitates creative incubation. *Psychological Science, 23*(10), 1117–1122.

13   Ritter, S. M., & Dijksterhuis, A. (2014). Creativity – the unconscious foundations of the incubation period. *Frontiers in Human Neuroscience, 8*, 215.

Chapter 17 – Unlock the power of rituals

1   Leong, L. (Host), & Ferguson, Z. (Producer). (2021, August 21). The power of everyday routines to boost your work life. In *This Working Life*. ABC Radio National. www.abc.net.au/radionational/programs/this-working-life/the-power-of-everyday-routines/13475998

2   Leong, L. (Host), & Werden, C. (Producer). (2021, April 2). Things we can do to bring meaning to our lives. In *Life Matters*. ABC Radio National. www.abc.net.au/radionational/programs/lifematters/things-we-can-do-to-bring-meaning-to-our-lives/13285726

3   Leong, L. (Host), & Tickle, M. (Producer). (2021, July 19). How to win at work through less, not more, effort. In *This Working Life*. ABC Radio National. www.abc.net.au/radionational/programs/this-working-life/effortlessness-burnout-greg-mckeown-v2/13446668

Chapter 19 – Mentoring Moments

1   Leong, L. (Host), & Tickle, M. (Producer). (2020, June 15). An angel on your shoulder, how finding the right mentor can change your career. In *This Working Life*. ABC Radio National. www.abc.net.au/radionational/programs/this-working-life/an-angel-on-your-shoulder,-finding-the-right-mentor-can-change/12350250

2   Leong, L. (Host), & Tickle, M. (Producer). (2021, February 22). The power of knowing what you don't know. In *This Working Life*. ABC Radio National. www.abc.net.au/radionational/programs/this-working-life/adam-grant-think-again-v1/13173280

3   *ibid*. n 1

4   Leong, L. (Host), & Jokic, V. (Producer). (2019, March 5). The power of a good mentor. In *This Working Life*. www.abc.net.au/radionational/programs/this-working-life/twl-22-january-2019/10867350

5   Pelly, M. (2019, December 12). Freehills rolls out reverse mentoring. *Financial Review*. www.afr.com/companies/professional-services/bossing-the-boss-freehills-rolls-out-reverse-mentoring-20191204-p53gls

Chapter 20 – The Second Renaissance

1   Leong, L. (Host), & Jokic, V. (Producer). (2019, April 9). Ottolenghi reveals rare recipe. In *This Working Life*. ABC Radio National. www.abc.net.au/radionational/programs/this-working-life/twl-22-january-2019/10976026

2   Leong, L. (2006, February 16). *Lisa's lentil slops (revived)*. ABC. www.abc.net.au/radio/recipes/lisas-lentil-slops-revived/9191624

3   Leong, L. (Host), & Tickle, M. (Producer). (2020, November 2). Harnessing humour as a superpower at work. In *This Working Life*. ABC Radio National. www.abc.net.au/radionational/programs/this-working-life/humour-is-serious-business/12830440

4   World Economic Forum. (2018, January 25). *Jack Ma: Love is important in business – Davos 2018* [Video]. www.youtube.com/watch?v=4zzVjonyHcQ

5   Utley, J. (2020, November 24). Convene a junto. *Jeremy Utley*. www.jeremyutley.design/blog/convene-a-junto

6   Leong, L. (Host), & Tickle, M. (Producer). (2021, March 1). Can Google teach us empathy? In *This Working Life*. ABC Radio National. www.abc.net.au/radionational/programs/this-working-life/empathy-at-work-in-artificial-intelligence/13196686